ALL THE WAY HOME

MARY SUZANNE LOPEZ

Scripture quotations marked KJV are from the *King James Version* of the Bible.

All the Way Home
ISBN: 978-0-88144-314-1
Copyright © 2008 by Mary Suzanne Lopez

Published by
YORSHIRE PUBLISHING GROUP
7707 East 111th, Suite 104
Tulsa, Oklahoma 74133
www.yorkshirepublishing.com

Printed in the United States of America. All rights reserved under International Copyright Law. Contents and/or cover may not be reproduced in whole or in part in any form without the express written consent of the Author.

LIST OF CHAPTERS

Dedication		5
Acknowledgments		6
Chapter One	It's a Jungle Out There	7
Chapter Two	Coto 47	39
Chapter Three	Independencio	66
Chapter Four	Promises and Other Scary Things	86
Chapter Five	Wishing Upon Stars	110
Chapter Six	Sound Advice and Hind Sight	122
Chapter Seven	Different? Dream On, Honey!	145
Chapter Eight	Safe in Tulsa?	155
Chapter Nine	Truth and Consequences	177
Chapter Ten	Storm of the Soul	196
Chapter Eleven	Bitter Vintage	212
Chapter Twelve	The Coward's Way Out	227
Chapter Thirteen	Silent	242
Chapter Fourteen	Santa Ana	258
Chapter Fifteen	Garrapata!	273
Chapter Sixteen	Life in the Burbs	291
Chapter Seventeen	Angels Unaware	301
Chapter Eighteen	Once Upon a Dream	307
Chapter Nineteen	Hope Deferred	319
Chapter Twenty	Gators and Tigers and Snakes, Oh My!	340
Chapter Twenty-One	With you	361
Epilogue		372

DEDICATION

To women and children who have no voice and suffer abuse all around the world.

For Alicia with lots of love! Mary Sue

ACKNOWLEDGMENTS

I'd like to thank my present husband, Arnaldo, who for the last nine years, has supported me in every way so I'd be free to write and without whose help this book could never have been finished.

Thanks to my children for all their support, especially Anthony, who lives nearby and helped me with computer problems and daily doses of encouragement. Thanks also to my cousin, Pat Thompson, whose extensive knowledge of our family history greatly enriched my story.

Thanks to friends at Tulsa NightWriters, who were always happy to answer my questions and to Peggy Fielding, author, professor at Tulsa Community College and Tulsa NightWriters Grand Dame who taught me so much.

Thanks to special friend and fellow author, Gloria Teague, whose encouragement, help and advice were indispensable. And last but certainly not least, my heartfelt thanks to kind and knowledgeable Todd Rutherford, VP of Yorkshire Publishing and Amanda Pilgrim, Director of Operations who with her expertise and wonderful sense of humor guided me through the process of putting into print the dream I've had for the last thirty years.

CHAPTER ONE

IT'S A JUNGLE OUT THERE!

Our plane swooped from the clouds along a shoreline thick with vine-draped trees that grew nearly to the water's edge. *We're coming in too low!* We banked toward a niche hacked from raw jungle and the village of Golfito clinging to the side of the hill. *There's no airstrip. I hate flying! I shouldn't even be on an....* Then to the left of town I spied an airstrip accessible only by sea, no bigger than an aircraft carrier. Overshoot that and our lumbering C-46 would never make it over those giant trees for another try.

The landing gear lowered; the plane shook and groaned. I braced myself: We were going to crash! The plane descended in slow motion over a long dock jutting into Golfo Dulce Bay, as a ship was being loaded with bananas. With my eyes squeezed shut, I white-knuckled the armrests remembering our Pan Am jet's landing in Costa Rica's capital three weeks earlier and how I'd held my breath as ice and cups tumbled toward the cockpit. The plane came to a screeching halt at the edge of the runway, the pilot standing on the brakes! Braving a peek out the window as we taxied to the terminal, I realized disaster had been

averted by mere inches as our wing passed over a precipice and the thick jungle below.

Bumps and thumps inside the C-46 cabin jolted me back to my present peril, landing in Golfito. Sure the plane was resting on solid ground and wouldn't summersault into the giant trees, I exhaled the breath I'd been holding and swore I would never fly again!

Pullets squawked from crates strapped near the exit, their feathers exploding through wooden slats, floating dust and debris everywhere. I held my nose, but the increasing heat and humidity only made the unbearable stench worse. The passengers choked and gasped for air as we gathered our belongings and shoved our way toward the cleansing salty breeze coming from the open door.

Atop the airstair, I caught the perfume of exotic flowers, their dazzling colors all nestled in cool lush shades of green and spotted in dappled sunshine. What a contrast to the drab gray January landscape of Oklahoma! Coto, too, must be like this, and my new husband awaited me there. I was finally where I belonged!

It was only mid-morning and I was already melting. Aunt Mozy had never liked the word "sweat." It wasn't ladylike. But sweating off makeup in humidity that dissolved sprayed hairdos like cotton candy would soon seem like a petty concern. Dabbing a tissue at my sweat-soaked face, I gawked like a tourist when I should have been looking for my ride.

"You must be Maria. I'm Aurelio, but everyone calls me Lelo (pronounced like J-Lo). My jeep's over here."

"You speak English!" I said to the man with the big smile.

"Studied in the States. Even married an Okie girl. Ever hear of Pryor?"

"Sure! Just east of Tulsa."

"Carol — I call her Carolina — is from Pryor and can't wait to have someone here from Tulsa. Same for our kids, Beer-HE-nia (Virginia), Lucita (Little Lucy) and Popo."

"Popo?"

"When he first started talking, he said 'popo' instead of perro or dog. Guess it stuck. You do speak Spanish?"

"Sure... *tortilla, sombrero, mañana.* I can even count from one to twenty. But I understand more than I can actually speak."

"Carolina (Caro-LEEN-a) can teach you. She sounds more *Tica* than a *Tica!* That's a Costa Rican gal. *Ticos* for guys. Most can't tell she's gringa. By the way, never call us 'natives.' It's 'nationals,' if you please. Ever read *The Ugly American?*"

"Sure, before I came down."

"Good, only you shouldn't use 'down' here, either. Ticos think you're putting Costa Rica below the United States."

Try looking on any map, I thought, my indignant look not wiping off on the tissue, only more sweat. Lelo whipped around like he'd read my thoughts. "We're Americans, too," he said. "CENTRAL Americans, unless you want only gringos for friends."

A little humility won't hurt, I thought. *This is his country!* "Guess I've got a lot to learn," I smiled.

"Know how to tell Gringos are in your restaurant before you hear 'em talk? Black pepper and ketchup on their table," he laughed, turning to pick up my bags. "Can't eat without 'em!" Unamused, I picked up my makeup case to follow. "Know how to pick 'em out in a crowd?" he added. "They never shine their shoes! Worst of all they take 'em off when they come to visit. *Patas hediondas!*" he said, squeezing his nose and pointing at his upheld foot. I took this to mean, 'stinky feet.' "Gringos smile too much with strangers, talk too loud in public and

storm in and out like they own the place!" I politely smiled but was fuming inside. "Don't *preocoop!*" he said, setting my bags down behind his jeep. "Married to a Tico, you're one of us." "You may look gringa but with the heart of a Tica!"

His "compliments" left me cold. Black pepper? Ketchup? Stinky feet? Americans storm in and out? You bet! Making the impossible happen even in the land of mañana! Gringos indeed! He looks pretty "gringo" with those sky-blue eyes, reddish-blonde hair and mustache! Americans talk too much? We smile too much with strangers? I'm a stranger to him and he hasn't stopped smiling or talking yet!

Throwing myself into his beat-up jeep, I reached for a door to slam. There was none. "You can hang on to the dash bar," he said, seeing my concerned look. The jeep swayed violently through basin-sized holes and jarred our teeth over washboard ruts left from the rainy season that had dried hard as concrete in the summer sun. (And we were still in the parking lot!) I'd seen a shoreline road from the air I thought must go to Coto. But we took another route out of Golfito leading where all roads did — into the jungle.

"No time for a scenic tour," Lelo said, "I'm needed back. A handful of shops, houses and a small hospital make up the biggest little town this side of the border. They milk snakes here for their venom. Costa Rica discovered anti-venom, you know. There's our botanical garden." I turned as the white blur of its office building vanished behind a ten-foot hedge of red hibiscus.

Once I got near Coto, I thought all things green would be glistening in the sun. But dry season dust had roadside plants as dingy as Lelo's red jeep.

The minefield Lelo called a "road" wound around Golfito's hills, then turned straight and smooth. I began thinking of a disturbing incident that had occurred three weeks earlier on the way into San Jose from the International Airport.

MARY SUZANNE LOPEZ

Roberto was glad to be back home. Things were always better between us when he was happy. Leaning toward the window of the speeding cab, he cupped the back of my neck to bring me forward, too. "Mary Sue, what do you see?"

He knew I didn't like being touched there. Stretching and straining, I pretended I couldn't see so I could discreetly move out of his grasp, then leaned back into him with the warmth of a new bride. "Trees and bushes?"

"Nothing more?"

"Undeveloped property?" I said of the jungle whizzing past.

"Hardly!" He feigned self-control in a voice that was unnaturally soft. "The fence, *pendeja!*"

"What's that mean?"

"Never mind."

Looking again to please him, I shrugged in syrupy sing-song. "Nothing I can see, honey."

"Posts! The posts!" he said, now more agitated.

"Those saplings?"

"So perfectly spaced?" he said, swiping his finger across the vinyl upholstery behind the driver's head. "Ash from the *Irazú*."

"The volcano your mother wrote us about a month or two ago that belched 4,000 degree heat that killed all those poor people and animals?" I winced, remembering the accompanying newspaper photo of a melted Coke bottle. "There's only one, right?"

"Only one?" he said. "Try a hundred. Don't *preocoop*. About thirty are active."

In tiny Costa Rica? But I was more interested in the new word. "Pray-o what?"

"*Preocoop?* We 'gringo-ize' Spanish words to sound like English. *No se preocupe* (no say pray-o-coo-pay) becomes 'don't *preocoop*.'"

"But what's it mean?"

"It means, 'don't worry.' We also use a lot of American first names and words like 'taxi,' 'okay' and 'wow,'" he said, touching the end of my nose. "And don't interrupt me again," he playfully added, pushing his finger against my nose.

"Sorry," I sweetly smiled in deference.

"Volcanic ash makes Costa Rican soil some of the richest in the world," he went on. "Those *saplings* were fence posts until they sprouted roots and started growing again."

"That's not possible," I cooed, snuggling in like a silly school girl then raised back up all wide-eyed. "Is it?"

"It is here!" he said in pride at my amazement. "Remember the blossoms dotting those flat-topped trees as we landed?"

"The dark orange ones?"

"The only flowers we saw from the air, dum-dum!" he said stretching across my lap. "Look!"

"Where?" I said, straining to see.

"Up there!" he pointed.

"The trees with the wide canopies?"

"Of course, *pendeja!*"

"What's that mean?"

"Never mind. See the small trees beneath them?"

"You mean those bushes."

"Don't contradict me, *bruta!*"

"How am I supposed to know what coffee trees look like!" I said, feeling the sting of his insult.

"Watch... your... tone!" he warned. "I suppose since you weren't born here, people will excuse your ignorance."

"Ignorance?" I said, more hurt than before.

"Didn't you pay any attention in school? Ignorance means 'uninformed or unacquainted with,' not 'stupid.'" (He was proud of his English, which was actually very good.) "You'd best pay attention to this. Men are different here. They won't approach you as long as you're with me 'cause I'll take care of them. Of course, if a wife 'puts the horns' on her husband with another man, he can take them both out!"

I lowered my gaze. I didn't like it when he talked that way. He sounded like a gangster!

"But you're too sweet for that. That's why I married you. Wait till I get you home..." he smiled excitedly. I looked back up thinking he was about to tell me more about his family.

"...I'll show you my German Luger. I keep it cleaned and oiled just in case." *In case of what?* "I've also got a pearl handled, twenty-two revolver. Wanna learn to shoot? You're always wanting to get closer as a couple. We could go way out in the woods and target practice."

The sudden twinge of fear surprised me, but I nodded to please him and changed the subject. "Tell me again about all those places you're going to show me."

"Well," he said, leaning back, "you already know that Costa Rica means 'rich coast,' because of all the pirate gold that was buried in caves at low tide along the Caribbean coast and that there's a mountain near San Jose, where on a clear day, you can see the Caribbean and Pacific Oceans. I've told you about the beauty of the rain forests and that cascading waterfall we can picnic beside someday, about the short drive to the sugary white beaches of Limón on the Caribbean, and near Coto on the Pacific, that beautiful spot where we can lie beneath swaying palms on warm golden sands and listen to the pounding surf."

This was more like it! "Sounds yummy!"

"What I haven't told you is about the wonderful food here. None of that frozen, canned or prepackaged stuff. And Coto's fruit? Few gringos have tasted, much less seen it. Our national flower, an orchid called the *Guardia Morada,* grows there." Pausing, he gazed at me so intently, I thought I'd die. "Your eyes are green as the sea. God, I love you! Our life together will be one long head-spinning adventure! The stories you'll have to tell our grandkids! Grandkids?" he asked himself, looking surprised. "I can't even imagine us with kids!"

―――――――

"...But kids will be kids," Lelo laughed heartily. "Maria?" he shouted above the road noise.

"W...w...hat? Uh, sorry. Kids? That's cute! I was just wondering, Lelo. How tall do you think those trees are around Golfito?"

"They say between two and three hundred feet."

Lelo was just opening his mouth about to go on, when I interrupted. "Define some words for me."

"Sure," he said with all interest.

"Roberto recited a children's poem and wouldn't tell me what the last word meant."

"Can you remember the poem?" Lelo asked.

"It goes, *Piña para la niña, mora pa' la señora y fruta 'pa...?*" I looked at him and shrugged.

"*Fruta 'pa la gran puta.*" Like most Latinos, Lelo proceeded carefully, ever respectful of a married woman. "That's no children's poem! And I wouldn't repeat it!" he added, clearing his throat in embarrassment.

"Why?"

His face turned red. "I shouldn't say this to you in either language but *puta* means slut or whore," he said, wiping the sweat from his brow. "Hope the next word's nicer!"

"I'm not sure. *Pendeja?*"

"That's a vulgarity for 'stupid' that nice women don't use either. Some hefty potty words for your first three weeks here."

"Think I guessed the last one."

"What's that?"

"*Bruta.*"

"A rough word for 'stupid'!" he laughed.

I was right!

"Sounds like 'brute' as in brute beast, doesn't it?" he added.

How could Roberto say those things to me?

"Many Spanish words sound like their English equivalent like delicious or *delicioso*, but especially modern ones like telephone or *teléfono* and television or *televisión*."

Language interested me. I leaned in to hear better.

"English words ending in 'ty' are likely to end in 'dad' in Spanish like tranquility or *tranquilidad*. And there's as many English 'ly' words that end in the Spanish 'mente,' like sincerely or *sinceremente*. Then there's the easy-to-guess words ending in 'ion' like affection or *afección* and decision or *decisión*. But they're not all that simple. You'll be doing the grocery shopping. *Pollo* (poy-yo) or chicken might sound a little confusing to you, since cabbage is *repollo*. *Carne* or meat is easy enough, as in *chili con carne; chili* being pepper. Melon is *melón* and banana is *banano,* unless you're talking about the tiny, sweeter *camburitos.* Learn shapes: a city block is *una cuadra* or square. Coto 47 is *un círculo* or circle. Then learn colors or better yet, numbers for telling time and counting change. Two words will have you instantly communicating: *tengo* and *quiero*. *Tengo* (pronounced, tango) means, 'I am or I have' as in *tengo catarro;* 'I have a cold,' *tengo hambre,* 'I'm hungry' and *tengo sed,* 'I'm thirsty.' *Quiero* (pronounced key-arrow) is 'I love' or 'I want.'" Lelo was hollering above the road noise, which wasn't as bad as in San Jose, where delivery trucks and half the cars seemed to have no mufflers. I'm sure Lelo had one, it just didn't sound like it! The hot wind in our faces was like a blast furnace. I tried remembering the word for "thirsty" as Lelo droned on. "*Quiero comer,* 'I want to eat,' *quiero ir,* 'I want to go,' *quiero tomar,* 'I want to drink' and... "

Bingo! "*Quiero tomar!*" I blurted out.

"Very good, Maria! Then *quiero ver,* 'I want to see' and... "

"No, I mean, can we stop? I'm awfully thirsty. I thought we'd be in Coto by now. How much farther through this jungle?"

"Over an hour with nothing in between. I hate to say this, but you shouldn't use the word, 'jungle' here, either."

Oh brother! I turned away and rolled my eyes.

"It's 'rain forest.' But don't *preocoop.* Jungle is what it is! Hey, *preocoop* is... "

"Thank you, I already know! It's..."

We looked at each other and shouted together above the road noise, "Don't worry," which broke the ice. Lelo's eagerness to please and giddy

cheerfulness was irresistible. I'd have warmed up sooner, but for his comments on stinky feet and black pepper. But what he said next made me wonder why I had ever come to Costa Rica!

"Yep, it's a jungle out there," he said. "Take the jaguar. We call him *tigre* (tiger). His thick neck, muscular shoulders and powerful jaws make him the pit bull of the cat family. Then there's the ocelot we call *manigordo* or fat paw, because of his large paws."

He could tell I was scared and began to lay it on thick. A natural storyteller, many took Lelo's yarns as gospel.

"Every night," he went on, "Coto sprays for mosquitoes from the swamp that fly in carrying malaria and yellow fever. Too bad we can't spray for boas that come onto the farms that are big enough to swallow a child whole!"

"Roberto's dad, Don Vicente," I excitedly interrupted, "said he read an article in the paper about a multi-ranch round-up in Ecuador, where they found a forty-two foot snake with two large bulges inside. They opened it up to see if they could tell whose calves it had swallowed and found two of their cowboys! ...Are those snakes here?"

"Sounds like an anaconda. Those live in the Amazon. We have something better than that! Snakes that slither to the tops of trees. When she spots a nest of baby birds or a mouse on the jungle floor, she hurls herself into the air and glides onto her prey."

"Snakes that fly? That's not possible. Is it?" Imagining one gliding in behind me, I let go of the dash bar and grabbed the back of my neck just as Lelo jerked the wheel. Knowing where each chug hole was, he merrily chatted away, geared down, swerved around obstacles, then zoomed on.

"Sure it is!" he said. "Like hooded cobras, tree snakes flatten out part of their bodies which enable them to glide like flying squirrels. You'll probably never see one. They live way out in the jungle. Don't *preocoop!* Snakes come in, but they don't stay. Company gardeners keep

the farm grounds nice and clean so there's no place for them to hide." *Is that supposed to make me feel better?* "There is one exception, however." *Oh brother, here it comes!* "The coral snake, with poison similar to a cobra's. Do you know her?"

"Sure."

"Her head's so small, if she grabs a toe or a finger, she must chew to get her teeth in, leaving you time to brush her off."

Brush it off? Chills went up my spine.

"Of course, they have bright colors like poisonous frogs the Indians used for the tips of their arrows and blow darts. I've never seen one of these myself," he said, "but there's a lime-green snake that flattens out like a blade of Johnson grass and coils around banana stalks to catch flying insects, bats and small birds that eat bananas. One bit a twelve-year old boy harvesting with his dad and uncle. The uncle grabbed the boy's hand whacked off his finger and saved his life. An experienced harvester has a sixth sense about such danger. If you're ever walking with them and they suddenly stop dead in their tracks, you'd better, too! Boas have a nasty bite but aren't venomous. They come onto farms to hunt Coto's gigantic rats. The bushmaster snake, who's skin is beaded, is the most dangerous in all the Americas. Except for her rounded head, she resembles an American diamondback without the rattle. We call her, *cascabel muda,* or mute rattler. At over eleven feet, she's the largest pit viper in the world with an 80% mortality in humans. Venom from one bite is enough to kill fifteen men. Her extra long fangs inject an enormous volume of toxins into their prey, including one that decomposes flesh (like the flesh eating virus). By the time she's gagged the animal down, it's already half digested, so she can easily slither back into the tall grass to sleep off her meal, safe from the gardener's machete. If one ever bites you, pray it's morning. If she's killed that night, she'll have less venom and you might survive. But with venom that gums up circulation and dissolves flesh, even a bite on the

ankle can get your leg amputated to the hip, that is, if you reach help in time. And the hospital in Golfito is forty kilometers away. The bushmaster pretty much stays out in the jungle, but her cousin, the *fer-de-lance* doesn't. I remember her name, because her long slender head is shaped like a spearhead. She's called *tercipelo* for her soft, smooth skin. But 'velvet' is too pretty a name for a snake that kills like her. Coto's *campesinos* call her, *matabuey* (mata-buay) or ox killer, because she can kill a full-grown ox in twenty minutes. Why, she can strike a running horse seven times before it passes!"

How can I ever run fast enough from a matabuey? But Lelo still wasn't finished!

"We also have big red monkeys that abduct small women and children, who are never seen again. Then there's the ten fuzzy kinds of tarantulas, three of which are deadly."

Eyes bugged out, my mind in a whirl from Lelo's tales, down the gravel road we flew at speeds I wouldn't try on a dry paved street back home. Ahead was a bridge, if you could call it that: a wobbly structure with tire-width planks laid across its single lane. My brakes were through the floor, and I wasn't even driving!

I pushed the sticky clump of hair from my eyes. "We're not crossing *that*," I said, shoving it back again and holding it.

"Sure we are!" Lelo laughed.

It was too late to jump out! I gripped the bar and braced myself for the cold plunge.

"I crossed here this morning, Maria," he reassured me.

We eased onto the narrow span. Wood groaned and nails squeaked as though about to pull loose. Mid-way across, Lelo turned off the engine. "Why did we stop?" I asked afraid to stir in the slightest; barely able to move my lips.

"To listen to the water. Nice, huh?"

All I could hear was my pounding heart now uncomfortably lodged in my throat. I swallowed hard. It wouldn't go down. "We're so high!"

"See the banana trees up and down this canal as far as you can look?" he asked, blind to my fear.

No doors to the jeep or sides to the bridge afforded me a perfect view of the swirling black water below. Vertigo must have greened me around the gills, because he started the engine. I was never more happy to reach the other side of something in my life! And this was only the first of many such bridges, which he took at break-neck speeds, merrily describing more morbid details. "Lelo, when do we get to Coto?"

"We've been in Coto Valley for some time."

"Really?"

"Yeah, the Indians named it for the huge Coto gators. This valley has a rich history."

I shifted my weight in the seat and prepared for more.

"For centuries, indigenous people have known about Coto Valley. Instead of warring on each other, every ten years, they'd come from miles around for Olympic-type games that lasted a year. Whole families came to cheer their young men on, who were sometimes accidently killed. The young and old also died of natural causes and were buried here with their jewelry, pottery, stone statuettes and replicas of gods they fashioned from pure gold. Sometimes on weekends, we go out and hunt for buried treasure. We find gold but mostly junk, but you're welcome to join us."

"I'll keep that in mind," I said with an uneasy smile, unable to imagine desecrating graves as a weekend pastime.

We'd been out for two hours with no sign of civilization. *Lord, where's 47?* God must have been listening.

"Look, Maria! The turn-off to 47!" Lelo shouted.

Barely enough time to grab the bar, we hugged the tight corner and sped down another road in a cloud of swirling dust.

Roberto didn't like explaining things like Lelo. Maybe I'd better find out more before we got there. "Lelo, Roberto's always mentioning 51 and 48, but especially 47. Why the numbers?" My hair was stringy now and whipping my face numb, when at about Mach one, Lelo slid it into final gear and said, "United Fruit sectioned Coto Valley into farms, giving each a number. Forty-seven is the hub we call the *Zone*; a slice of paradise and the closest thing to civilization within forty kilometers. That's about twenty-seven miles to you."

I looked around in dismay. *This* was civilization?

"On the Zone are company office buildings, a school for the kids of management, pilots and mechanics. Some *campesíno* kids, who go elsewhere, have the brains to go further, like Enrique Villalobos, who started with us washing choppers. He showed mechanical aptitude and was sent to the States on the same government program as Roberto. He's due back with his American wife, Billie, any day.

"Next to our school is the cantina and dancehall we call the American Club, where we set up chairs for movies on weekends. Next to that is a small park, gardens, swimming pool and tennis courts, where we sometimes hold dances out under the stars. We have a restaurant, a church with an itinerant priest, a commissary and a grass airstrip next to our maintenance hangar and chopper pad, where single prop planes fly mail in and out with an occasional passenger brave enough to tag along. Roberto should take you up, sometime. There are no doors or dash bar to hold on to. But he'd fly safely and you wouldn't fall out."

No more flying! I thought, politely shaking my head.

"From up there, you'd see that 47 is a circle with a two-lane road and railroad tracks running through its middle. Opposite the half with offices, school, club and a few homes are most of the two and three bedroom houses on asphalt streets. Our restaurant is there, too, and two buildings that each have four one-bedroom apartments. Down the street, near the hangar, is another building with single rooms and private baths but no kitchens called the bachelor quarters for unmarried guys. Inside walls are studded and look unfinished here, because there's no need to insulate. All but bachelor and *cuadrante* housing are on stilts to keep out snakes, iguanas and other jungle animals."

"Iguanas? Are they very big?"

"Some about five feet long," he casually said. "Carry a flashlight when you're out at night. Concrete slab walks stay warm throughout nights that can plunge to three-blanket cold; snakes coil up there to keep warm. That's pretty much it. Carolina can tell you the rest."

There's more? I rolled my eyes.

Lelo pulled into the Zone circle and parked in front of a building surrounded by manicured grounds, the smell of flowers clearing the sting from my nostrils of newly asphalted roads. "We're here!" he said. "Don't forget lunch with us tomorrow and we'll see you at the movies on Friday." Leaping from the jeep, he whistled and waved, shouting *"Benny, por aca!"* (over here!) Roberto was called Benny, mostly by Americans, who couldn't prounounce his last name, *De Benedictis*.

Wind-blown and caked with grit, I was hardly the fetching vision I'd planned to be. But I was there! Practically rolling out of the jeep, my heart burst with joy as I took Roberto's hand. His look was troubled, though I hadn't been there long enough to do anything wrong.

"Our house won't be ready for two weeks," he confessed, "but I couldn't wait! Hope you won't mind staying at the bachelor's quarters."

"No, of course not!"

"I waited for you to have lunch. Hungry?"

"Try thirsty," I sighed.

"The restaurant's got pop, coffee, milk, beer and ice tea."

"I could drink it all!"

"Heat affects gringos that way," he casually said.

The next few weeks, we were invited to lunch with some of the pilots and mechanics Roberto had studied with in Tulsa. One of the wives loaned me her electric skillet and dishes. About as averse to a sunrise as Dracula, it was a major shock for me to get up at four-thirty to fix breakfast and see Roberto off.

Pilots were to be at the hangar by five-thirty, take-off by six, fly to assigned farms, where they filled thirty-gallon tanks on each side of their chopper with fungicide, then sprayed, refilled and sprayed until noon. There was no flying after lunch as the heat affected the helicopters.

I didn't mind that the tiny three-quarter bathrooms at the bachelor quarters had no shower curtains, but I did mind not having hot water! You'd think as sweltering as the days were, the water wouldn't be ice cold. The sink was too small to wash clothes in, so we paid Lelo's maid. The next day, it was back all ironed, folded and ready for the next load. Maids were no luxury even for wives like Carolina who had wringer washers. (No one had dryers.) Appliances cost double in Costa Rica, so Americans brought theirs from the States. Americans often drove to Panama for Stateside priced canned goods and clothing.

When Roberto left for work, I'd wash the skillet and dishes in the miniature bathroom sink and hang his bath towel to dry. It was frustrating having no broom or cleanser to scrub the sink and shower stall. Worst of all, I was bored with no radio or TV for company. When Roberto got back at noon, he'd clean up and we'd eat with friends or at the restaurant.

Lately, I'd been sleeping constantly. I'd just dozed off around six that first morning, when there came a loud thud that shook the room. An earthquake? I'd have been petrified to know it was probably an iguana falling out of a tree and onto the roof. Grabbing the .22, I sat up in bed, wedged it between knees drawn to my chin and listened for every sound. From then on, gun in hand, I'd stay awake until dawn to take care of anything that jumped through that window. It's a wonder I wasn't startled awake and blew my dang foot off!

Except for snakes, electricity and heights, I really wasn't afraid of much of anything. I hated the fainting heroine in movies, who when fleeing the monster *in heels,* would invariably sprain her ankle, forcing the hero to carry her to safety. None of that clinging vine stuff for me! Well, most of the time.

Cuadrante shacks and the bachelor quarters were the only ground-level buildings without window screens to keep out wild animals. On one occasion, while at the window frying eggs in the electric skillet, a face suddenly appeared out of the dark. It was Enrique Carr, one of the Costa Rican pilots, who was staying at the bachelor quarters until his wife and two boys arrived. Having crashed once, much of his forehead had been replaced with a metal plate. This sweet and gentle man had large bulging eyes and long deep creases down his face which by our room's dim light, made him look like the Frankenstein creature. "Enrique, you scared me!"

"Sorry, Maria," he said. "I smelled the eggs and wondered if you had a couple to spare?"

"Sure! How do you like 'em, hard yoke or over easy?"

"Just the eggs, please."

Cracking them on the windowsill, he swallowed them raw. I nearly gagged as I watched the slimy bulges slide down his throat. He thanked me and disappeared into the pre-dawn darkness.

Knowing no one in 47 gave me plenty of time to dwell on things that should have sent up red flags from the very first. I romanticized everything, including the incident that happened before Roberto left for Coto. He said it wouldn't happen again. But he had made that same promise after punching me on our wedding night.

―――――――

The first of the "head-spinning experiences" he'd promised (as if finding out about his guns didn't already do it for me) was the look on his mother's face when I stepped from the cab. He hadn't told them he was bringing home a wife, and a foreign one at that! I wanted the ground to open up and swallow me whole! After her initial shock, Doña Lydia couldn't have been nicer, indicating her welcomes in charades as she invited this stranger into her home. Roberto had already told me how proud she was of her French/Lebanese heritage.

Don Vicente, who spoke English with an Italian accent, offered a warm greeting. Roberto's teen sister, Andreina (Ann-DRAIN-ah) was cool and stand-offish. But ten-year-old Sandra made up for it with lots of laughter, hugs and kisses. A man in the shadows, beneath the eaves of the apartment building, was waved over to join us.

"Honey, this is my mother's brother, Tio Palanco. *Tio* is uncle. *Palanco*, not his real name, is masculine for *palanca*, meaning 'influence or pull.'" Tio Palanco nodded and extended his hand like he'd understood everything said about him in English. He didn't look influential in his wrinkled sports jacket, head full of thick curly hair needing cutting and his five o'clock shadow. He forced a smile, revealing several missing front teeth. His brooding, almond-shaped eyes held a strange sadness. Later on, I asked Roberto about him. "*Tio* had an American wife who lived here for several years. One day, she took their three children and left. Nobody knows why. He never talks about it."

Within an hour, the whole family was over for a welcome home party Doña Lydia had organized. My pocket dictionary proved useless; by the time I found the right word, the conversation had changed. Understanding some Spanish, but unable to answer quickly enough, I mostly smiled unless Roberto or his dad were there to translate. Everyone pronounced Mary, *Mah-dee* but couldn't get the "Sue" part, mistaking it for the Spanish word, *su*, meaning his, hers or its. When I wrote it down, they pronounced it *su-way*. (I wish I'd known at the time to tell them it was like "Susana.") *"What kind of name is su?"* they seemed to ask as they shook their heads and walked away. When someone finally called me Maria, people chummed up like long-lost friends.

How lucky was I? Here I was with a handsome husband, an exciting new life and a beautiful last name. I loved Roberto's full name: Roberto Rafael (Christian names) de Jesús (baptismal name) DeBenedictis (his father's last name, meaning, "of the blessing") Mongue (his mother's last name, which was French and I didn't know the meaning). Latino names tell who your parents are. If I'd been born Latina, my full name would have been Mary Suzanne de DeBenedictis Hoover, the "de" (of) meant I was married, or belonged to my husband.

An older woman standing nearby at the welcome home party introduced herself to me in English. "Your name is Maria?"

"Uh, yes, Maria."

"*Encantada*. I'm Inéz. How do you like it here?"

Recognizing *encantada* (enchanted) from movies like *Roman Holiday* and *West Side Story*, I returned, "*Encantada, Señora.*" Then in English, I said, "I love it here! Everyone's so nice."

"Good pronunciation," she smiled. "I hope you know more. Not everyone here speaks English, you know!"

"I'm trying, ma'am."

"English is a terrible language: their, there, they're; ... two, too, to; since, sense, cents. I thought I'd never learn! Practically no one spoke Spanish where I lived in the States," she said. "It had the funniest name. People were called rednecks, whatever that is. Now I remember. Oklahoma! Where are you from, dear?"

"Sand Springs, a small town west of Tulsa."

"And that's in...?"

"Oklahoma."

"Yes, well," she said, obviously embarrassed, "languages can be difficult *and* discouraging."

"Yes ma'am, I'm somewhat discouraged, myself."

"Well, don't worry, dear. Some people never learn another language. There's one word you'll hear a lot here, though. *Preocoop,* from the Spanish word, preo...."

"Thank you, I already know that one."

"Good! And do you have your *cédula?*"

This word I didn't know. "A what?"

"*Cédula,* dear, an ID card with your picture, thumb print, nationality and physical description. If you can't produce it when the police ask, you can be arrested. It's the law!"

Listening nearby, Roberto stepped over and in English said, "Doña Inéz! So good to see you. You mentioned *cédulas?* You know she doesn't need one with our connections."

"But I don't want to break the law," I said, looking up.

"Then tell them who you are," Roberto said.

"Who am I?"

"*La* (the wife of) *de* DeBenedictis, who they won't dare touch!"

He knew best. After all, this was his country.

The next day, my first full day in Costa Rica, I learned that mornings were when people came to call. First to call was the wife of one of the four fixed wing pilots the Costa Rican government sent to the States for rotary wing training. Don Vicente's political connections got Roberto in.

Nena was already seated when Roberto ushered me into the living room and sat down beside me. Nena (Nay-nuh), meaning "baby" was a good name for her. Though in her mid-thirties, Nena had a girlish way about her and an infectious smile that lit up the room with her energy and vivacity. She awkwardly balanced a gift for me (a common gesture on first visits and special occasions) on one forearm and picked at the lid of the flimsy box. Finally opened, she shoved it under my nose, speaking sixty miles an hour with Roberto translating as fast as he could. "Hi, Maria, I'm Alan's wife, Nena. Sorry to bring something from a bakery, but my oven's out." (Home baking was more prized.) The cake, in the shape of an oversized ear of corn, was frosted in autumn golds, burnt oranges, russets and greens.

"It's wonderful!" I said. "Fall's my favorite season, when the air's cool and crisp and trees are ablaze with color! Guess I missed my first Costa Rican autumn."

"There's only two seasons here," Nena laughed: "dry and rainy. It's summer now, when everyone goes to the beach. Do you have nice beaches where you're from?"

"The closest beach is Galveston, about eight hundred miles away!" I laughed. "Besides, there's no swimming, now."

"Why?"

"Because back home, January is snowy and freezing cold!"

"I've never been freezing cold. Are snowy days like they show in movies, really cold?"

"Not while it's snowing. It's colder the next day."

"Gwow!"

'W's' were pronounced with a hard 'G' sound. But being the foreigner there, I didn't laugh or even smile.

"Does your breath smoke or is that a movie trick?"

"It's no movie trick only we call it, 'fog.'"

"Gwow! I'd like to see snow, someday. What does it taste like, Maria? Is it good?"

"I don't know, I suppose it tastes like rain. When I was little, Mama would go out and put snow in a pan, add sugar, vanilla and milk and make snow ice cream."

Nena got a dreamy look. "Gwow, ice cream from the sky! What a wonderful place your home must be! You must tell me more when you get to Coto. It's hot there. In San Jose, it's summer heat and mosquitoes and later, winter colds with drenching rain and flu!"

It was how she said it that made me laugh. My hand flew to cover my mouth. "I'm sure you're exaggerating!"

"No, I'm not! You'll see."

When Nena stood to leave, I saw she was nearly my height in black patent heels that accentuated her long, plump legs. In Latin America, thin wasn't "in." Nena, the typical full-figured woman in her tight leopard print dress, had an earthy cleavage bursting from her plunging V-neckline, dangly earrings playing peek-a-boo through frizzed, fly-away hair that framed a face where the wrong shades of make-up had been improperly applied. She put on no airs. What you saw was what

you got: her friendly, cheery smile and sincere loving heart made it hard not to like her. But our friendship was never to be.

Maybe it was because her husband, Alan, spoke with a lisp that he thought he had to constantly *prove* his "manhood." He wasn't bad looking, even with his quarter-moon profile and protruding chin. His Elvis sideburns and the strand of hair that fell over his forehead gave him a "bad-boy" look. Other than his one physical detraction, a heavy five o'clock shadow, he was always immaculately groomed in American Western shirts and cowboy boots he kept to a spit shine. Quiet and sullen, he had banished Nena's older son from a previous relationship to her mother's house in San Jose. It broke her heart, but she stood by her man. When they moved next door to us on 51, rumors of abuse were confirmed. Everyone heard her being knocked around early one morning and heard the perfume bottles hitting the wall. Later, those fragrances drifted into the other houses. Nena kept to herself for weeks until the bruises faded.

It's hard to think of her any other way but smiling as she did the day she brought the "corn" cake. After she left, Doña Lydia got out her baby pictures and Don Vicente translated. Roberto was so cute. And our baby would look just like him!

Sitting next to Roberto on the arm of the rosy pink easy chair, his arm tensed and mood changed as he scrunched into the vinyl chair dingy with volcanic ash.

"I gave him diluted Jell-O to drink," his mother began. "Strengthens the bones, you know." I didn't contradict her, though Stateside doctors were now trying to change this misconception. "Not wanting sticky furniture or stained school clothes, I kept giving it to him in baby bottles."

Roberto's teeth were grinding. Didn't they hear it?

"Baby bottles were ruining his teeth and braces would cost us a fortune. He was sixteen when I brought him his last bottle. I thought his friends who were there would never stop laughing!"

After lunch, Doña Lydia napped and Roberto sulked. I tried comforting him but he pushed me away, so I watched a TV soap opera set in Chile in the 1500's called, *"Fray* (Fry) *Escoba,"* using Old Spanish thees and thous. (I was surprised to later find that *vos sabeis* (bos-sah-VASE, "thou knowest") was used in Costa Rica. *"Fray Escoba"* was a story about the son of a Spanish Conquistador and black slave, who loved God and grew up to be a Franciscan Monk. Monastery "brothers" gave him menial jobs like peeling potatoes and sweeping floors, which he cheerfully did. Thus, the name, *Fray Escoba* (Brother Broom). After supper, he'd take table scraps to the poor down in the village. Opening his basket, he would discover that the peels, cores and crusts had become whole potatoes, fruit and fresh loaves. Doña Lydia said he was the saint of the hopeless.

Roberto suddenly tapped me on the shoulder. "Let's get out of here." We walked a block or two. "She shouldn't have told you all that. For Christ's sake, I'm twenty-two! I'm a man and my friends still call me, *Chilindrín* (Chee-leen-DREEN)!

"What's that?"

"Everyone here has a nickname. Baby Rattle's mine." He turned away in shame.

"How could she humiliate you like that?"

He didn't answer.

"I'm leaving for Coto tomorrow. *Avenida Central* (Central Avenue) is close. Let's go downtown and look around a while."

He was still fuming on the way back, when I suggested we stop at a cute, sidewalk café. He led me to a back table next to a man reading a newspaper and sipping coffee. The waiter reeled off a list of soda pops, local and foreign beers, and fresh juices, then took our order and left.

Roberto sat quiet, tense, and distant. I was so childishly innocent, never realizing he was fuming about how I'd pushed him into marriage and that he now felt trapped. Roberto knew his mother concealed her objections to our marriage around me. I was about to mention how nice the café was when he said, "You ordered *piña*, didn't you?"

"*Piña?*"

"Pineapple. Next time, ask for *fruta*."

"Why? Is *fruta* better? Silly! Why didn't you tell me, sooner?" I laughed. Then my face turned as serious as his. "What's *fruta?*

"Mary Sue, consider this your first Spanish lesson:

> *Piña para la niña,*
> *mora pa' la Señora,*
> *Y fruta pa' la gran puta!*"

"This is fun! I think I got 'em all, except for *mora*."

"Blackberry," he answered with indifference.

"And *fruta* is fruit, right? Okay:

> "Pineapple for the little girl,
> blackberry for the married lady, right?
> and fruit for the big 'what'?"

"I'll tell you, later," he said flatly, without looking up.

"You're not going to leave me in suspense, are you?" He did the "guy thing" and ignored me. Exasperated, I flopped back in my chair and just as quickly flew forward again. I wasn't one to give up that easily! "Please!" I begged.

"Later!"

I had to know what *puta* meant! I tried tickling him. I confess I was cutting up and laughing too much in public. "Come on, what's *'fruta pa' la gran puta'* mean?"

"Keep your voice down, *bruta!*"

Bruta? Sounds like brute. Surely he wouldn't say that to me! I'm only trying to cheer him up and learn a new word.

He clammed up, so I glanced around to soak up the local color. The place was decorated for tourists with Indian pottery, stone statues, wood carvings and a big conga drum next to a bushy potted palm. On the walls hung guitars, maracas, and oil landscapes, while on the ceiling hung twisted crepe someone had forgotten to take down from Christmas. I loved it! I happened to glance past Roberto's glowering, blood-red face. His eyes were riveted on me. "What's wrong?" I asked with a nervous little laugh.

"You know!" he growled, teeth gritted.

"No, I.... "

"Look, stop it!" he shouted.

Embarrassed, I looked around to see if we were disturbing others. "Stop what?" I whispered.

He motioned with his chin at the man sitting behind him. "See that guy?" he loudly whispered.

"I do, now," I said, looking over Roberto's shoulder.

"Stop staring, will you?"

"But you said...."

"I don't care! Stop!"

"Okay!" I shouted back in a whisper. I'd answered too sharply. But my real sin was my indignation at his jealousy. His eyes narrowed.

"You're not in the States. Everything here is flirting!"

"You're kidding!"

"Keep looking at him and I'll have to take care of this!"

"But...."

"Shut up! Our drinks are here." Chugging his, he slammed his glass down so hard I thought it would shatter. Impatiently drumming his fingers on the table, he waited until I finished sipping mine through the tiny paper straw. Then shooting to his feet, he shoved his chair against the wall with the backs of his knees and slapped some coins on the table. "Let's go!"

I quietly followed. We'd gone about half a block, when I thought I should say something. "Honey, I.... "

He looked behind him, then all around; the coast was clear. With clenched jaw, he grabbed the front of my blouse and hustled me into a wall. "Shut up, and listen! You're in my country, now! Don't ever make eye contact with *any* man! Got it? From now on, you will bow your head, fold your hands and walk next to walls like a nun." Leaning into me, he pinned my shoulder to the wall. "Like this! Got it?"

I nodded, trembling.

"Another thing. You called me 'silly' a minute ago. Don't do it again!" He backed-off and walked away.

Eyes welling, I tried swallowing the growing lump in my throat, when Daddy's words broke through the deafening silence like thunder. "Mister, soldiers don't cry!" I snapped to attention with chin up and shoulders back. *Ow, that hurt!* Mama always said "put one foot in front of the other." My feet obeyed as I solemnly followed Roberto back to the apartment.

I would soon learn that it wasn't what a woman did here, but what others *said* she did that got her beat up or killed. Her own word meant nothing; she needed a witness to her integrity. That's why girls still took aunts and little sisters as chaperones on dates, and married women went places together whenever they could. So I learned to go nowhere without Roberto's mother or sisters; a major drag for an American used to her freedom.

Gossip was a national pastime. Doña Lydia gossiped about everybody, including Nena's husband, Alan, whose mother had worked on a plantation as a maid until she turned up in a family way. It didn't matter that the father, a British gentleman, had done the "right thing" by marrying her, had actively participated in the rearing of their son and provided for and kept his family together all those years. One thing about it, no one could gossip about me walking "improperly" down a street with Roberto around to teach me. What a load off!

Emotionally drained upon arriving at his parents' apartment from our walk downtown, I went in to lie down. When Roberto came in, I pretended to be asleep. He contoured his body behind me and held me close. "Look, I'm sorry. Something just comes over me. I go nuts! I've dreamed of punching her in the face! Better yet, putting a bullet between her eyes."

"Who?" I asked, spinning around in astonishment.

"Mamá!"

When I gasped, his demeanor changed as quickly as a switched-on light. He was real good at that.

"Of course, I can't do that, so I yell and cuss or punch a wall! Look, I took my frustration out on you and I'm sorry. I should've gone out alone. Walking helps me cool down." I didn't answer. "I've never needed anyone, before. I thought I could walk off the anger and show you around at the same time — you know, like killing two birds with one stone."

Kill? Stone? He has such a way with words!

"Look, I was lonely. You make me feel strong, powerful; like I can do anything! All I can say is I'm sorry and it'll never happen again. I promise! When my uncle dies, I'm next in line for the family title. You'll be a baroness someday. I know you don't care about all that, but stay anyway. I can make you happy. Look, I can't go to Coto thinking you might leave me. A pilot must keep his mind on flying. They'll have me in the air the minute I get there." I said nothing. "Don't do this to me, Mary Sue!"

Did it always have to be about him?

"I know it's been hard on you. But it won't always be like this. Give me another chance. Please?"

If I believed what the church taught about marriage, why was everything inside me screaming to run? Was he sorry? Could he really change? Could I forgive him, and the real question: Should I? But wasn't "to err human and forgive divine?" Wasn't the husband the head and the wife his helpmate? Wasn't marriage a holy state before God and vows not to be taken lightly? Mama always said "A woman worth her salt keeps her marriage together no matter what!" But if staying was right, why did it feel so wrong? If I only had time to think!

"I can't leave all worried!" he said. "Tell me, now!"

"Okay!" I'd raised my voice to him. My eyes shot to his. I prefaced my intention to stay with, "Don't *preocoop*, I...."

"You mean, you forgive me? My God, how did I ever get a girl like you? Now, I'll never let you go!"

Though his words lacked the comfort he'd intended, perhaps it was nobler to stay. Mama had been a trooper through a difficult marriage. I would be, too. He didn't mean it. He was just on edge with his new job and needed to blow off some steam. Men have to do that, you know. Wives must make adjustments and give their marriage time. I tried to

cheer myself up by remembering what Aunt Mozy would say, "Chin up, my girl! We're pioneer stock!"

That night, we were invited for drinks and hors d'oeuvres at Roberto's cousin's. Conversation began in English but soon changed to Spanish, leaving me to my coke and piles of boiled shrimp, which I'd never had before. Lately, I'd been so hungry, I was eating anything that wasn't nailed down or getting up and running away from me! Maybe it was the zesty cocktail sauce that had me hooked. Like everyone else, I wolfed the shrimp down as fast as they came only to get an all night tummy ache.

Next morning, I was glad Roberto didn't leave from El Coco International, where we'd landed a few days earlier, but instead from the old airport within the city they now used for small aircraft. My eyes welled with tears as his plane gathered speed down the grass field for take off, then disappeared into the dreary haze.

Without Roberto, life lacked color as I rode back with his parents beneath bleak skies. What gray volcanic ash wasn't on cars and buildings had been swept into piles along the streets. Everything looked so drab. The nearly unbreatheable San Jose air was nauseatingly sweet like maple syrup. I covered my nose with the empty sleeve of my sweater. But even inside the apartment there was no escaping it. That smell was everywhere!

Montezuma's Revenge left me with the unsavory dilemma of rushing to the bathroom, not knowing which end to point at the john first. What was worse, the commode not only overflowed, it backed into the shower stall. Too sick and weak to clean it up, I shivered beneath my covers, mortified by the terrible impression I was making on my new in-laws.

Doña Lydia was sweet, bringing one-liter glass bottles of hot water to lay against my tummy, followed by gelatin and chicken broth when I was able. She even sat with me while I recovered and brought photos of Roberto to keep me company. Family visited; even a friend of Roberto's.

I'd never received company in bed before. Doña Lydia ushered him in like it was the most natural thing in the world. Knowing the rules women had to follow and that her son had a hair-trigger temper, why let a man in my room at all? Latino mothers and sons have a special bond. I didn't know it then, but she considered me an intruder who had just robbed her of her precious son.

CHAPTER TWO
COTO 47

The two weeks in Coto's bachelor quarters passed quickly, and we were finally notified of the availability of a house on Farm 51. With nothing but luggage, moving into a furnished house was like falling off a log. Lelo made out like a bandit, ending up with our guestroom dresser and twin beds as his reward for helping us move. Lelo's large family also needed a bigger fridge, so we traded ours for his smaller one that barely made enough ice, kept ice cream soupy and would need defrosting every week. I didn't buy much ice cream, so it really didn't matter. The only flavor was *ron con pasa* (rum raisin). Nasty!

Farm 51 originally had six houses but one of the four with two bedrooms burned down. The two with three-bedrooms stood at the curve of the sidealk on the far end. Two by two concrete slabs formed a horseshoe-shaped sidewalk around an immense center yard that led to every door. Another walk down the palm-lined middle which led to a dirt road out front, must have been for show, for it was only used by gardeners, maids and strangers on foot. Residents and guests always entered from side parking.

In the pre-dawn light of our first day there, I watched from the front door as Roberto walked towards Lelo's to ride to work. Out front, *campesinos* walked to fields, machetes slung over their shoulders that nearly dragged the ground. Rumor had it that there was strife in Panama and people were being hacked to death. Even though our house was high on stilts, I continued to take the revolver to bed with me. I didn't know it yet, but *campesinos* were some of the gentlest people I would ever know.

The day we moved in, the grass was short as Lelo said it would be, especially around the sidewalks and bushes pruned from the bottom so nothing could hide beneath them. Shade trees surrounded each house. An avocado tree in a back corner towered over a fragrant citrus orchard. Flowers were everywhere, even wild orchids!

On the long trek from parking around the "horseshoe" to our house, we could see three teenage boys bending over, their bare-backs glistening in the blazing sun. They made level swings across the grass with a long object, then would stand and rub it against a stick in their other hand.

"Why are they beating the grass with sticks?" I asked.

Lelo glanced up and chuckled. "Those aren't sticks, they're machetes and a metal rod to keep them razor sharp for cutting grass!" Lelo replied nonchalantly.

"You're kidding!"

"Nope. They're the gardeners on 51."

"Aren't there any lawn mowers down... I mean, here?"

"No need for 'em."

"But it's such hard work."

"They're young, healthy and used to hard work. Boys around here would give anything for this cushy job to help support their families until they're old enough to move up."

"Move up to what?"

"To real work in the banana fields or the box factory. Out here, kids start working at twelve."

"Shouldn't they be in school?"

"Public school is free through the sixth grade. Boys don't need brains to rake leaves, do field work or pack bananas. Girls work as nannies until they're strong enough to be live-in maids. It takes muscles to wring-out towels, sheets and blue jeans. You'll be needing a maid soon."

Giving the boys a last glance, I followed Lelo and Roberto around the horseshoe, shaking my head and clicking my tongue. *If a son of mine ever complains about having to cut our grass, I'm going to tell him how lucky he is to have a mower!*

Our house was no wider than a double-wide mobile home and half as short. From the front bedroom where we set the luggage, we could see a second bedroom connected by a three-quarter bath. In the combined living/dining room was a bamboo loveseat and an easy chair in green fabric. With that heat, I was just glad it wasn't vinyl. Everything looked so bare, now that the American pilot Roberto was replacing and his Italian wife had moved out. Aurelia had framed photos, knick-knacks and potted plants on tables, the floor and along the window ledges running the length of the combined living and dining rooms. In a corner by the front door, was a small cascading fountain surrounded by various plants. There were no drapes to collect mold and dampness on the huge screened picture windows in the main rooms. Rain was kept from blowing in by an outside canvas that could be rolled down from the inside. We only used it once during a hurricane Lelo said knocked down over a million banana trees. Cutting one down merely took one swipe of a machete through their scroll-like trunks.

The main rooms of our home afforded a lovely view of jet black orange-winged orioles. I'd never seen such intense colors!

The sturdy nutmeg dining room table and chairs were unpretentious and mismatched with an old-fashioned ornate black buffet.

ALL THE WAY HOME

The kitchen table top, sink and countertops were metal. A modern cooking range stood next to the screened-in porch, complete with a propane cylinder delivered to the tenant about every six weeks (I believe) for about ten dollars or eighty colones. (Roberto always paid.) On the countertop was a heavy ceramic cylinder which held a couple of gallons of water. Although it wasn't there for looks, I liked its stylish cream glazed finish and wide sage stripe. Its top half had a five-inch thick stone that fit the bottom like a glove. Water seeped to the bottom half, where drinking water was dispensed through a turn spout. About once a month, pea-size chunks of a black, fishy-smelling sediment would sputter from the tap. Some joked our water came from the swamps. A clean cloth tied to the faucet caught most of it. The stone filter got the rest.

Water had to be boiled anyway, so I'd keep pitchers of cold tea in the fridge. Never having liked the taste of water, I'd long since pronounced it only fit for bathing. It never occurred to me I might actually need it in all that heat! I thought I got enough fluids each day downing a pitcher of tea, six to eight bottles of pop from the commissary and the daily two or three quarts of milk delivered to our house. In 1964, who knew about proper hydration? Eating well was my measure of good health. Every two weeks, the company would hang a free stalk of bananas and half a stalk of *plátanos* (plantains) on a tree next to our backdoor. The rest, we bought at the commissary.

Thanks to Lelo, I'd already learned the names of many foods. I even practiced by writing my first grocery list in Spanish, which was a good thing, because the commissary wasn't self-serve. Humidity made the paper bags so wet, they easily tore, so women brought their own bags called *bolsas,* made from woven strands of rope. *Bolsa* was also the word for purse and wife, as in "old bag." Grocery items came in only one brand, many of them American. Pronouncing familiar products was nearly as hard as learning a new word. Colgate was *Col-GAH-tay* and Ajax, *Ah-HOCKS.*

Carolina was the first to take me shopping. Even though she was multi-talented and capable, she was disorganized and slow as molasses. "The kids will be home from school, soon," she said. "We'd better hurry. Do you have your list?"

"In my purse," I said

"Good! How was your first night in your new house?"

"Fine, except the water was so cold, I had to wait till eleven to shower."

"Wait till you roll over in bed and the sheets stick to you," she laughed. "Humidity even gets into the saltshakers. Better keep yours dry in the oven with the pilot lit."

"I didn't know they had saltshakers down…, I mean, here. Roberto's family dips the end of their butter knife into a tiny bowl of moist salt and taps it over their food. I've gotten pretty good at it."

"At fancy dinners," she commented, "there's a salt bowl at each plate. Make sure you keep your cookies, crackers and dry cereal in the oven, too, to keep them fresh and crispy. By the way, we keep closet lights on at night, so our shoes and belts don't mildew. Speaking of shoes, shake 'em out before putting them on. You never know what might have crawled in at night!"

Shuddering, I asked, "What's at the commissary?"

"Like old general stores, everything! Dry goods such as…."

"I mean food," I interrupted.

"Main staples and a few canned goods."

With its unpainted plank exterior, weathered and gray, the commissary was nothing like the Safeways back home. Four-feet off the ground, it was no bigger than a convenience store today. Doors were open from sunrise to sunset for workers living in back, in the *cuadrante* (quarters).

Refrigerators were luxuries, so perishables were bought just before cooking on their kerosene stoves.

Inside, we clomped across wide, dusty plank floors that were splintered and worn. Hanging from twelve-foot ceilings were all kinds of tools, iron skillets, pots and pans, oil lamps and long and short machetes in leather sheathes with colorful plastic fringe. These dusty items were tangled in wispy webs like they'd hung there for years.

"Don't they rotate merchandise with sales like they do in the States?"

Carolina didn't hear me. She was already at the long wooden counter, reading her list to the clerk. Behind him were floor-to-ceiling shelves covering the entire wall with cans of juice, tomato paste, canned sardines, squid, octopus and an assortment of Campbell's soups. I'd have bought tomato soup, but they wanted six colones a can (one whole dollar) instead of the eleven cents it cost in the States!

There was no dish washing liquid. Instead, women had to play slip and catch with the laundry powder some of the luckier wives used in their ringer washers. Everyone bought the huge bars of lye soap for scrubbing clothes by hand.

Sandwich bread in wax paper wrappers with faded, black print were plentiful and stacked on the shelves. Most, however, preferred the unsliced round-top in the old-fashioned wood and glass case next to the register. The clerk would remove it with his bare hands, wrap it in small, thin, square, brown-paper sheets and tie it at the top with the ends sticking out. Except for French loaves for garlic bread, I'd never seen unsliced bread before.

I'd also never seen five-pound rolls of *mortadela* (bologna), or tasted salami. Remember the Popeye cartoons on TV? "Salami, salami, bologna." The salami was great with mustard. I bought a roll of each every week.

It was a good thing Carolina was there to help me count the "Monopoly Money," because merchants often short-changed kids, simpletons and foreigners.

Unlike in the United States, in Latin America lunch is the main meal of the day. Roberto only wanted meat, potatoes, rice, black beans and salad. If I dared serve anything "fancy," he'd curse the air blue and knock me around. As I learned to cook, and often burnt our meals, he said nothing. I think he liked the restaurant's *bisteks* (beefsteaks), which were nothing like those served in an American steak house. The dish he always ordered came in a sauce from sautéed onions, bell peppers, tomatoes and *Salsa Inglesa* (English sauce: a runnier local copy of Lea and Perrins) ladled over steaming rice. It smelled wonderful, but I couldn't chew it. The meat there was tough because without commercial refrigeration, it had to be sold the day of slaughter. Or it might have been that the thin *bisteks,* cut along the length of the muscle, made them tough as shoe leather.

As time passed, I began craving foods like cashews you couldn't buy in Coto, and was happily surprised when within reach of our back steps grew a *marañon* tree. At the bottom of each small, pear-shaped fruit was a quarter moon-shaped growth. When the maid told me what it was, I shouted, "Cashews? How do I roast them?"

"No, Doña!" she warned. "If not processed in a factory, they're poison." What a disappointment!

But I was pleasantly surprised to find some favorites: glazed donuts, thousand island dressing, peanut butter, marshmallows, powdered sugar for cakes and donuts, all made by Coto's women in their own kitchens! But, one thing I couldn't buy or make at home was popcorn. To satisfy my craving, I came up with what became a big hit among our friends. I fried tortilla strips with butter and salt and voilá, we had corn chips! But I did more at the movies than just munch a bunch. Pointing and asking, "What's that?" at the open market had taken me only so far.

ALL THE WAY HOME

Weekend movies in German, French, English, Italian, and even Hebrew with Spanish subtitles expanded my language skills even further. My favorite film, *"Orfeo Negro"* (Black Orpheus), a Brazilian tear-jerker, involved an electrocution, which got my immediate attention. It won the Golden Palm at Cannes. When watching British and American films, I listened and compared English dialogue to Spanish subtitles and before long, I could fully enjoy any film they showed. Not only did my vocabulary increase, but my sense of tone, inflection, sentence construction and grammar, too. Films from Spain and Mexico helped me understand Costa Rican cultural norms and the hand gestures used in speaking. I also learned that while men could smile in public, it was taboo for a woman to do so. Men considered a woman's innocent inadvertent smile or eye contact to be an open invitation. And if a man was rebuffed, he could retaliate by smearing her reputation, that is, unless she was accompanied by a respectable woman. Except for flirting, men who smiled excessively in public were thought to be either fools or con artists. American Missionaries from the language school must not have known this, because they were always ignored when trying to talk to people in grocery lines or at bus stops.

Unlike the women in Costa Rica, people expected men to be blatant womanizers! Men were gossiped about as being homosexual if they didn't have a lover stashed away on the side somewhere. It was common for wealthy men to buy houses and apartments for their *paramours* and wives forced to put up with it. I was naive to expect cultural differences and no cultural shocks.

Gossip was a way of life. Through the grape vine is how I found my first maid. Carolina put out the word and a middle-aged woman showed up at my house the very next day. Carolina even helped me interview and hire her. After the next day's washing, the maid came upstairs and started talking. After a futile attempt to communicate with her using the dictionary and sign language, I asked Carolina to come over to help. "She wants to know," Carolina asked, "if you want her to hang the clothes out to dry now?" I had to wonder, *what else do you do with wet laundry?* Misunderstandings like this were common occurrences over the next few days, and finally, she just didn't return. So, Carolina put out the word to neighbors again. Mid-morning a few days later, a couple and two adult family members escorted a fifteen-year old to my home. This would be her first live-in work away from the watchful eye of her parents, and I soon discovered it was I who was being interviewed for the job.

With Carolina's approval, the family took the girl and her meager belongings to the maid's quarters under our house on stilts. That Lilliputian room, now her home, had a small cot and dresser, a stool and tiny bathroom, its toilet inches from a pint-sized curtainless shower.

With the girl comfortably settled in, her family said good-bye and began the long walk home. Nearly lunchtime, it was too late to get much wash done, so I showed her around the kitchen so she could get a bite to eat. Roberto didn't like maids using ketchup or steak sauce, but I let them have it on the sly. Dressed and ready to go with Roberto to lunch at the restaurant, I watched her cook, hoping to learn something.

A pretty girl, Cecilia had thick, short, black hair in soft curls; gorgeous eyes, perfectly formed ultra-bright teeth and a smile to die for. She not only was polite, sweet, considerate, cheerful and eager to please, but worked quickly and quietly, never wasting food or cleaning supplies. She took special care of our meals, clothing and meager possessions as if they were the crown jewels, and seemed to almost caress the furniture as she polished it.

Carolina had mentioned to me that by law, maids only got Sunday afternoons off, but I gave her half of Saturday, too. When her parents came that first Sunday to walk her home, they couldn't thank me enough. But, I couldn't get away with paying her a *centimo* over a hundred colones as it would have forced the other wives to increase their maid's pay, too.

"Fifteen dollars per month seems so little!" I argued with Carolina.

"Stop thinking in dollars and Stateside pay scales!" she replied. "Income fits the cost of living anywhere in the world."

Food was certainly a bargain. A week's worth of groceries and supplies were a hundred colones. The best prices in meat and fresh produce were in Villaneily (Vee-ya-NAY-lee), about six miles east, across the "big" intersection. I expected it to be a paved highway; instead it was a dirt road with near zero traffic. North went to San Jose and south to Panama. On the southeast corner of Villaneilly's entrance was a big red sign, familiar the world over: *Tome Coca Cola, bien fría!* (Drink ice cold Coca Cola!)

Before Villaneily existed, before the farms were numbered, before banana fields were planted, United Fruit had called nationwide for field workers. But the response was minimal, despite high pay and free housing. The biggest objections were twofold: living in the boonies, and no women. So the company built two and three story buildings along the highway, furnished them, brought in prostitutes from the cities and Villaneily was born, along with many babies! Men began marrying these women and moving their new families into free housing *cuadrantes* behind the commissary and outlying farms. These unpainted, dilapidated shacks with only shutters to keep out rain and vermin dotted the landscape.

As cantinas sprang up, couples began dancing Friday and Saturday nights, leaving children and infants home alone. Often parents would return home to find their baby's fingers, toes, nose or ears chewed off by rats. Housecats didn't survive in Coto because the chemical sprayed on bananas did something to their nervous systems, leaving rats to grow as big as housecats. Even with all this, disadvantaged women looking for a better life and a chance to marry flocked to Villaneily. With all this growth, the buildings continued to go up, some with storefronts so tenants could start their own businesses. It was a great opportunity for many.

Villaneily had a small *mercado* (market place) with meats and produce. Customers weren't the only ones buzzing around the butcher's stand. You had to get there early to beat the flies, as animals were slaughtered that morning and their meat hung in the open air. Popular *lomito,* the most desired cut, was our favorite. Roberto loved meat, so I bought a whole *lomito* about every week. The cow's head was even hung up. *Who would buy that?* I often wondered, until I heard that boiling the eyes and inhaling the broth up the nose was a remedy for epilepsy. Sounded more like a prescription for drowning to me!

The local butcher was a "full service" kind of guy, who even ground hamburger then handed it to me wrapped in a leaf! There was no heavy, white butcher paper. Strong and supple *plátano* (plantain) leaves are unlike banana leaves that tatter and tear, so people remove the center vein, cut them into large squares, wipe them with a damp cloth and use them for wrapping foods. *Plátano* leaves also lent a wonderful flavor to hot tortillas and Christmas tamales.

Plátanos look like giant bananas and are eaten green or ripe. Green was my favorite. I would score them and pry off the peel, slice them thin with a potato peeler, then fry and salt. They were great plain or with guacamole and other dips. But I never did develop a taste for ripe *plátanos,* which can be flattened into a pancake, fried in butter and served for breakfast with honey or maple syrup. Starchy ripe *plátanos* are also boiled in black beans like potatoes.

Another local delicacy was *mondongo* (cow stomach). It was boiled and the smell could knock you over! Even its name is awful!

Cooking in Coto not only took acquired skill, but a strong constitution. Before eating anything, you had to clean, and I do mean CLEAN it! Without pesticides, worms were in practically everything. Some Americans soaked fruits and vegetables for thirty minutes in a washtub with a third cup of Clorox, which must be more dangerous to your health than eating the worms! I meticulously split green beans and sectioned broccoli and cauliflower to rid flowerets of little green worms. Rice worms looked like grains of rice with tiny black dots on each end. You nudged each grain. If it moved, you got rid of it, unless you didn't mind a little extra protein on your plate! With such tedious cleaning, preparing lunch was a three-hour chore.

I slept most of time, thinking it was the oppressive heat. It could get hotter than blue blazes in the dry season. With a fan, I could have done like my grandmother and blown air through a wet towel but I had never even seen a fan anywhere. I only knew of one person in Coto who had an air-conditioner. He must have been a VIP! How else could a bachelor get a three-bedroom house smack-dab in the middle of the Zone? I never told Roberto how much I wanted to sit in that house a moment. But the unit was in a bedroom window, so Roberto would never have understood.

Heat that didn't bother *Ticos* sure worked us gringos into a lather! With no physical exertion, we'd sit and drip. By mid-February, heat and humidity had me so drained, I was sick as a dog. I was even nauseous when it was cool, especially mornings. An appointment was made in Golfito that would confirm my suspicion.

Public transportation was by train, automobile or motorcar. The big silver motorcars looked like old streetcars without the overhead hook-up to the power lines. Anyone could get a private one, so Roberto put in a request. Those looked like a smaller version of the World War II troop transport trucks. With leather bucket seats and three wooden benches facing forward for passengers, it had tram openings for doors and roll-down canvas to keep out the rain. But why call them *motor*cars, when they had no motors? Fitted with railroad car wheels and mounted on tracks, they ran on batteries and glided silently down narrow swaths cut through tall, vine covered trees. Riding along, you could see jungle birds

of brilliant plumage flitting from branch to branch and parrots gliding gracefully above. Bright flowers and orchids of every size, color and variety dotted lush foliage, all covered with dew that sparkled like fairy dust in the morning sun.

Not even these breathtaking scenes could quell all the apprehensions about my coming exam at the doctor's. Growing up, the word "pregnant" was considered vulgar and seldom if ever used. One was "expecting" or "in a family way." If you wanted to be daring, racy or modern, you used the term, "PG." I was about to see how *Ticos* dealt with this, or at least how the doctor a friend had recommended would.

Dr. Silva was a soft-spoken, older gentleman with silvery white hair. His office and examining rooms in an upper story of the hospital, were spacious with plantation doors opening onto a veranda that overlooked *Golfo Dulce*. Through the gauzy haze of its floor-length sheers that moved in soft waves of a gentle breeze, I could see potted veranda plants against blue sky and water.

Since I'd never had a baby, it was important to me that I have a doctor who spoke English. Dr. Silva didn't rush things but held my hand as I lay there and talked. His voice was kind and gentle, his accent pleasant to the ear. "The nurse says you think you're expecting. Is this your first?"

"Yes," I answered, nervously.

"Do you want a little girl, or a little boy?"

"My husband wants a boy, but I don't care as long as it's healthy."

"How old are you?"

"I'll be twenty-one next month."

"That's a good age to have a child. Now, let's see what we have here."

I closed my eyes tight and clenched my jaw. But instead of pulling his little stool up to the "business end" of the table, he stayed by my side,

blindly reaching in to feel the forming child inside. He not only believed in preserving a woman's modesty, but that she not be subjected to the embarrassment of collecting stool samples for parasites and amoeba. It can't have been good for the baby or me, but I wasn't about to object!

Because of all the pop and tea, I had a slight bladder infection, for which he prescribed an antibiotic and sent me on my way, saying he'd see me in one month and that the baby should be born September eighth. Eight was good. It was the number of new beginnings.

Roberto got a few days off to fly up and tell his parents. We took a motorcar to Golfito. Roberto didn't want to wait for our flight in the large building, which was slightly farther from the airport but in walking distance. I needed to be there for a cool place to sit down and a ladies room. It annoyed Roberto that I had to go so often.

Doña Lydia was overjoyed at the news that she was to become a grandmother, and smiled the whole time. Everyone made such a fuss over me. She even made a special dish. Roberto handed me some with a proud smile. "Try this. You'll love it!" It smelled incredible! I recognized the onions, cilantro and bell peppers, but not the white stuff in all that lime juice. "It's expensive. We only make it on special occasions."

Spoons poised, they waited for the guest of honor to dig in. It wouldn't be polite to be finicky, so I tried it. It was delicious! *"Como se llama esto?"* I asked my mother-in-law, using the little Spanish I knew.

"*Ceviche,* mi amor."

Mi amor means "my love." I felt warm all over.

"Honey, ask her what it's made of," I said.

"Chopped vegetables and lime juice," he said, "but mainly raw fish."

I was going to be sick!

"Don't *preocoop!*" Roberto laughed. "I didn't say what it was before, 'cause I knew you wouldn't try it. Mamá bought it fresh this morning. Have some more. It's sea fish. Good for the kid's brain or something."

"But raw?"

"Its not raw. Lime juice "cooks" it. Good, isn't it?"

"Yes?"

"Give me a big smile then and tell Mamá, 'thank you.' She made it for you."

"Muchas gracias, Doña Lydia."

"Por nada (for nothing/you're welcome)," she smiled.

After siesta, we went downtown. He was glad his parents were excited about the baby, glad there was no trouble with his mother and even glad I was his wife. He said so. Passing a pet store window, we stepped in to see a black kitten with four white paws and a white patch on her chest. It didn't take much for me to fall in love with her. I hadn't yet found out that what they sprayed on Coto's bananas affected a cat's nervous system. But Roberto knew, and wanting to please me, he got the cat anyway. I held her close as he and I embraced in front of the store. I'd never been so happy.

"What'll you call her?"

I loved how Tweety Bird said, 'I taht I tah uh puddy tat.'

Puddy? Nah. I gazed at the tiny kitten snuggled in my arms, buried my face in her soft fur and cooed, "Her my iddy, biddy pushy caht. *That's it!* Come on Push, let's go home."

I wasn't going to add this to the story, but Roberto took me to see a shocking movie called, "Goldfinger." Shocking, because violence like that had never appeared on the screen. I liked how Sean Connery pronounced Miss Galore's first name. I wasn't going to exclude this because I'm prudish, but because a book on movies lists *Goldfinger* as being released nine months after we bought Pushy. Keeping Sean Connery's pronunciation in mind, I couldn't have come up with that on my own, could I?

The addition of Pushy made us a real family. But the birth would be soon, and I knew absolutely nothing about babies.

"Do you know how to fold a diaper or change a baby?" Carolina asked.

"I babysat an infant, once. It slept the whole two hours."

Carolina lent me a life-sized doll and a diaper to practice. With luck, I'd learn before the birth!

Speaking of luck, *campecinos* (country folk) had some strange beliefs. As I ate breakfast one morning, something else was eating Cecelia. For weeks, she'd stood behind me at the kitchen door. A younger woman, especially a maid, never offers opinions to a *Doña*. She thought I was endangering my baby. I had to be told, but how? She inched closer everyday until she stood beside me, silently waiting to be recognized.

"Yes, Cecelia?"

She was naturally timid but didn't hesitate, spitting it out in a tone that was dead serious. "Excuse me for bothering you, *Doña,* but if you keep using black pepper, your baby will be born red!" There! She'd said it, and respectfully stepped back to be reproved.

I all but lost my mouthful in a gagged spray! She stepped over to slap my back. I wasn't choking but trying to keep from laughing out loud into my napkin, so as not to embarrass her.

"You see, *Doña?* Pepper is bad for you!" she proclaimed, pounding away. (I remembered Lelo, Americans and black pepper.)

Another time in front of our house, it was getting dark and I didn't have a flashlight. Wanting to show off my Spanish to Carolina and the

others, I called, *"Cecelia, traeme 'la foca,' si me hace el favor!"* (I'd meant to say, "Bring me the flashlight, if you don't mind.")

They politely sniggered. I looked at Carolina.

"Your pronunciation is good, Maria. Only one thing. We're nowhere near a colony of seals."

"Huh?"

"You asked for *la foca* or 'a seal,' when you should have said, *el foco* or 'flashlight.'"

"Estoy TAN embarasada!" I said, one-upping myself. Everyone howled with laughter! Carolina, maintaining her serious Latina look, barely cracked a smile. "Are you really?"

"Am I what?" I asked, perplexed once again.

"If you're trying to say you're 'embarrassed,' the word is *avergonsada*. You just said, 'I'm VERY pregnant.'"

Cecelia came with *el foco* and I got safely up the back stairs. The next day, I mentioned my fear of snakes. *"Doña,"* Cecelia said in wide-eyed innocence, "snakes won't bite *you*." I had to ask why. "Because," she smiled, "God won't permit a serpent to harm a woman carrying new life."

I had to believe in something. "How do you know this for sure?"

"Because one cold morning, a local woman stood by a corral to watch her husband work a horse when something slid around her ankles. She looked down. It was a *matabuey!* She froze as its head inched up her leg. When the serpent saw she was expecting, it slid back down and slithered away. So, you see? God will protect you."

Her face shining with the faith of a child. Having conveyed her beliefs, she turned without waiting for my nod of approval. I would adopt this notion until I found something better.

Cecelia didn't keep her innocence. A neighbor's maid began visiting her after work. Like a *matabuey*, Yolanda "injected" Cecelia with poison that corrupted and destroyed her from within. A little older than Cecelia, Yolanda had lived fast and hard and it showed. Her first words to me were, *"Soy pervertida."* I'd never heard anyone call herself that before and ran to look it up. Pervertida (fem., ie pervert): to turn or be turned from the truth. I never knew why she said that. I only know that Yolanda changed Cecelia's life for the worse and destroyed her future.

Yolanda worked for Jim (a pilot) and Shirley, who lived directly across from us. En route to visit Shirley one day, I got the scare of my life, one that could have dealt my baby and me a most unpleasant death!

I was big as a barn and constantly craving lemons, salt and Tabasco sauce. Drinking all that pop and tea instead of water had me so swollen, I couldn't wear shoes. Thongs cut into my pudgy feet and my legs looked like an elephant's. Unable to walk around the horseshoe to Shirley's, I took a short-cut across the yard. The grass looked invitingly soft and cool, so I left my thongs. Being broad daylight, I figured it was safe to go barefoot. Maids did all the time, even at night. Then, too, I was expecting, so God would protect me.

Nearly across, I caught sight of movement in the grass. To my horror, it was a twelve-inch coral snake with three babies following, a third its size. One more step and I'd have been on top of them! Would I have had the nerve, much less been able to bend over, to brush them off before they got their teeth in? I doubt it!

My feet didn't swell so badly in San Jose, so it was the only place I could comfortably wear shoes. In the States, I never liked admitting to being a size nine. In Costa Rica, I was the highest size for women: a thirty-nine. The only drawback to being in San Jose where it was cool, was frequent nightly trips to the bathroom. Andreina suggested the local remedy of wearing socks to bed. To my surprise, I did get up fewer times!

There were other remedies, some bordering on voodoo, like the one they used on ten-year-old Sandra, who was suffering with an earache. "Mamá is going to give Sandrita a *cartucho*. Don't say or do anything," Roberto warned.

Does he think I'm an idiot? What's a cartucho, anyway?

Doña Lydia rolled a newspaper diagonally into a narrow cone. Tearing off a piece of the small end, she placed it in Sandra's ear and lit the other end. My eyebrows went up! Sandra lay quietly, then began to squirm and complain about the heat. Undoubtedly! It burned half-way down. Sandrita loudly complained, but her mother held it firmly in place. She began to wail, begging her mother to take it out. My hands went to my cheeks. This had to stop! Smoke suddenly puffed once from the burning end. She stopped crying and her body relaxed. I never used this practice on my kids.

I did use the remedy I learned for hiccups: a tiny piece of cotton with alcohol stuck to the forehead. A minute or two and hiccups were gone. Convinced it was the power of suggestion, I dismissed it until I saw it used on a newborn.

But there was no slick remedy for Roberto's antics. I think he teased his little sister just to hear her scream. I'd just arrived in Costa Rica and was about to learn a new word.

"*No me molestes* (Don't molest me)!" Sandra yelled from the next room. Horrified, I ran to her defense and was relieved to find that *"No me molestes!"* turned out to be, "Don't bother me!"

Not knowing at first that I could get a better deal in Panama, I made the long trips to San Jose to shop for the new baby. Roberto's family was always glad to have me and ran me all over town. I made three or four trips there during the pregnancy. Roberto suggested we take the mail plane, which was more convenient, taking off from Coto and landing at the old airport inside San Jose. The grassy fields were uncomfortably

bumpy, and also scary to me. I didn't tell my pilot husband my fear of heights was worse in small planes. He'd already stereotyped me as a "typical woman, scared of everything." My fear of heights annoyed him as much as my endless trips to the john, so I said nothing. It was better that way.

Morning sickness would have been bad enough in the States with its familiar smells. I quietly suffered Coto's putrid stench of rotting vegetation rolling in with the morning fog. But what affected me most the whole nine months was the sickeningly sweet smell from what turned out to be a winery across from the Presidential Palace that dumped its waste products into the city sewers.

At least the smell wasn't quite as bad when it rained. On one rainy day, Andreina and I went shopping downtown. I learned to jaywalk instead of crossing at corners, where cars would plow right into you! But topping the list of the things I learned that day was that my American accent would have to go. "People think Americans are all rich," Andreina warned. "If you open your mouth, we'll get charged double or even triple, if they can get away with it." She said not to speak in the taxi either, but I forgot. The driver pulled in to our destination. "Six-seventy-five, Señorita."

She never batted an eyelash. "Maria, step out while I pay the fare." I was safely out, when boy, did she let him have it! "It's not worth more than two-thirty-five!" she said, slapping some coins in his hand and stomping away. I was shocked! In the States, you didn't argue prices. You paid! I was so embarrassed, I didn't follow her. I couldn't. My mouth was still open, when she stopped to look back. "It's okay, Maria! He won't molest (bother) us." I cringed, expecting any minute that he'd run out, take her by the scruff of the neck, turn her upside down and shake out the rest of the owed fare. But he only muttered something unrepeatable under his breath and drove away.

I learned another lesson in line at a frozen custard shop. A woman in her forty's sat on a bench against the wall, making eye contact with no one, licking her cone behind a napkin. Was she threatened by her husband? "Why's she eating that way?" I asked Andreina.

"She's just an ignorant *pola!*"

"*Pola?*" I repeated.

"A country person. Like the hillbillies on that TV show. Women don't do things like this, anymore."

Oh, really? Has anyone told Roberto?

Voting age was twenty-one. This was my first presidential election. Excited, I made my way to the American Embassy and voted for LBJ, who promised an end to the Vietnam war.

One place in Coto looked like how I imagined Vietnam to be. It must have been April, because I was in my fourth month when two couples invited us to go into the hills surrounding Coto Valley. I was more accustomed to the smell of tar they sprayed on the main "highway" to keep the dust down and had learned the hard way to wear an old shirt of Roberto's over my clothes to protect them from tar spatters while riding in the back of Lelo's old Willis Jeep. They weren't built for comfort and you could feel every bump. But today, we were going in style in the most popular and desired vehicle in Coto: a Land Rover. It not only had doors and a suspension ride, it was air-conditioned! Roberto and I rode with Roger and Carol in their pea-green Land Rover, while Alan, Nena and their son followed in their light blue one. It was to be my first and last long car trip, until the baby. Well, nearly my last. Those awful bridges no longer bothered me. Soon, we were out of the plantations and in thick jungle. An hour later, we parked in a roadside space big enough for both cars.

The narrow path cut along a cliff with a sheer drop into lush flora. Covering the cliff wall were the same flower in hot pink and firey coral with large, thick, waxy petals and leaves like magnolias. Lagging behind, I casually strolled the shaded path, enjoying the ambrosial fragrance and brilliant color against the verdant mantle until it opened onto a meadow.

The others had already crossed a suspension footbridge spanning a deep gorge. Roberto waved me to hurry to help me across. The meadow went up a grade on the other side to a modest cabin belonging to a young couple of humble means.

The refreshments they offered were pieces of sugar cane, another new experience to be relished. I mostly kept quiet, chewing the sweet cane and listening to them talk as I still couldn't keep up in Spanish. After initial greetings, we women seated ourselves on the porch for pleasant conversation, while the guys huddled in the yard for more manly topics.

With no moon that night and certainly no streetlights, leaving at four would give us time to reach the plantations before dark. Jungle nights were dark as a cave.

Lelo used to lend us his motor scooter to get us from 51 to the club and back on weekends. Riding home from the movies in the dark, frogs would hop through the scooter's headlight and disappear. "Watch this," Roberto said, turning off the lights. I'd never seen such pitch black and was glad we weren't walking.

Still deep in the jungle, edging the curves above Coto, my mind was on sugarcane, coral and pink flowers and suspension footbridges. I was gazing at the sun's hazy red sphere sinking into the jungle mist, when Roger suddenly spotted a large snake slowly making its way across the road.

Like cowboys bulldogging at a rodeo, the boys hooped and hollered, lit out of the cars and made for the slithering serpent. Trying to grab the tail of what might have been a boa but could have been a *matabuéy*, the minute they touched it, it zoomed into the underbrush. The more sensi-

ble gender waited in the car, marveling at their men's utter stupidity and hoping they wouldn't go in after it. They didn't.

I learned about the frail male ego that day at our picnic along the riverbank. Lelo and his family went, Alan, Nena and their six-year old, Roger and Carol and Roberto and me. The women were getting the food ready and watching the children play, while our the men challenged each other to a little target practice. Many men in Coto had guns. Roger and Alan sure carried theirs often enough as well as short machetes. Roberto brought both of his.

Crossing the dry riverbed, Lelo found a round flat rock and placed it upright on a boulder. Shots cracked as each fired and missed. When Lelo suggested I try, Roberto handed me his German Luger. I preferred the .22. The wives got wind of it and stopped to watch. The target was about the distance of a four-lane street. Taking no aim, I raised the gun and fired. Having retrieved the sandstone rock, Lelo walked back with a Cheshire Cat smile, his finger wiggling around the half-dollar sized hole through dead center. "Look at this!"

Roberto's face turned pale. The rest of the day the guys teased him about living with Annie Oakley and that he'd better watch his step. They seemed oblivious to the fact that he wasn't amused. Roberto, who was an excellent shot, couldn't face losing to a woman in front of his friends. He sulked and pouted for days until a trip gave him time away to lick his wounds. It was the most miserable week of my life.

He must have missed me too, because when he returned, he was more loving and affectionate. We knelt by his suitcase, so he could surprise me with each of the goodies from the U.S. I'd been craving. But I wasn't interested in *things!* What I wanted and needed was him! When he looked up and saw the longing in my eyes, he dropped the lid. Shoving the bag aside, he took me in his arms and we knelt there for the longest time, locked in a sweet embrace. It was wonderful!

ALL THE WAY HOME

By the time I was seven months along, I'd made about four trips back and forth in small planes from Coto to San Jose. It was during that forth visit that Don Vicente made a comment that changed all that.

He'd worked for Pan Am Airlines for some thirty years, and I believe had reached the position of chief mechanic. Everyone either knew him or knew of him as the legendary mechanic who'd flown into a rage and bitten the edge of a wing when the engine wouldn't work! What probably seemed like standard shoptalk to him put the fear of God in me!

"Ever since I can remember," he began, "planes as big as World War II troop transports, have crashed along that same route you take on their way to ships in Panama and were never found."

If huge planes could disappear into the undergrowth, how would they ever find a mail plane? I cancelled my return flight opting to take a bus back to Coto.

Don Beh (Bay), as he was often called, (the Spanish "V" pronounced like a "B") didn't say how long the trip would take, so my decision was made in consideration of my baby's safety. Flying was out and that was that! A bus trip might be nice. (And I thought I was scared of heights, before!)

Costa Rica is known as the Switzerland of Central America. Slow as an ox cart, the old American-style school bus laboriously chugged ever upward. A mist hung on top of the mountain and the air was crisp and cold. It was strange to see what looked like frost on tropical ferns. The driver pulled over to let us catch a view of both the Pacific and Caribbean Oceans, which you can see on a clear day. Unable to see either, he pulled back onto the road and began the long descent around hairpin curves, through muddy ravines until ascending another formidable mountain that rivaled the first.

It was getting humid and sticky the farther south we went. Nearing the crest of the last mountain before the coastal plains, the jungle crowded in, gradually narrowing the road to the width of a country lane. Pushing our way through shrubs and weeds that overlapped the road reminded me of Humphrey Bogart and Katharine Hepburn prodding the African Queen through reed choked tributaries on their patriotic quest.

Until now, the ride had only been rough and bumpy. Now, it was bone jarring through enormous chug holes that could swallow a Volkswagen Bug whole!

A canopy of tall jungle trees blocked the afternoon sun. Sapling limbs violently thumped and scraped the side of the bus on the cliff side, whipping past windows and covering passengers with leaves and twigs. At first, I was glad to be on the left of the aisle in case a snake dropped into the growing pile of debris, but left was now no advantage. Outside my window was a sheer drop into the tops of jungle trees with no visible bottom.

The back wheels skidded in the mud when the driver braked and spun when he accelerated, slipping and sliding this way and that, as the bus hugged the precipitous edge of the cliff. A huge tree was growing off-center of the narrow lane. Unable to go between tree and cliff, we squeezed within inches of the abrupt drop. One false move and we'd plunge to a fathomless death. With the bus loaded to capacity, how much more could it take and for how long? Our saving grace were tree roots that held the rain-soaked soil together. Several roots at the base of the tree were way above ground, the tallest about eighteen inches. How would we ever get through the slippery mud and over those roots without caving in the cliff and bringing the mammoth tree crashing in on top of us?

Fear of heights kept my eyes away from the window as the driver raced toward the edge of the cliff and geared down to cross the first obstacle. If he went at the root too slowly, he might not clear it and the rear might slide too close and over the edge; too fast and we'd plunge on over. The lower roots were first, at a speed that made me cringe! Holding on to the handle on the seat in front of me, I cradled my tummy with the other hand as we cleared the low roots, smacked into the taller root with a thud and rolled back. The driver geared into first to goose the bus over, when the back wheels began to slide toward the edge. The older lady next to me took it all in stride. Suddenly, the thought of flying thousands of feet above all this didn't seem so bad. In fact, I could have been home hours ago! Fear turned my belly hard as a basketball. *Why didn't I fly?* Outside my window was nothing but thin air. I didn't want to die; not on a day when the sky was so blue! *Please God; my baby!* I was afraid of airplanes and now was about to fall from a great height anyway, smashed to smithereens and lost forever!

The bus rocked and swayed to the sound of grinding gears. Metal, pulled this way and stretched that way. It creaked and groaned toward that last defiant obstacle. Tires clawed to reach the traction of wooden roots within inches of its tread, spinning wheels slinging mud, the rear sliding sideways toward the edge. The driver gunned it over the tallest root in a series of jarring bumps and thuds, then drove on as if it was all in a day's work. Yikes!

As we started down the mountain, undergrowth opened and the road widened at the crest overlooking a valley; a pink one! This was no illusion; not the sun shining at an angle making the valley *look* pink. It *was* pink! *Toto, I have a feeling we're not in Kansas, anymore!* I turned to the older woman and asked in Spanish. "What's down there? Why's it all pink?"

The tiny lady strained to see over the seat in front. "Piña," she said with a kindly smile. "Before the fruit comes, the plants are pink."

After miles of rosy fields on the valley floor, the road became a straight stretch lined with tall prairie-like grass. Gone was the shade of jungle trees. The sun beat down relentlessly. If not for our speed, the metal bus would have been an oven. We hadn't seen another vehicle since leaving San Jose nearly ten hours earlier.

The sun's coral sphere hung suspended above jungle mist on the horizon as we reached the big red Coke sign in Villaneily, her gray, dilapidated buildings now a dusty rose in the last rays of sunset. The sting of tar in my nostrils wasn't as bad in the cool of late afternoon. Evening would bring the pungent smell of fog rolling over rotting jungle vegetation. These smells were welcome now, for these were the smells of home. We turned right at the intersection into the sun, up a road I knew well. Soon, I'd be with Roberto and Pushy; home, where I belonged.

I nearly forgot! This wasn't any old dirt road we'd been on all day. Lelo said it ran all through Latin America. And the name of this marvel of modern engineering? Why, the Pan American Highway, of course!

CHAPTER THREE
INDEPENDENCIO

Roberto ran into the house in a snit over something that had happened at work. I followed him to the bedroom. Pushy, who we'd only had a few weeks, preferred quiet, cozy places and would often climb inside drawers from underneath the dresser to nap. When Roberto opened the drawer and saw her curled on a stack of one hundred colón bills, he grabbed her by the scruff of the neck and threw her against the wall. I'd never heard an animal howl like that in pain. Trying to pull herself up and run, her front paws scrambled on the polished wood floors so she could stand. Her back legs only twitched. Finally giving up, she cowered and trembled and stared up at Roberto.

"How could you?" I screamed, running to her.

His answer? He stormed from the house.

With no vet in Coto, I applied hot and cold packs and massaged her when she could tolerate it. I even held her up to do her business when out to potty. Because she was so afraid and couldn't move, I put her food, water and bedding under that heavy dresser, where she'd feel safe. She slowly got better. Finally able to jump, I put her bed on the dresser, so she could watch iguanas climbing to the top of the *pejiaye* (peh-hee-VI-yea) tree for the clusters of plum size, bright,

pumpkin-colored fruit. The *pejibaye* palm has needlelike thorns on the trunk, three to four inches long. While Pushy stalked iguanas from her bed, I marveled at how those heavy creatures could get to their favorite treat without a scratch.

I had no camera, so I'd draw and color pictures to send home of these incredible sights. One rainy day, I drew one of Pushy sleeping at the window on her aqua blue pillow against a background of thorny palms and gentle rain.

A one-bedroom apartment was finally available next to the restaurant, half a mile from the commissary and half a block from the hanger. We could now walk home from movies on lighted streets and Roberto could walk to work in the pre-dawn darkness. I'd be able to stroll the baby down shaded walks, and have access to the pool, tennis courts and neighbors. Life couldn't get any better!

Lelo helped us move to our apartment on stilts. It was an end apartment so it had extra windows. A crib would fit in the corner of the tiny bedroom, beneath the window that faced the restaurant.

The bedroom opened onto the living room with the dining room by the front door and its tiny, screened-in porch. A large serving window into the kitchen gave a perfect view from back door to front. Later, I would use the serving window for Pre-Columbian statuettes and clay pots vendors sold door to door. Larger than 51's kitchen, it also had a pantry. The company moved our furniture and added a big rocking chair for me to rock the baby.

Our maid, Cecelia, didn't come with us. She was offered a secretarial position. I was happy for her chance to move up. (How naïve could I be?) I later saw her at the commissary, nicely dressed and smiling unashamedly. She now lived in Villaneily and had become a "lady of the night."

I don't remember the name of the next maid, who only stayed a couple of weeks. I spent that time with Push on a blanket, under "our" tree, in the cool of morning. She'd softly purr as I sang to her and scratched her under her chin. She liked best to be scratched behind her ears. She'd sometimes go into fits of pain, where she'd howl, chase her tail then lay very still. Progressively worsening, these "fits" would strike without warning. She scratched me once without meaning to. When she could no longer chase her catnip toy on a string, she found another amusement. Her ears perked up at butterflies flitting overhead and her large blue eyes now honed in on tiny lizards zipping through the grass. She'd groom her sleek black fur where she could without pain, then snooze in dappled sunshine. Near the five-foot tall grass in back, I watched for four months as ants stripped a large tree. I'd heard of flesh-eating ants and never left Push alone.

Mid-morning, I'd take Pushy in and go shopping or visiting. Maids preferred when *doñas* were gone to get more done. It poured on rainy-season afternoons, so I sometimes spent mornings swimming. One day, some of the Latina wives of company executives waded over and introduced themselves.

"So, you're the expecting wife of the new pilot?"

"You can't be very far along," another added.

"She just found out," a third chimed in.

"I'm five and a half months," I smiled.

"You can't be," the first said. "You're not even showing!"

"That's 'cause it's a boy," said the second.

"When are you due?" asked the third.

"September eighth."

"You ARE going to San Jose to give birth?" one smirked.

"No, the hospital in Golfito."

Several sniggered. *Gringos are a bunch of cowboys! She'll end up in Coto's dispensary like the last one.*

"Better order a motorcar now. Independence Day's on the fifteenth with the big dance the night before."

"My doctor said the eighth."

"What do doctors know? The fastest way to Golfito is by motorcar. People for miles around will be here for the dance with parked cars blocking tracks jammed with motorcars. With all the drinking, no one will know whose motorcar is who's to make way for yours."

Regrettably, I ignored their advice.

Lelo's family had already moved from 51 into a two-bedroom house on the Zone, near the school and club. After settling in, Carolina helped me make a maternity outfit. It was at the commissary I learned that asking for *una feria* would get me extra fabric or a free spool of thread. This applied to food, too. Though akin to our baker's dozen, it wasn't automatically given. You had to ask.

Roberto bought a turntable and stereo speakers while we lived on 51. I loved the three record album of Handel's Messiah he bought me for my birthday. We'd listen to Frank Sinatra's album, "Let's Fly Away," and Cecelia loved Simon and Garfunkle's 45, "Cecelia," which I played for her often.

Music was all we had until we moved to the Zone, where I discovered entertainment outside our bedroom windows. Flying insects and mosquitoes swarmed around streetlights like the one next to the tree the ants were stripping. With Roberto gone at night, I'd sit on the bed, watching bats fly in from the jungle. They'd fly straight for the back window, zigzag our building and sail past the side corner window, giving me two fascinating views. They weren't there for entertainment, but to devour thousands of mosquitoes that carried malaria and yellow fever. It's amusing what entertains one in the absence of TV. I'd sway to Strauss' "Die Fledermaus" (The Bat) playing in my mind as I watched. It was a favorite of Aunt Mozy's. I'd imagine her stories of nineteenth century ballrooms and lovely gowns the ladies wore. Mama hated my daydreaming and notions of "escaping into music," though she did it often enough herself. Aunt Mozy also taught Mama about classical music, but Mama preferred pop songs like "You Made Me Love You, (I Didn't Want To Do It)," "You Always Hurt the Ones You Love," "(One of These Days) You're Gonna Miss Me, Honey," but especially, good looking Billy Eckstine's "Prisoner of Love." (Though many considered him the black Frank Sinatra, he was ordered not to make eye contact with white women in his audience.)

> *Alone from night to night you'll find me*
> *Too weak to break the chains that bind me*
> *I need no shackles to remind me*
> *I'm just a prisoner of love.*
> *For one command I stand and wait now*
> *From one who's master of my fate now*
> *I can't escape for it's too late now*
> *I'm just a prisoner of love.*

Mama "escaped into music," though it can't have helped. I always remember her so sad and unhappy.

My days of leisure with Push ended abruptly when the maid quit. And I can't blame her. It was all my fault.

"I work in that heat all morning," Roberto complained at lunch one day, "and come home tired with no steak knife at my plate!"

"Sorry, honey. I'll get you one."

"You're slow as molasses. Hope you get in shape after the baby." (I actually looked good with a little meat on my bones.) Back with the knife, he slid into his chair. "Remind that girl about the ketchup and steak sauce."

"But she uses so little."

He stared daggers, his nostrils flaring!

"Roberto, we can afford it! She deserves...."

"I'll tell you what she deserves. I pay her plenty. As a servant in my house, she'll do as she's told!"

The oppressive heat had me worn out and nauseous. A nap after lunch would fix me up. My head had no sooner hit the pillow, when Roberto's arm snaked around my middle. "Ready for a little action?"

"Not now, honey. I don't feel well."

"Come on; just a little." He rolled me on my side.

"Later," I said, moving his other hand away from the back of my neck. Taking this as a personal rejection, he flew into a rage. "Later? You're no fun anymore! All you do is lay around like a fat sow! You should be taking care of me. I need this! It's your duty!"

"If I could just rest in your arms I'd probably...."

"You rest all day! I need it now!"

"Try a cold shower!" I said, turning into my pillow.

Both his feet connected with my backside, knocking me out of bed. He flew on top of me, punching and slapping, his arms flailing like a windmill. "I'll teach you to say no!"

The pummeling alternated from slaps to my head to punches to my arm and hip. "Roberto; the baby!"

"The baby, the baby!" he whined. "What about me? I need things back to normal!"

Missing my hip, he struck my tummy, then froze. Jumping up, he pulled on his dirty khaki pants and tee shirt and ran down the front steps. The muffled sound of boots hitting hot asphalt ran toward the hangar. Everything throbbed with pain. I limped to the kitchen for some ice tea.

The maid was eating at the kitchen table, below the serving window, when I walked in trembling and rubbing what hurt. Under the table went the A-1, but I'd already seen. In raw reaction to Roberto's abuse, I slapped her. I instantly came to myself with her look of horror! What have I done? What am I becoming? "Please, I'm sorry! I didn't mean to!" I sputtered in broken Spanish. The bottle slid from her lap and onto the floor as she jumped up and flew out the back door and down the stairs.

Too great with child to run after her, I dropped to my knees, my face to the floor, and wept bitterly. I wouldn't blame her if she never came back. She didn't. Not even for the two weeks pay we owed her.

Word quickly spread of the cruel tyranny of *la doña brava en la zona* (the angry lady in the Zone). From then on, notices to hire went unanswered. And I, who couldn't imagine washing the "tough stuff" by hand was doing just that!

At seven months, my stomach muscles had weakened. Sheets and towels were hard to ring out and stiff blue jeans nearly impossible. Roberto was no help. "Washing is women's work." One question I had for God someday was, why give the lion's share of upper body strength to men when it's women who really need it?

I was still washing by hand when September eighth came and went. Skinned knuckles or not, I'd get the stiffness out of my baby's new things to protect his tender skin if it killed me!

Beneath the stilted housing were utility sinks called *pilas* that had built-in concrete washboards on one side leaving the other for rinsing and soaking. Ironing boards, the size of diminuitive *Ticas*, came with each house. It was strange that maids were afraid to iron with a toothache, but would iron all day long on the concrete floors flooded with one inch of water! Since it was so cool there, some tenants stained the floors red, polished them and put out patio furniture and potted plants. Ours had nothing. I had no strength, and he hadn't the money!

August and September afternoons were cool and rainy, so getting soaked down the front while washing kept my tummy perpetually hard. It was sweater-weather with nights so cold, sometimes three blankets weren't even enough. Social evenings in friend's screened-in living rooms could be downright chilly. But weather wasn't all that was uncomfortable.

Not until moving to Costa Rica did I find out that Roberto once belonged to the Young Nazis. He often argued politics with poor Carol, whose Jewish parents escaped Holland just before the 1939 German invasion. Roberto's views were annoying and disgusting but no one could dissuade him. He privately told me that when the "prophecy" said over him as an infant came true then he'd deal with those Jews.

In Latin America, *brujas* (BRU-hass, witches) or mediums are common and their advice followed by many. Doña Lydia was friends with one, who came to see the newborn Robertico.

Babies are enthusiastically welcomed into family-oriented Latino families. Friends and relatives coo over a new arrival with lots of compliments and congratulations to the parents.

Taking baby Roberto in her arms, the *bruja* said something Doña Lydia never let Roberto or anyone else forget. "This child will be President of Costa Rica. He will walk with kings and princes will call him friend. He will bring glory and fame to Costa Rica and history will revere his name forever."

Because Doña Lydia was rearing a child who was destined to change history, she made allowances for Roberto's outrageous behavior and failed to correct his tantrums.

I believe Carol's maiden name was Bregstein (I never saw it written down) and that her parents were originally from Holland. They escaped to the U.S. where Carol and her brother were born. I believe Carol was five when they immigrated to Costa Rica and her father entered the coffee business. Carol had a duel citizenship until twenty-three. The year before I met her, she'd elected to remain Costa Rican.

Carol not only spoke Spanish and excellent English, but her parent's native tongue as well. Well educated, cultured and refined didn't mean she wasn't down-to-earth. She made even the most humble person feel important, loved and accepted.

Carol met Roger at twelve and instantly fell in love with the tall, good-looking guy with golden eyes and medium blonde hair, vigorously pursuing her dreamboat with the California tan and creamy complexion until he "caught" her. In Latin America, lengthy attachments and even longer engagements are the norm. Eight years later, they had a storybook wedding with all the trimmings.

They brought their own furniture to Coto, the kind you see in expensive stores in the States. She covered each shelf and table with photos of their grand wedding. She was truly beautiful holding her huge white rose bouquet, a delicate lace veil cascading over a white satin, form-fitting floor length gown encircling her feet in scalloped lace.

I had no white wedding and secretly envied her, but even more so, I envied Carol and Roger's loving, easy-going relationship. They had a calming influence at weekend gatherings, when Roberto got into heated political arguments. My Spanish wasn't good enough, although I did understood words like *Auschwitz, campo de concentración* and *gas* (pronounced, "gahss.") To think that mothers hid their babies inside clothing left on hooks on the way to the showers, hoping some miracle

would save their child. I'd have done the same. My baby wasn't born, but he was alive. I could feel him now! I'd never seen or held him, but he was no less precious than those little ones. I began to wonder if I'd married a monster.

As a seven-year-old, I learned from the film, *The Thing*, that you couldn't reason with a monster and wondered how that silly, pointy-headed scientist thought you could! Carol didn't judge me for Roberto's faults and I was glad. I valued her friendship.

Carol's cheerful tact at weekend gatherings kept controversial topics from turning ugly, along with Lelo's accordion music and jokes that kept us in stitches and defused Roberto's negativity. One of Lelo's jokes had three Spanish words to the punch line; *Bruto,* "stupid," *civíl,* "civil" and *iglesia,* "church," like Julio Iglesias. (See, you knew more Spanish than you thought!) Latinos have their civil wedding ceremony at the court house and a week later, a religious ceremony in their church. At this particular weekend gathering, chairs were set in a circle in the living room. We were chattering in small groups, when Lelo shocked us with a personal revelation that hit everybody like a two by four.

"*Me casé tres veces* (I married three times)!"

A hush fell over the mostly Catholic crowd and people began to look at each other. Carolina lowered her eyes, knowing what was coming, which only confirmed suspicions. When he repeated it, you could hear a pin drop.

"*Me case tres veces: por civíl, por iglesia y por bruto!*"

The next one hit closer to home to us Protestants.

"Oh, Carmen," Lelo began, "I can't face family and friends."

"What happened," Carmen asked? "What did you do?"

"Not me! My daughter!"

"What did *she* do?"

"My priest will deny me Holy Communion."

"What did she do?" Carmen asked, again.

"She's a… a…"

"Spit it out!" Carmen demanded.

"She's become a prostitute," the evil word tumbled from Lelo's lips.

"A what?"

"A prostitute!" Maria said in shame.

"Thank God!" Carmen cried, "I thought you said she'd become a Protestant!" There were lots of laughs on that one!

Lelo had another. "A man comes home drunk, takes a wrong turn and ends up in the barn. He lies down with the old sow, wanting to make love to his wife. He squeezes her tight, making her grunt. Oink, oink, oink! Insensed, he backs off. 'Como que no, no, no… (What do you mean, no, no, no)?'"

The last one I remember is, "*Esa no es vida. Es un bidet!* (This isn't life. It's a bidet!)"

Not only was Lelo the life of the party, he played background music while we talked. If Roberto was leading the conversation into an unsavory subject, he'd play some rousing tune everyone could sing. I could sing in Spanish to lots of "oldies," even though I didn't know what half the words meant, yet. One day, Lelo struck up not only a rousing tune, it was Rebel Rousing!

Among those at Farm 48 that evening were five women from the American South. I happened to see Lelo smile and wink at a *Tico* husband next to him and whisper in Spanish, "Watch this!" Without missing a beat, he struck up a lively rendition of "Dixie." Mississippi jumped to her feet, followed by the mother and daughter from

Louisiana. He'd never played an American tune. When I recognized it, I stood with the other Okie.

"Dixie," written in 1859 as the finale of a minstrel show, was an immediate hit. When Abraham Lincoln ran for president in 1860, "Dixie" was used as a campaign song against him. He personally liked the tune, and five years later asked a band at the White House to play it.

I liked it, too. To me, it had nothing to do with the evils of slavery. It was simply a song from home. Unless you've lived abroad, it's hard to understand how reminders of home are blown out of proportion in new fervors of patriotism, even for a song now as offensive to some as "Dixie."

Keep in mind that in 1964, attitudes were still in flux on the subject of race. I can remember when African-Americans weren't allowed in movie theaters, restaurants or swimming pools. Was it wrong? Of course, but it's all we knew.

The late 50's or early 60's were the first time I saw a couple of "color" at the movies. Playing was either "Ben-Hur" or "The Ten Commandments." In the back row, quietly waiting for the crowd to thin out before getting up to leave, was a middle-aged couple in their Sunday-go-to-meeting best; she in a hat, he in a suit and tie. My response was one of surprise, not because I didn't want them there or thought that they didn't belong, but because I'd never seen it.

I had nothing on which to base a derogatory opinion of colored folks (the "polite" term my mother *insisted* I use out of respect—she thought Negro sounded too harsh; too much like the "N" word). I'd heard white trash using the "N" word in high school, but was fifteen before I actually met a colored person. With both parents remarried and busy with their new lives, this good woman took time to befriend a confused and lonely teenager. Clarice was one of the kindest people I've ever known, who talked like she knew God and Jesus and they lived right down the street from her.

ALL THE WAY HOME

She worked for my stepmother. She was "just a maid" but never lost her smile; "just a servant" but walked in dignity. She suffered slurs and insults, had her share of money troubles, teenagers and a "no-good husband," but walked in love. I wish she'd told me her secret to life then. It might have saved me some trouble and heartache down the road. But she was what they called a "silent witness." She didn't speak about her faith, she lived it.

Three years later, Roberto introduced me to a friend of his of African descent in a movie theater in San Jose, who sat right down beside me. This was confusing, because Roberto was jealous of other men and would vehemently argue with anyone that there was nothing good or noble about the "Negroid" race, that they should reinstate slavery and literally wore out a stale one-liner of that day: "Haven't got a thing against niggers. In fact, I'd like to own a couple of 'em!"

The few blacks that lived in San Jose spoke English, which was good to know if I ever got lost downtown. Most lived on the Caribbean coast, had been owned by the English and were descendants of slaves. Roberto's black friend must have been from one of the islands, because he spoke several languages including Papiamento, something African slaves cleverly invented by mixing Spanish, Portuguese, Dutch, English and French with some Arawak Indian and African influences to confuse and frustrate their white captors. They did such a good job at playing "poor dumb slave," who couldn't quite understand you spoke one language at a time, whites had to learn Papiamento to communicate their wishes and demands.

Months later, in a hot debate on race at Carol and Roger's, I'd learned enough Spanish to add my two cents. "Once this proud race cuts the last tie of its devastating past," I said, "there'll be no stopping them! Once they begin to study and discover how smart they really are, they'll run rings around the rest of us like they already do in sports!"

MARY SUZANNE LOPEZ

By Roberto's daggers, I knew I was in for it when we got home. "Keep your stupid opinions to yourself," he warned, "and don't embarrass me like that again!"

My legs were becoming numb. It's a good thing the baby's arrival was near. I didn't know the phosphates in soda pop pulled calcium from bones and put it in the soft tissue. While my body desperately scoured cells for what fluids it could scavenge to change the amniotic fluid eight times a day, I was blithely dehydrating both baby and me at break-neck speed! Though my ankles disappeared, the doctor never told me that caffeine in coffee, tea and pop held in fluids and water flushes cells out. Maybe doctors didn't even know that until the health craze thirty years later. Company doctors saw me at the movies every weekend and never mentioned the possibility of pre-eclampsia.

The eighth of September came and went. Roberto bought a color TV, so I gave up bats and watched U.S. shows translated into Spanish. I especially liked two new programs that came out before I left the States: "The Adam's Family" and "The Beverly Hillbillies." Roberto was always gone, so I watched alone and waited for the birth.

Monday, September fourteenth, dawned like any other workday. That morning, I'd washed some new baby things and hung them to dry. Sunny said expectant mothers have a surge of energy toward the end. She said to remember when it started and three weeks later, I'd have my baby. But I forgot. By six that night, I was still ironing. Twelve hours on my feet had me too tired to attend the Independence Day Dance. Roberto didn't even go, which surprised me. Not much stood between *that* boy and a good time! With three tiny shirts left to iron, I called it a day, quoting Scarlett O'Hara, "After all, tomorrow is another day!"

I'd eaten, showered and tucked myself in with a book, when my tummy tightened like a drum. It had done that a lot lately. Twenty minutes later, at about 9:20, it happened again. It didn't hurt, so I didn't wake Roberto. It happened again and I timed them for the next hour.

When Lucy was expecting on "I Love Lucy," Ricky, Ethel and Fred were so excited they forgot to take her with them to the hospital. I hadn't planned to go until the contractions were five minutes apart, as first births can take longer.

The dance started about seven. Out of the three company doctors, two were drinking while the third abstained in case of an emergency like when the field hands had drunken machete fights on weekends. With Independence Day dances going on all over Coto, there would probably be a lot of those that night.

Sophisticated Dr. Menendez spoke several languages, was well read, well traveled and on call. So the evening wouldn't be a total loss, he'd planned a little something to liven things up. He went into the men's room, removed his shirt, shoes and socks, pushed his pant legs up and donned a grass skirt. He then put on a carved wooden painted witch doctor's mask, and bead and feather necklaces he'd paid *campesino* artisans to make for him. With his short machete in hand, he gave the signal and started for the dance floor, people making way in surprised anticipation. The record he brought began playing. Through huge speakers came the throb of jungle drums which electrified the room. Leaping onto the dance floor, he landed square on his bare feet. The wide swath opened to a circle as he swung his machete within inches of screaming celebrants delighted with the colorful, innovative show. Around he swirled in a dizzying display of untapped talent. Dipping to a squat, he jumped high flailing both arms in wide circles over his head. Drunk with applause, he spun faster, swinging the machete all around, aspiring to feats trained dancers wouldn't even try, when: he cut his thumb. An inebriated Dr. Nuñez took his colleague to the dispensary to sew him up.

By eleven thirty, contractions were five minutes apart. Roberto hurried to warm up the jalopy he'd dubbed, *la uva*. Lord knows why he named that old black car "the grape!" He'd been under that clunker's hood since he bought it and it had only run once. This time, it wouldn't even start. It was just as well with forty kilometers of pitch black jungle to the hospital. He hurried back upstairs. "Don't move!" he ordered. "I'll be back!" I wondered where he thought I was going to go?

Contractions were getting harder when headlights hit the window over the crib and raced around the curve toward our apartment. The bag I'd packed was by the bedroom door. I was dressed and sitting on the bed, when I heard men running up the front steps.

Lelo smiled as Roberto nearly hyperventilated with new father-to-be panic. "We're here," Roberto said out of breath! "Don't worry, everything's under control." He reached out his hand then pulled back, afraid to touch me. "Man, how do I do this? Uh, how do you feel? Can you walk?"

"I'm fine," I said, standing up. "Let's just put one foot in front of the other."

"Oh, yeah." Putting an arm around what was left of my waist, he began walking me to Lelo's jeep. "Be calm, now. Here's the stairs. Step down. Careful! Step..., step...."

"My bag," I called over my shoulder.

"Lelo, get the bag!" Roberto ordered. "Slowly; that's right. Now, step down..., down...."

The dispensary parking lot was so full of frogs that we had to take huge steps to get over them. I'd never seen so many in one place! It wasn't air-conditioned and I already dreaded going in. I should have bought a fan in Panama. Too late now! We walked through the large waiting room and down the long hall. The dispensary had an operating/delivery room across from the only private room, in addition to a small men's ward, a women's ward and one for children.

Lelo was still grinning when Roberto said goodbye at the delivery room door with a tortured look like he'd never see me again. The nurse in a white uniform and head full of curlers ushered me in and closed the door.

I got along well in Spanish, now. Not knowing what to expect, I was still concerned about not having an English-speaking nurse.

"What's your name?" the nurse said in Spanish.

"Maria."

"I'm Flor. Take everything off, put on this gown and I'll be right back."

I did as she asked then sat on the end of the table.

The nurse returned and helped me lie down. That's when I saw them. Directly overhead was a tangle of webs that covered the ceiling with fuzzy gray spiders the size of a thumbnail. They stared down at me with all eight eyes sparkling! Dinner was served, and I guessed I was it!

"Those things up there don't ever… ?"

"… Come down? No," Flor laughed, "they catch flies and mosquitoes that carry diseases."

Webs were in all the public buildings. Why not over delivery tables?

"Is this your first?" she asked, trying to take my mind off of spiders.

"Yes."

"When the contractions get harder, we have aspirin and chloroform."

"Thank you." I'd hated objects over my face since I was five and Daddy held me down so the dentist could give me gas and pull a tooth. At seven, it took five nurses to hold me down before my tonsillectomy. Grit would get me through this!

"See that?" Flor said, pointing to window screens fifteen inches down from the ceiling all around the room, where the spiders had attached their webs. "Ventilation screens are in each room," she contin-

ued. "You can hear a pin drop anywhere in the hospital. Being so late, everyone's asleep, so you'll have to be quiet during delivery."

Nurses and doctors were part of the authority figures I'd been taught to obey without question as a child. In my strict upbringing, complying wasn't optional. Besides, it seemed like a reasonable request. How bad could it get?

Labor was getting "uncomfortable," when the doctor came in. He told Flor something in Spanish then went to his office. I chatted with Flor to get my mind off things.

"I've never heard the name, *Flor*. What does it mean?"

"My full name is, Flor de Maria. My grandmother named me."

"You have such pretty names, here. Does 'Flower of Mary' refer to Jesus?"

"I've heard some say so!" she smiled.

Contractions were getting closer and harder when something moved in the corner of my eye. A spider was attacking something that had flown into its web. If one of those things came toward me on its silk thread, I didn't care what stage of labor I was in, I would be off that table and out of there!

Another contraction. "Flor, it hurts."

"Do you want something for pain?" she asked.

"No. Here it comes, again!"

"Don't push."

"I'm so hot," I said, turning my head back and forth in pain as huge drops of sweat poured onto the pillow.

"I'll turn on the fan, honey."

I raised my head, my eyes following her. There WAS a fan in Coto! How did I miss seeing it? I would later pay dearly for those few minutes of relief. I contracted a cold and would spend three weeks in a mask, before I could kiss my baby's velvety forehead.

Friends waiting in the hall listened to everything, quietly cheering me on. Roberto got tanked on some booze they brought from the dance and they had to run him outside, where he ran all over the parking lot kicking frogs and barfing.

Dr. Nuñez returned wearing sunglasses. He leaned back in the chair, folded his arms and snoozed, leaving everything else to Flor.

I was secretly afraid to take pain killers. I hadn't taken aspirin or any other drug throughout the pregnancy, because of pictures I'd seen of the poor thalidomide babies, born without arms and legs. I knew aspirin wouldn't do that but didn't take it anyway. Doña Lydia made up for it by taking any drugs her kids or husband didn't finish. A bit of a hypochondriac, she complained about every ache and pain. I learned the parts of the body in Spanish from her.

I'd been worried about spiders, when the real danger was that the dispensary had no blood bank, silver nitrate, and a seven-month preemie occupied the only incubator.

The next contraction took my breath away, bringing Dr. Nuñez up from his chair. Neither he nor Flor wore masks or gloves. "Here it comes!" I groaned.

"Push!" Dr. Nuñez ordered. "The head's crowning."

It seemed to last forever. I'd just laid back exhausted on the soaked pillow, when here came another.

"Bear down! Don't stop till I say!" he said. "Good, good! Now, stop!"

Dr. Nuñez said something to Flor in Spanish I couldn't understand. "Now, push," Dr. Nuñez exclaimed in English!

Holding my breath, I bore down.

"Keep pushing!" he ordered. "Don't stop! Hard! Harder!"

My face turned red as I gave it all I had. One last ounce of strength then the world seemed suspended as a limp baby was laid across my stomach. All was quiet.

"You have a beautiful baby boy!" he smiled.

"He's not crying," I said. "Is he okay?"

"Don't *preocoop*, he's fine," Dr. Nuñez laughed. "Babies don't always cry at birth."

They do in the movies, I thought. The baby lay perfectly still, his eyes moving around his bright, new surroundings. Finally fixing them on me, he gazed into my eyes in amazement. He recognized my voice and stared more intently. At that moment, I fell in love and have been so ever since. So he is what's been kicking me all these months, this tiny, beautiful person! Tiny? How did he ever fit in there? With a miracle like birth, how could anyone doubt the existence of God?

At that time, U.S. hospitals didn't let fathers near babies until they went home. But this wasn't the States! When things were cleaned up, Roberto was called in to see his new son. I'd have died to know an open bucket with the placenta sat on the floor as our friends filed by with hugs and hardy, but quiet, congratulations.

"A boy!" Lelo exclaimed. "And born on Independence Day! Like our Popo, he must have a nickname!" Amused friends cooed in agreement as it was pronounced.

"Welcome little Independencio! Welcome to Coto!"

Chapter Four
Promises and Other Scary Things

I was taken to the private room about four a.m. A metal bassinette lined in white linen was wheeled in front of the open window next to my bed, looking a lot like an Easter Basket. Its off-center "handle" probably used to drape a mosquito net, was an ugly tube with a drippy paint job. Beneath its arch lay a pink, plump bundle blissfully asleep. Up for nearly twenty-four hours, I should have been tired but couldn't take my eyes off the miracle that was part Roberto and part me.

At Independencio's first six a.m. feeding, I opened the receiving blanket and we played our first game. I recited the familiar nursery rhyme, "This Little Piggy Went to Market," as I gently wiggled and counted each of his perfect tiny toes.

His tummy full, the nipple slipped from his mouth, still gazing into my eyes. I was overwhelmed with love for this tiny person. He began to squirm. Instinct told me he needed to be burped. No sooner was he on my shoulder than two huge sounds erupted that could have easily come

from his father! Wiping his mouth, I cradled him in my arms and cooed. "What a bubble! Feel better now, Sugar?"

Taken with the sound of my voice, he looked like he was thinking, *So this is the one I've heard all these months!* At this tender moment, in walked a nurse speaking to me in Spanish. "*Buenos dias, Señora.* We have a new baby! Have you named him?"

"Not yet. I'm waiting for his daddy."

"*Por cierto* (for certain/of course)! Fathers like to name their sons! Has he nursed?"

"Just finished."

"Good! Time for his first bath."

I suddenly felt protective. I'd seen no nursery window last night. She reached for the infant. Not at all concerned about my less than perfect Spanish today, I pulled away. "Where are you taking him, Mrs. uhh…?"

"Sorry. Isabela Alvarez, head nurse."

"*Sra. (señora)* Alvarez," I repeated.

"Babies stay with their mothers," she continued. We only take them to the nursery next door to be bathed and changed. It's also our neonatal intensive care unit. We finally got an incubator. There's a seven-month preemie in there, now. Don't *preocoop,* your baby will be back before you finish breakfast."

I pulled the covers away and sat up on the edge of the bed. The swelling was completely gone and my legs were once again sleek as a thoroughbred's.

I was cleaned up, and my breakfast sitting there, when the baby was returned. Eyes glued to my beautiful newborn, I held him until he fell asleep then carefully placed him in his tiny bed on wheels. I stared at him, eating my cold breakfast.

Sra. Alverez had just taken the tray, when Roberto swept into the room with a big smile. Bending down, he kissed me on the forehead. "How's Mama?"

Mama! I smiled. I couldn't wait to hear the baby say it! "Mama's great! How about Daddy?"

"Flying all morning and nowhere near a chopper!" We both laughed. "Everybody's off for Independence Day. Independencio!" He bent over to kiss the baby then turned to me. "Got some exciting news!"

"What?"

"A name for the baby!"

"Wonderful!"

"Christopher Lee."

"The vampire?"

"No, the English actor who sometimes *plays* a vampire."

"I thought it would be Roberto Rafael."

"I never liked Rafael."

"Robert's nice. How about Robert Christopher?"

"Hmm," he pondered, "not bad. Robert Christopher it is!"

We planned our son's future in a playful tug-of-war between a military career and medicine that ended on a good note. I had Roberto place the heavily ruffled peignoir of my white negligee over the bassinette tubing to block a gentle breeze that had picked up outside. Our baby looked like a little prince asleep in a royal bed. Roberto kissed his son goodbye then gave me a peck as he left for the restaurant.

That afternoon, Carolina and some friends dropped by with some lovely red flowers. With them was an old woman. Customary to her station and generation, her eyes were lowered in humility. Except for darker hair, she was a dead ringer for Granny on "The Beverly Hillbillies."

"I didn't think you'd be up to interviewing a new maid," said Carolina in English, "so I put out the word."

"Good!" I said.

"Margarita?" Carolina paused and motioned. The old woman stepped forward and nodded with a grin, the sparkle in her eyes outshining the gold in her teeth. "She's raising two grandkids and looking for day work. She lives behind the commissary, so she can walk to work and be there by six. She'd like to leave before dark and can start anytime."

I was barely keeping up with general cleaning, cooking from scratch, washing by hand, hours of ironing and now a baby? I looked the old woman up and down. Margarita smiled over the tops of spectacles then lowered her gaze. I needed help but was she physically up to it? Barely five feet tall, she was wrinkled as a prune from years in the sun. Her leathery skin covered a boney frame, and with her hair pulled back tight in a bun it accentuated her hollow cheeks and round sunken eyes even more. This diminutive woman belonged in a rocking chair telling stories to her grandkids; not wringing out sheets, paste waxing and hand-buffing floors and running up and down stairs all day. But her eyes sparkled with energy, and a salt of the earth smile creased her lips as if she was hiding a secret. "I'll do a good job for you, Doña," she assured me in Spanish.

She looks seventy. I should be calling her "Doña." Maybe she'll do till I can find someone younger. "Thank you for coming." Her expression was hopeful. "You may start Friday morning."

"Okey-dokey!" It was the only English she remembered from American GI's in the Panama Canal Zone during World War II. Her wry smile turned serious with a look you could take to the bank. "I'll be there, Doña. Muchisimas gracias."

Margarita left and the ribbing began.

"You're certainly living the life of Riley!" said Carolina.

"Enjoy it while you can!" another laughed.

"Yeah," Carolina added. "Life as you know it is over!"

"After leaving here, you can forget about sleeping through the night!" the third friend joked.

"When he's a teen," said Carolina, "it'll be even worse!"

"Your kids are still small," one said. "How do you know?"

"'Cause I used to be one!" she quipped then added. "By the way, fess up! How did you do it?"

"Do what?" I asked.

"Six hours on a first birth! Back labor without a peep! What'd they give you?"

"Nothing."

"Nothing?"

"All the wards were asleep, the nurse said…."

"To heck with that!" Carolina interrupted. "I'd have yelled my head off like Sunny did!"

"Don't *preocoop!*" I laughed. "I'll make up for it next time."

I admired Sunny, the wife of the chief helicopter mechanic. She was five months along when she first came to Coto, expecting a modern medical facility offering epidurals. Instead, she got a rudimentary frontier clinic dispensing bandages and aspirin. This modern-day pioneer, who adjusted well to Coto's hardships, brought four children to live on a remote plantation and had her baby there, got her name from her sunny disposition. She and Carl had been married about thirteen years and were as in love as newlyweds. A good Catholic, Carl took his religion seriously and nurtured his children in the faith. They had never a missed Sunday mass. Five p.m. at a potluck cookout on a farm one Sunday, Carl told the kids to get changed for mass. They were not only cooperative but cheerful. With all the food, fun and games, they were going where? What about the homemade ice cream? Couldn't church wait? Not to Carl, and off they went! I was secretly impressed.

Sunny, a Baptist, never went, figuring if she couldn't be a good Catholic, she shouldn't attend mass. I never questioned it. She was a loving wife and mother and a good friend to me.

After my friends left the hospital that day, I spent most of the rest of the day talking to the baby and watching him sleep. Tranquil evening hours bathed in silence, I lay beside his little bed, my hand on my flat tummy, reliving the day's events. It was late when I came off my "joy high" long enough to relax and fall asleep.

Thursday, after paying the combined doctor/hospital bill of seven hundred colones, or about one hundred and ten dollars, Roberto had a surprise: He'd worked on *la uva*. There would be no bumpy ride home in Lelo's open jeep.

Carol and Roger waited outside our apartment with a homemade dessert. We were in the kitchen, cooing at the baby, when Pushy hobbled in. She hurried across the room to greet me when her back went out. Howling in pain, she chased her tail in one of her fits. Before I could put the baby down and go to her, Roberto grabbed her by the scruff of the neck and headed out the back door with Roger in hot pursuit, his hand on the gun strapped to his belt. Heavy boots pounded like an earthquake across wooden floors and down the back steps. Then silence. I froze. Roger followed Roberto as far into the tall grass as they dared and pulled his revolver. "Do you want me to...?"

"No," Roberto said, "I should do it."

I was still standing there when the shot rang out. My heart sank. If I had thought physical exertion from the ride home from the dispensary was too much, the sad loss of Pushy was my *coup de grace*. I spent the rest of the day in bed. Roberto sent out for lunch and supper at the restaurant and showed true remorse for what he felt he'd been forced to do.

Ants will get Push after all! I can't think about that today! I'll think about it tomorrow.

Friday dawned. I got Roberto's breakfast ready then jumped into an icy shower for my first day at home as a new mother.

I'd just dressed when the baby began to fuss. I already had water boiling for his sponge bath in the kitchen, cushioning the cold metal counter top with towels for a soft place to lay him. His clothes laid out on my bed, I sat in the rocker to nurse him.

After he was deliriously full, I went to the kitchen to fill the baby tub, when someone knocked at the back door. It was six o'clock. I showed Margarita the pile of laundry and returned to get the water to a perfect temperature for little Robert Christopher. After his bath, I laid him on the bed to dress. This was going to be fun! Doing exactly as the nurse had instructed, I carefully cleaned around his umbilical cord with that strange-smelling Costa Rican alcohol. After it was dry, I tied the *fajero* (fah-HAIR-o), a bias-cut cloth, tightly around the baby's middle, essential for a nice belly button according to Costa Rican tradition. Who was I to argue? I knew nothing!

Next, I applied baby lotion, dressed him in a tiny tee shirt, and then a miniature shirt I'd so meticulously ironed. As I reached for his tiny socks and booties, a stream shot into the air. I grabbed a diaper to cover the yellow fount but kept missing as he continued to squirm! Like a loose fire hose, the stream hit clean clothes, pillows, me and then splashed across his own face, startling him as he gasped for air! Flailing his arms, he rocked from side to side so I just missed covering the geyser

every time! Finally able to cap the gusher, I dabbed the warm fluid from a stunned little face that was as surprised as mine!

I reheated the kettle, got the water perfect, bathed him and found a dry spot on the bed to dress him, this time keeping a diaper over the offending member. For the second time, I cleaned around the cord, leaving it to dry while rubbing on lotion. Then I dressed him in a fresh tee shirt, ironed shirt, socks, booties, *fajero,* diaper, plastic pants and a lightweight receiving blanket. But, as I turned to change his bed, a sound came from behind me that only babies can make in polite society. His red, puffy cheeks morphed into a satisfied look, followed by a sweet odor found in nurseries.

Unpinning the diaper, I got my first gander at baby poo. What looked like "curdled mustard" was everywhere: tee shirt, edges of his ironed shirt, even socks and booties where he'd kicked himself in the buns. *This isn't as easy as I thought!* I threw the soiled clothing onto a growing pile in the corner, and turned the kettle back on for the third major overhaul. It ended up taking me four times in all and completely wearing me out. Exhausted, I laid down for a moment and fell asleep. When I awoke, Margarita already had the wash on the line and the house swept and straightened, so I looked for something to fix for lunch. As I stepped into the kitchen, she rushed over and insisted I get back to bed. "Señora, you shouldn't be up. You must observe *la quarantena.*"

Sounded like 'quarantine.' "Observe what?" I asked.

"*La quarantena.* Forty days of bed rest after giving birth."

Forty days! In bed? I'd go crazy!

"Pardon me, Señora, but you must. A woman must maintain her health."

"I've got baby things to wash and iron."

"But that's why I'm here, Doña," she answered softly.

"Thank you, I'll do it." I didn't trust *anyone* with baby things that had to be done just right.

"But Doña, you can't go up and down stairs, yet!"

"I'm fine. You may straighten the bathroom now."

On the way downstairs, I noticed my underwear discreetly hung inside sheets on the line. I liked that. Mama did it that way. What I didn't like was one sheet on that weathered, beat up *lata!* (A lata is a corrugated metal sheet nailed to four-by-four stilts about two feet off the ground). Cecelia never used ours on 51. If not for our next door neighbor's laundry on hers, I'd have never known what the ugly thing was for!

I carefully washed the baby's little duds and hung them to dry. Going back upstairs got to me, so I paused to rest a time or two. Margarita was at the back door shaking her head. "Your bed is changed, Señora. Come and lie down."

"No…, gracias."

"A *short* rest," she insisted.

"I can't."

"You must, Señora; for the baby."

She was right. If bath time was a sample of things to come, resting while he slept was essential. As she walked me to my room, I asked, "Why are there sheets on the *lata,* Margarita?"

"That sheet needed whitening," Margarita answered.

"I don't have any bleach."

"Don't need it," she said, covering her laugh. "I soap them real good with lye soap, add lots of lemon juice and leave them in the sun all day."

The backyard was full of lemons for Roberto's lemonade and to squeeze over his fish and pork chops, but to whiten clothes? Our lemon

tree was spliced with orange, grapefruit and lime. My favorite tree had two pound avocados and grapesized seeds. I saw myself sitting under it with some limes, salt and a spoon!

When we had first moved in, there were four pineapples in our garden ready to pick; but Angela next door had gotten to them first. She was stealing our milk, too. When Margarita noticed the water ring under one of the empty bottles, she started arriving for work before the milkman and the pilfering stopped.

Margarita was right. After I'd rested, she knocked on my door. In her hand was a cup of something hot that smelled wonderful. "It's *sustancia*," she said.

"What's that?"

"A sort of beef consommé to regain your strength. Lunch will be ready at twelve, Doña."

I ditched the spoon and drank it down. It was delicious! Freshly made *sustancia* twice a day, plus glasses of *avena* (ah-VAY-nah) made from two tablespoons of cooked oatmeal, sugar, cinnamon and milk, blended to the consistency of a milk shake made me strong as ever. Margarita took excellent care of me. But good food wasn't all she dished up!

"Señora, permit me to say, but you should never go barefoot outside."

"But, it's just to the clothes line," I responded in defense. Then I winced, remembering the coral snakes.

"I know Señora, but there are worms that bore into the bottoms of feet and cause all kinds of health problems later."

She must mean hook worms. "Does a doctor cut them out?"

"No, Señora. We get off our feet for a day, wrap the foot with bacon and...."

"Bacon?"

"...and wait. Worms back into the bacon and we throw it away. But why waste good bacon and lose a whole day of work, when you can just wear shoes, okey-dokey?"

Margarita knew everything, even the exact time it would rain, and she had clothes off the line before it even started sprinkling. She spoiled me rotten. I'd never been so pampered! Anticipating my every need, she took perfect care of the house, washed and ironed the baby's things better than I could and saved us money by conserving food and cleaning supplies. What a treasure!

After settling into a routine, I shopped for groceries and cooked breakfast and lunch. With most of my time spent caring for the baby, when I got free to clean the kitchen, she'd already done it and was downstairs ironing. Margarita loved holding the baby and would rock him for hours.

Margarita would have known what to do that night Roberto was at the movies and our two-week old baby started crying. I'd just laid him down and started reading, when he began fussing. I burped him and he fell back to sleep. Minutes later, he began crying and flailing his arms. He wasn't wet or soiled, so I held him over my shoulder a while then laid him back down sound asleep. In no time, he was screaming. Unwrapping the blanket, I checked the pins. Everything was fine. I held him to me again and he fell asleep. I was drowsy; I put him in his crib and had nearly dozed off, when he screamed again. As I was getting him a hot water bottle, I heard a knock at the front door.

"Good evening," the woman in a robe said in Spanish. "I live across the street and heard your baby. Do you need help?"

"Come in," I said. "I think he has a tummyache."

"I've had six of my own," she said.

I'd never met anyone with six children before! She nodded with pride as if to say, "Yes; *six!*"

"It could be colic," she said, "but I doubt it. You can tell by the cry. May I see him?"

"Sure. The bedroom's back here." By this time, the baby was hysterical and I hurried to pick him up.

"Please; let me. You sit there."

To give her room in the narrow space between bed and crib, I swung my feet onto the bed. She gave a disapproving glance at my bare, unshaven legs. I must have looked like a werewolf! I pulled my gown and cotton duster down as far as they'd go, which was barely below my knees.

On her shoulder, the baby stopped screaming like before. "Are you nursing?" she said, looking me up and down.

I nodded.

"That's it. Your milk's bad."

How could this be? At that time, babies were put on formula and nursing discouraged. But I'd read about it and chosen to nurse, beliving mother's milk was best.

"Bad?" I asked. "How can you tell?"

"Your legs!"

Where was this leading?

"You shave them, no?"

"Yes; but...."

I was embarrassed for her when she opened her robe and showed me her hairy legs.

"You see?" she said in triumphant pride. "Always plenty of good milk. No razor has ever touched my skin. My husband would never permit!" She didn't hang around long and never came back. Boy, was I glad!

Days later, it was a normal Monday morning when Roberto left for work. Drearily overcast and cooler than usual, I got under the warm covers to nurse. The baby full and sleeping, I went into the kitchen for a hot cup of coffee, when someone knocked at the door. Margarita, who always let herself in the back, had been downstairs washing since six. Still in my gown and duster, I was glad it wasn't a door-to-door vendor, but instead, I spied several women through the half-closed plantation shutters.

"Maria, it's Carol," one strained in a loud whisper. "Let me in."

Fine time for company! I'd left breakfast dishes on the table to run feed the baby. I unlocked the wooden door to the screened-in porch and then the outer screen door. In rushed Carol with a plate full of cookies, smiling from ear to ear, followed by the others. Carol presented herself as positive and cheerful, when truth was, she was scared to death! She insisted on seeing the baby, then they all cooed and complimented me on how cute he looked that early in the morning and what a happy baby he was. I changed him and we passed him around until he was so worn out he fell back to sleep. So I put him to bed and they suggested we have coffee. As I poured the last cup, the phone rang.

"I'll get it," Carol said, sprinting to the living room wall unit by the bedroom.

Others stopped talking and strained to hear, some seemingly nervous. Margarita even came upstairs and stood at the door, drying her hands on her apron.

"Yes, Margarita?" I said.

"Nothing, Señora," she said without moving.

I was seated at the table when, visibly shaken, Carol returned to the room. The others tensed as she got down on one knee cupping her hands over mine, which were folded in my lap. "Don't be alarmed, Maria, but there's been an accident."

"Roberto!" I tried jumping up but she held me down, the others moving in to steady me with their hands on my shoulders.

"He's okay!" Carol blurted.

"What happened then? Where is he?"

"Well, about thirty minutes after takeoff, he crashed and landed upside down. After Roger phoned, I called the others and we rushed over. They're bringing him in, now."

I didn't allow myself to cry. *Stiff upper-lip as Aunt Mozy would say.* Besides, there wasn't time! I had to get dressed. What if they had to fly him to Golfito? I thanked them and ran to get dressed while they waited.

Within minutes, Roberto walked in, dazed and holding his black helmet which had a deep, silver gash in it. Though pale and visibly shaken, there wasn't a scratch on him. I helped him to bed as friends quietly left and Margarita returned to work.

As I held him he trembled and repeated over and over, "My whole life flashed before me. I swear on my son's head. It flashed before me and I'm going to hell!"

Unknown by us wives at this time, the Costa Rican pilots had been going into Villaneily for "entertainment." I hurried to get him some hot *sustancia*. When I returned, he was holding his son and weeping, his face buried in the receiving blanket. I set the cup on the nightstand, eased onto the bed, held them both and we wept together.

For a period of time after this close call, Roberto was more loving, attentive and considerate. But it wasn't long before he returned to his old self and worse. Mild insults that became vile threats had escalated to

murderous bluster. It was in Coto that I first noticed these seemingly psychotic episodes manifesting like clockwork about every two weeks. Was it caused by a chemical imbalance or some trauma in his past? I tactfully approached his mother, who excused him as having "special" needs. What need could be more special than to be loved? I had tried that, believing love could heal any hurt he had and I could help him be all he was meant to be. Instead he'd become an out-of-control, man-sized brat! Later on, I would discover that the source of his rage was in front of my eyes the whole time and I never even knew it.

The truth is, no one had forced me to marry Roberto. I had picked him and now this man was the father of my child. I had so wanted to help him; to save him. But now, the question was: Who would save me and my baby from him and his "special" needs?

Of course, Roberto's most imminent "special need" was resuming intimacy after the baby was born. When I told him the doctor had recommended that we wait a full six weeks, you'd have thought he was condemned to death! As usual, he dealt with this problem by first smacking me around, and afterwards folding in remorse at what he had done.

"God! What was I thinking? Are you all right?"

I took his offered tissue and dabbed at my blurred, tearing eyes. Falling to his knees, he held me tight around my waist. "I swear on my son's head; I'll never do it again!" I could hardly breathe as he squeezed me so hard. "I don't know what happens," he blubbered. "I just lose control! Please, Mary Sue, if I ever do this again, slap me!"

"What?"

"Yeah, right in the face."

"But I'll hurt you."

"A little slap from a woman can't hurt me, but it'll shock me into seeing what I'm doing. That's all I need to stop and think!" My long

silence had him begging. "Don't turn your back on me, please!" He buried his face in my lap. I stroked his dark wavy hair. My husband needed me. He raised his tear-stained face and I nodded. Next time, I'd slap him, just like he said. But, there was no need, because the next few months passed by without a whimper from him. He seemed to be keeping his word.

Baby items in Costa Rica cost double, so getting a stroller was out of the question. Roberto made plenty of money, but he just never saved it. I began snagging his pocket change (which he never missed), while he was showering.

The baby was only three weeks old when my milk dried up. If I had just known to rest twenty-four hours and drink water and juice, it would have come back like gangbusters! As a result, the doctor put the baby on that nasty smelling formula, which he said would double his birth weight in ninety days. Instead, he tripled it in sixty! So, a stroller was no longer a luxury.

Doña Lydia had a crib built, painted white and shipped to us before the baby was born. Smaller than a standard U.S. crib, it fit perfectly in his little corner, only the sides didn't go up and down and the mattress was stuffed with straw. She called the baby, *Crisanto* (Holy Christ) from his name Chris and said "he would be like the Holy Christ Child, sleeping in a manger."

It was during a particular hot spell that I was able to keep my promise to "help" Roberto with his temper. Roberto had been grumpy for days. Chris was now sitting up. I was feeding him in his walker because we couldn't afford a high chair. (The money was going to girls in Villaneily.) While spooning food to the baby Roberto angrily slammed his glass on the table resumed eating. I was to pour his tea, add sugar and stir it for him. With the baby hot and fussy, I was having trouble getting him to eat. I didn't want to stop, as I might not get him eating

again. "Could you pour your own, honey?" I asked Roberto, trying to deal with the baby. "The pitcher and sugar's right there."

Without looking up, he slammed his glass again.

"A few more bites and I can put him to bed," I said, bending over the baby with another bite.

"Do as you're told," Roberto ordered.

Stalling for time, I stirred the silver baby spoon around the jar, trying to jolly Roberto into a better mood. Maybe if I were cheerful, he'd "get my drift." But being affected by the heat, and not exactly thrilled at his attitude, I resorted to sarcasm and stalled for time with a little humor. "Do as I'm told? I heard no nice request only a glass slamming." Thinking I'd been clever, I chuckled as I fished around the jar for the last bite.

His heavy chair scraped the floor then fell with a thud as he sprang to his feet. "I don't have to speak! Here, I'm king!"

"Get your own tea, Your *Majesty*. The baby's still eating."

"Pour it or else!" he warned.

Dropping the spoon in the jar, I scooted the baby back and confronted Roberto nose to nose. "I thought you said I wouldn't have to take this crap, anymore!"

He punched my arm. I was stunned but not hurt. I paused. *Should I? I should! He had told me to.* I slapped his face! His surprised look is the last thing I remember. I "came to" in the corner, curled in a ball. The baby was in his walker a few feet away, his back to me, head slumped over. "What have you done?" I screamed. Roberto never blinked. The irony was that beside his plate was a full glass of tea. Sugared and stirred, no doubt!

I scooted to the walker on my elbows. The baby was only asleep. I put him in his little Jesus bed. Appetite gone, I lay across the bed watching him sleep, gently massaging my bottom where Roberto evidently kicked me. I rarely bruise with one exception: being on the receiving end of heavy flight boots. I was twisted around examining the big purple bruise forming, when he walked in. "Why make me do it? All I wanted was my tea!"

I didn't answer. The pain was more than physical. My very soul was bruised. This time, an apology wasn't enough.

"Look, I'm sorry. I've had a hard day."

"And I haven't?" I blurted out.

"Your lunch is getting cold."

"I'm not hungry."

"You've got to eat! What if you die?"

I stared daggers. *If it were up to you, I WOULD be dead!*

"Eat!" he reiterated.

"No thank you, I...."

His tone was soft and controlled but nonetheless menacing. He gritted his teeth. "I said, eat!"

The delicious lunch I'd looked forward to had no flavor.

A month later, his temper flared again, only this time, he'd make sure I died. On this particular Saturday night, after the movies, he and his friends went whoring in Villaneily and he'd come home drunk. Nearly noon, Sunday morning, he stumbled to the bathroom door, holding his throbbing head and pointing a finger at me. "You; a glass of milk!"

"Be with you in a second," I sing-songed. "I'm changing the baby." I wanted him receptive when I talked to him about his drinking.

Hanging on to the doorsill, he took a step back and clenched his fist. "Move it, *pendeja* or else!"

ALL THE WAY HOME

Hurriedly fastening the last pin, I put the baby in his crib and rushed to the kitchen for the milk (their remedy for hangovers). I chose a plastic tumbler. Premeditated? You bet! Still, I paused at the shower door. *Dare I? Why not?* The milk would all go down the drain. He must have seen me through the fogged glass door, the light streaming in behind me. "Are you going to stand there all day, *bruta?* Give me my milk *NOW!*"

(Can't say he didn't ask for it!) Tearing the shower door open, I threw the ice-cold milk on him, glass and all! Not waiting to see what he'd do, I grabbed the baby, tore down the back steps and into the thick bushes under the apartments. The only thing louder than my breathing was my own heart throbbing in my throat. A screen door softly slammed and steps creaked as he descended the back stairs. Like a fawn in the thicket, I stayed perfectly still. Moving with cunning, he passed my hiding place, slowly hunting me as though I were an animal. In his hand: the German Luger.

God, what can I do? This is Sunday. Everyone's in church... undoubtedly where I should be!

His footsteps softly faded down the asphalt road toward the helicopter hangar. I'd managed to evade him for nearly an hour, hoping neighbors would start filtering back from church. The baby, now unbearably heavy, began to fuss. Past his naptime, he was wet and wanting a bottle.

I slipped up the front steps and locked the doors. If I had to wait, why not in my own home? I changed the baby, got his bottle and sat in the rocker to feed him. Afterwards, I'd just put him on my shoulder to burp, when I heard the bottom front steps creak. Someone was coming. I wanted to run, but where? Besides, my arms were so weak and shaky from carrying the baby so long. I could hide in the bedroom, but he'd just break in and corner me. He might even stand downstairs and randomly shoot through the floor. My staying calm might at least save the baby.

I rocked and patted, waiting for a bubble, when I heard the click of a weapon being cocked. From the corner of my eye, I saw him stiff-arming the gun and trembling, pointing it straight at my head. It was so close, I could smell the oil he used to clean it. I waited to die, hoping and praying he'd miss the baby. *God, please save him!*

"Get up and open the door," he calmly ordered out of breath.

Hearing that familiar voice, the baby bobbed his head from my shoulder with a bright smile to greet his daddy. Roberto rushed through the unlocked door like a commando. Figuring it wouldn't do any good to burst into tears or plead for my life I did as I was told. "Go to the bedroom and don't try anything," he said waving the gun toward our room then pressing the barrel against the base of my skull.

"You don't like my hands touching the back of your neck. How about cold steel?" He shoved the barrel in farther.

I took long, deep breaths, believing each to be my last then stopped at our bed.

"Put the baby in his crib," he motioned.

I put Chris on his tummy facing the wall, so he wouldn't see what was about to happen. But he scrambled over and sat up, ready to play.

Roberto ordered me to turn around.

I turned in obedience thinking *what a color contrast bright red would look on the sunny yellow curtains I'd made.* With a wildness in his eyes that turned my blood cold, Roberto asked, "Why do you make me do stuff like this? You know I love you!"

His weapon was pointing toward the crib. As he talked, I took two fingers and pushed it away from the baby's direction. I would have lowered my hand, only he gave no resistance, so I pushed until it pointed out back, toward the jungle. Because this was like disarming a delicate

ticking bomb, when he spoke, I nearly jumped out of my skin! "I could never hurt you!"

My composure regained, I curled my fingers gingerly around the barrel.

"You're the mother of my son for Christ's sake!"

Slowly, gently, I twisted the gun from his fingers. He crumpled onto the bed and wept bitterly into his pillow.

With no idea how to uncock or lock it, I carefully laid it on the floor, scooted it under the bed and sat down. My heart wasn't in it, but stroking his hair, I attempted to comfort the one who'd just nearly killed me. Whipping around, he grabbed me around the waist with both hands and buried his face in my lap. My heart skipped a beat!

"If you can't forgive me, I'll use the gun on myself right now and rid the world of the good-for-nothing trash that I am!"

"You mustn't say that. Self-murder would be your last act on earth. You could never ask forgiveness. You'd end up in...."

"I don't care about that!"

I said nothing, more out of shock than rejecting him.

"Then I'm lost!"

I still couldn't answer.

"I'd cut off my arm before I'd really hurt you!"

Suddenly, it all hit me in a flood of emotion. *Bright red on sunny yellow? That would have been my blood! I might be dead now! Who would take care of Chris?*

As I burst into tears, he pulled me into his embrace.

"Oh, thank you! Thank you! It'll never happen again. I swear: On my eyes (a Latino oath), on my mother's life, on my son's head!"

Roberto's promises to me had become as terrifying as he was. He'd always promise there'd be no next time, but his lies were more sure than his word. Over time, I got real good at ducking on a dime, a survival mode I had learned in childhood; now perfected as an adult. Only a few weeks after this incident, something else happened that was scarier than any gun. It wasn't human, either!

At six months, we began calling the baby "Chris," about the same time as an outing we went on with friends to the beach. All our cars made up quite a convoy. *La uva* wouldn't run, so we rode with Roger and Carol. After about an hour's drive, we arrived at a beautiful beach in Panama with miles of yellow sand and shady palm groves. As I spread our blanket, Lelo came by to talk.

"How's Little *Independencio?* Is he ready for a swim? This is a nice place, Maria, but I should warn you that we're next to a river that empties into the sea. Sharks look for prey at the mouths of the rivers; most of their attacks occur in shallow water only a few feet from shore. So don't go out too far, and pick out a landmark — a tree, or a car — to keep from drifting. The current can push you toward the river without your even noticing."

You could depend on Lelo for a dose of gloom and doom!

"Thank you," I said. "I'm not taking Chris in, anyway." He's too young to be out in the sun, but not me." I turned to Roberto. "Mind if I go in for a dip?"

"Go ahead," he said, taking a drag off his cigarette.

I took the shorts and top off I'd worn over my suit and went in to cool off. I wasn't gone long. Wrapping a towel around my wet hair, I played with Chris on the blanket, while Roberto went off somewhere with the men. Chris kept trying to crawl off the blanket, so I picked him up and walked to the shore's edge to sit where he could splash in the shade of the umbrella I had brought.

ALL THE WAY HOME

An offshore reef kept the waves calm like a lake. Unlike in travel magazines, the water wasn't clear, but clouded and murky.

Bored sitting in mere inches of water, I went out a little bit farther, holding the umbrella over us for protection. Fascinated, Chris leaned over as far as possible to watch the sunlight playing on the water as I splashed along. Now ankle deep, the water was still too shallow to sit down and play, so I continued walking.

I loved when Chris saw something new and different. Having a child was as new to me as the ocean was to him, so I had to see his giddy smile and excited reaction to every new discovery. The water was still so shallow, what harm could it do to go out a tiny bit farther..

"Like it, Sugar? Pretty, isn't it? Can you say water?" Bending over, I lowered him in, watching his face as he kicked and splashed in the warm waves. I first thought mid-calf would be about right for us to really enjoy ourselves. By the time we were there, though, I was so hot, I walked farther to more easily dip myself, still holding tightly onto Chris. Then we'd go back to the shallows and play under the umbrella. Watching the wonder in Chris' face, I paid little attention to direction, walking until the water was mid-thigh or a little over two feet.

That's when Lelo's advice about landmarks hit me. Thinking the beach only a few yards behind, I turned to find out that we were more than a block and a half away from shore. I'd gone too far! What's worse, I'd drifted toward the mouth of the river. Something long swished a current of water against my leg. *Lord, help me!* Fearing for my baby, I wanted to bolt back to shore, but I had heard that splashing attracted sharks. *Stay calm!* Clenching my jaw, I held Chris close, ready to punch or kick anything that came near. This time, my eyes were fixed on the shore instead of Chris, who laughed at the sparkling water, joyfully unaware of any danger.

MARY SUZANNE LOPEZ

If Daddy had been here, he would have said, "a soldier can make it if he stays calm," and Mama, "put one foot in front of the other." And that I did, all the way to shore.

CHAPTER FIVE

WISHING UPON STARS

While visiting Roberto's family in San Jose, I was so preoccupied with Chris, I forgot it was Thanksgiving. Doña Lydia served roasted *tepezquintle*. (And no, it didn't taste like chicken, more like pork roast.) Roberto said *tepezquintles* lived in the jungle, grew three feet long, a hundred pounds, were excellent swimmers and the favorite food of jaguars. But did he have to tell me that the same animal Americans call "capybaras" were the largest rodents in the world? (Rodent? Yuck!) Doña Lydia tried to make up for my shock. "Instead of coming here for Christmas, Maria, how about we visit you in Coto? I can bring a small turkey."

They were both such sweet, doting grandparents. Doña Lydia couldn't believe how beautiful Chris was! She invited family and friends who all brought gifts, over to see him. Not being from a "touchy-feely" family, myself, this was how I'd always dreamed a family should be. Mom did send me a nice Christmas card with a check for fifty bucks (over three hundred *colones*). Now I could finally get a stroller and give my back a break. Knowing of no banks near Coto, I put it away to cash it in San Jose. The nearly one year I'd spent in

Costa Rica, Roberto had never put his money in a bank. He didn't trust them. Having been ordered to never open the money drawer in our bedroom, I was surprised when Roberto came home and showed me we were nearly broke. (I still didn't know about his nocturnal visits to Villaneily and how they were adding up.) "What happened to all the money?" I said.

"You spend it all on food. What do you need, now?"

"Money for Christmas gifts." I'd planned to shop in San Jose. If I'd only remembered that they'd be coming here for Christmas, I could have shopped in Panama. If Mom's check had arrived here sooner, I could have bought the stroller there, too. But I'd saved hundreds of colones from Roberto's pocket change; maybe thousands! I could use that for presents and pay myself back later. *La Uva* wouldn't make it to Villaneily, much less Golfito, which left the commissary. There, I found a party ice bucket with little tongs for Don Vicente, who liked having friends over for drinks and I'd seen him serve ice from a cereal bowl with a tablespoon. I found a lovely pink blouse for Doña Lydia and a more youthful white one for Andreina. Eleven year old Sandrita still played with dolls, so I got her a large dollhouse in a tattered, dusty box; the only one left.

Margarita mentioned how cold she'd been at night, so I got her a blanket in a colorful Indian design with enough left over for a huge bag of hard candy for her grandkids. Tears streamed down her face as she left for home Christmas Eve, bearing gifts.

That dingy white tissue paper and faded ribbon to wrap it all must have been on the commissary shelves for years. The eight *colones* left bought me that can of Campbell's Tomato Soup I'd been craving all through my pregnancy. Home I raced, my *bolsas* stuffed with goodies!

I'd found a garland and some discolored glass ornaments in Panama, but didn't have a tree. In Latin America, elaborate Nativity Scenes were used. But this was Chris' first Christmas, so things had to be just "right."

ALL THE WAY HOME

I taped the sparkly silver garland in the shape of a tree in the biggest section of bare wall, which was next to the front door. I then hung the ornaments from it and placed our presents beneath it on a white sheet representing snow. I made a star for the top, but had no tin foil to cover it with, since that was an imported luxury, along with paper towels and wax paper.

The Christmas toys purchased in Panama for Chris were: a kiddy car shaped like a saddled palomino and some inflatable toys, including a Santa, which I kept hidden in the closet until Christmas morning.

When Roberto's family arrived from the ten-hour bus trip, I offered them our bedroom, but they wouldn't hear of it. They'd brought bedrolls and were really sweet about the discomfort and inconvenience.

Doña Lydia had the turkey in the oven, bright and early Christmas morning. Roberto's folks couldn't afford gifts for us, but seemed pleased with what we'd gotten them. I was hurt that Roberto had forgotten to get a little something for me. Carol sort of made up for it later that morning when she came by with a three-bar box of fancy soap from Spain, wrapped in nice paper and ribbon. I still have it to remind me I wasn't completely forgotten.

I got a little teary-eyed that first Christmas in Coto, listening to Elvis croon, "I'll Be Home for Christmas," from our stereo's speakers. I was pleased that I could keep up with his family in conversational Spanish as they sat around cracking jokes, and all making the baby's first Christmas one to remember. Later on, with leftovers and dishes put away, Chris asleep hugging his inflatable Santa and the family watching TV, I slipped outside to be alone a while. It was my first Christmas away from home.

Evening was settling over Coto Valley. It was summer in Costa Rica, so there would be no pungent smell coming in on the jungle fog to spoil the fragrance of the citrus trees and flowers. Houses on stilts, wild orchids, ten-foot hibiscus and palm leaves glistening green against a clear blue sky were now commonplace. But even with all this beauty, it wasn't

home for me. They say home is where the heart is, but if you don't feel loved, your heart and mind will take flight to find it.

My mind wandered to Christmas back home. I could almost feel the frigid blast of an Oklahoma winter and see snow glittering like a million diamonds by day and a soft blue by moonlight. I could smell the fresh baked gingerbread, chewy fudge brownies and taste hot chocolate brimming with miniature marshmallows and a steaming mugs of apple cider; our reward for an evening's joyous caroling. I felt the warmth of our cozy kitchen after we'd built our carrot-nosed snowman and made winged snow angels. And it just wasn't Christmas without Aunt Gladys' annual gift box of chocolate covered cherries, the scent of freshly-cut firewood, the wintery smell of chimney smoke on the cool air and the faint sounds of children playing out in the cold.

What I wouldn't have given to escape home to Tulsa that night! It wasn't strange at all that the word "escape" should remind me of home. I can't have been more than three when Aunt Mozy first played that piece with the funny name.

———————

"Repeat it," Aunt Mozy coaxed, never allowing baby talk. "Good! 'The Gordian Knot Untied.' And it's not a 'song,' dear. In serious music, it's called a 'piece.' The English composer, Henry Purcell, wrote this nearly three hundred years ago. Pay close attention to the harmony, honey. He was the first important English composer to use harmony in the Italian style. He changed the music of his time, setting the stage for such future musicians as William Boyce, J.S. Bach and George Frederic Handle."

I knew what harmony was. Mama and Daddy sang on those four-hour trips up highway 66 to visit family in Tulsa. I loved all of Aunt Mozy's music, because of the stories. "Aunt Mozy, does this song, uh, piece, have a story?"

"Everyone and every piece has a story," she said with that familiar twinkle in her eye.

I sat up straight on the divan and crossed my feet at the ankle like I'd been taught. My hands folded neatly in my lap meant I was ready and she could begin.

"This story is of the Gordian Knot from Greek Mythology, which was a skillfully crafted knot tied by a peasant named Gordius, who used it to tie the ox yoke to his chariot. Gordius became king of Phrygia because an oracle — which is a wise man or a prophet — said he would. A legend grew, that the man who could loosen the difficult knot would become ruler of all Asia. Many tried without success. When Alexander the Great could not solve the riddle of the intricate knot, he severed it with his sword, declaring he had fulfilled the prophecy."

"That's a funny story," I said.

"Well, I'm not finished," my Aunt replied. "Remember King Midas whose touch turned everything to gold, even his daughter? Gordius was his father."

"I like the story of King Midas! Will you tell it to me?"

"What do nice little girls say?" Aunt Mozy reminded me.

"*Please...?*"

"Hear the end of this one, first. Always remember that 'to cut the Gordian Knot,' means to solve a difficult problem in an unexpected way."

───────────

Her sage wisdom was too subtle for a child my age. My Aunt Mozy brought fun and magic into my drab little world, not swords to cut future Gordian Knots. If I'd only understood, my ordeal with Roberto might have been over sooner. But hind-sight is always twenty-twenty.

The name Mozy might sound strange. Her real name was Audrey Mozelle. Rather elegant, don't you think? She was elegant, in her own way. She tried rubbing shoulders with the upper crust, but she was happiest with her hands in the soil of her huge garden on 15th and Memorial, which is now in Tulsa's city limits. Later, her Victory Garden on Quebec Street took up the whole backyard, where she grew everything from apples to zucchini. I can still see her in a bib apron snapping green beans, the smell of fresh greens mixing with the ashy smell of a summer fireplace. Her applesauce in the fall simmering with candy "Red Hots," hot apple cake topped with homemade whipped cream at Christmas, chocolate cake with a dash of cinnamon, potato salad and Southern fried chicken in summer, were the smells of home.

She could do anything! One year for each of her six nieces, she made red velvet Christmas stockings cuffed in white satin. On each of them she put felt cut-outs of snowmen and candy canes all outlined in beadwork; she filled the empty spaces with large sequins of bells and snowflakes. For the finishing touch, she even lined them with heavy plastic. This was quite an innovation for the 1950's, since Santa's candy back then didn't come individually wrapped.

Each stocking had something special to set it apart. Mine had a pony on it and my sister's — a Christmas giraffe? It's nubby horns were probably what was left of reindeer antlers she had accidently cut too short. Not wanting to disappoint Linda with this glaring mistake, Aunt Mozy dubbed the animal a "whatnot." Too young to know it was a joke, Linda bragged that her stocking was best because it had the "whatnot."

Aunt Mozy knew everything about flowers and trees. As they bloomed, she would point out to us her majestic purple iris, trumpeted daffodils and the tiny crocus that broke through crusted snow to bloom in early spring. I helped plant her rose moss (portulaca) among the rocks in back and begonias along her front sidewalk. By age three, I could recognize and properly pronounce the bright bougainvilleas, dazzling azaleas, willowy forsythias. I could distinguish the stately elms from maples before they turned gold and red in autumn; discern silver maples, their leaves shining like coins as they twisted and fluttered in the summer wind; the symmetrical pine oak and gnarled scrub oak, so plentiful in Oklahoma; and the sycamore with leaves that turned pungent after a rain. But I loved mimosas best for their fern-like leaves and sweet-smelling, powder puff blossoms. Maybe I loved them because "mimosa" sounded like "Mozy." Her mimosa had a branch as wide as a pony's back, where I'd ride through forest and field, dreaming of adventures in far-away places. Wide enough to lie on, I'd lie there on summer afternoons munching salted green apples and watching fluffy clouds lazily drift through imaginary tropical skies. Mama discouraged daydreaming, but not Aunt Mozy. Her stories sparked my imagination and gave me joy, hope and courage.

One night when I'd had a nightmare, she didn't hold me, but sat on the bed telling me to have a "stiff upper lip! You're from pioneer stock!" Suffering from night terrors, she understood my fear and reached for an old 78, Tchaikovsky's "Dance of the Sugar Plum Fairy," saying, I must learn to "escape into music."

"Ex-cape," I repeated in baby talk?

"It's pronounced, 'escape,' dear. It means to run; to get away from. From now on, close your eyes, listen to the music and imagine sugar plum fairies dancing above your head, and bad thoughts will vanish." Aunt Mozy was high strung and wanted me to learn to relax sooner in life than she had.

I peeked through pudgy fingers to see if they were there.

"Eyes closed," she scolded. "Fairies fly on the wings of imagination and can only be seen through the mind's eye." I didn't know what that meant. I only know my Aunt Mozy had said it. "Relax, listen and watch them dance."

Aunt Mozy made fantasy seem real. I was about six and my sister four, when Mama took us to spend the summer in Tulsa with Aunt Mozy and Uncle Joe. We couldn't wait until the Fourth of July, when Uncle Joe had promised to buy a grocery bag of fireworks and lots of sparklers to write our names in the sky like Aunt Mozy taught us.

Watching from the patio, Aunt Mozy sipped her coffee after breakfast, pretending to read her newspaper as we played in the backyard. "Aunt Mozy, come see what we found," we said, pointing at two sparklers sticking out of the ground.

"Well, I'll be!" she said in animated surprise. "I've read about this but never expected to see it!"

"What?" we asked in wide-eyed innocence.

She looked around, making sure we were alone and no one else could hear, then bent low.

"There's magic afoot here, girls," she said then added in a whisper. "Fairy dust was sprinkled over this very spot."

"Really?" we whispered back. "Can we pick them?"

"*May* we?" she corrected. "'*Can* I?' asks, *am I able?*, while '*May* I?' asks permission. You know you're strong enough to lift them, so what do you say?"

"*May* we pick them, please, and write our names in the sky?"

"Wonderful idea!" Aunt Mozy smiled, "But let's experiment. This is a miracle you may never see again!" Glancing suspiciously around, she pretended to make sure no one was near, then leaned in to whisper. "Let's leave them another night to see if they grow." Her expression was dead serious and so was ours. "Okay," we whispered, our eyes filled with wonder.

The next day, they'd grown to a medium size. She persuaded us to wait another day. The third morning, we were up at dawn, running past

ALL THE WAY HOME

Aunt Mozy, who was picking tomatoes. "Come see," we squealed, jumping in place! "They grew! They grew!"

"Adult sparklers!" she pronounced, rushing over.

"You mean they're all grown up?" I asked, astonished. "May we pick them, now?"

"One more night," she said. "They might have babies."

"Babies!" we exclaimed, our faces wild with excitement.

"Pretend they're not here," she whispered. "To have babies, they need peace and quiet."

"Yes Ma'am," we said with our aunt's same gravity of voice.

Next day, the Fourth of July, *adult* sparklers stood tall in the morning sun, surrounded by dozens of *babies!* Aunt Mozy said all of heaven would be able to see our sparklers that night.

Years later, she confessed it nearly killed her getting up at the crack of dawn to get sparklers in the ground before we got up, then staying up all day to make sure we didn't fall on them and get hurt.

The phrases "Make hay while the sun shines," "The early bird catches the worm," and "A penny saved is a penny earned" we learned from Aunt Mozy. But more than learning those or her wanting us to learn the value of money, she also insisted we grow up using correct grammar, finally resorting to bribery. We got twenty nickels each Saturday, which we couldn't spend for a week. In return, we were to put "-ly" on the end of nearly every word, stop splitting infinitives, and especially cut out the double negatives we were picking up on the school playground. Noncompliance meant our nickels went back to her. "Working at Brown Duncan," she would lecture, "when fellow clerks went to the drug store for Cokes on break, I took my nickel to the bank. That's why we can now afford Pig Dinners at Hawk's (about ten scoops of ice cream with every gooey topping you can think of, served in a

wooden pig trough that I think cost about eighty cents). "Wow," we said, "you must be rich!" Too cheap to buy her own, she took bites from everyone else's. When she found that keeping ice cream at home in the freezer saved her even more, we'd serve ourselves big bowls on summer nights, listen to the hum of Katydids we called locusts, rock in her iron patio chairs, count the stars and gaze at the Tulsa skyline.

Even sweeter than ice cream was the love of music she passed on to me. In her day, Russian composers like Tchaikovsky, Rimsky-Korsakov and Rachmaninoff were all the rage. She never liked Vivaldi, saying much of his music was frantic and repetitious. (I think it made her nervous.) She praised the talents of Josef "Papa" Haydn, the father of the symphony, as well as the genius of Mozart, the cleverness of Bach, the boldness of Beethoven, the spirit of Liszt and the passion of Chopin. From her old 78 recordings, I heard everything from the fire and splendor of Old Spain in Georges Bizet's "Carmen" to Rossini's light and sparkling, "Barber of Seville" (remember the Bugs Bunny and Elmer Fudd cartoon?); from the terror of Mussorgsky's "Night on Bald Mountain" (the mountain that's really the Devil, unfolding its wings in Walt Disney's Fantasia) to the charm of Mozart's wind divertimentos. But Tchaikovsky's "Dance of the Sugar Plum Fairies" I reserved for Aunt Mozy's escape technique.

My first Christmas away from home, and it felt more like summer. I was separated from everything I loved. Could God see me under all these trees? Aunt Mozy wasn't there with sparklers so He could or bowls of ice cream to fight the jungle heat. This Christmas, there were no red velvet stockings cuffed in white satin, no felt ponies or "whatnots," no crunching snow, blazing fires or chocolate covered cherries. As for escaping into music, I couldn't even conjour up a little Scarloti, Albononi or Corelli. Instead, still ringing in my ears was the line from "I'll Be Home for Christmas"—"Please have snow, and mistletoe, and presents on the tree."

ALL THE WAY HOME

Where had the family gathered for Christmas this year, at Mom's in Sand Springs or Aunt Mozy's in Tulsa? Christmas was over there, too. Weeks of preparation were only refrigerator leftovers and empty gift boxes stuffed with crumpled wrapping paper. The kitchen would be clean by now. Mama and Aunt Mozy would be serving pumpkin pie and hot apple cake piled high with whipped cream in a room filled with family and laughter. The fading fragrance of spruce lingers around warm sparkling lights on a tree bare of gifts. On the floor, next to a crackling fire, lay the crumpled stockings that Jolly St. Nick had filled last night with candy, fruit and trinkets. Carolers are indoors with their pie and coffee and tonight, the fogged breath and rosy cheeks belong only to neighbor boys building a snowman out front.

Standing there in Coto's darkening shadows and stifling heat, I hear birds settling high in the avocado tree and the first bat silently fluttering by overhead. Frogs begin to chirp in the citrus trees and croak from the shoulder-high grass as iguanas climb thorny palms to feast on clusters of pumpkin-colored *pejibehes*. Delicate flower petals close for the night as scruffy rats scurry to hide and nibble stolen morsels away from the fatal embrace of boas and fanged death of *matabueys*.

Palm trees stretch toward a vermilion sun, casting their lacy, black silhouettes against a scarlet sky. Soon, the evening star will appear in the indigo canopy above. Playing in my mind is a variation by Mozart we all now recognize as "Twinkle, Twinkle Little Star." Soon, I'll whisper the children's poem Grandmother Hoover taught me so many years ago.

> "Star light, star bright
> first star I see tonight.
> I wish I may, I wish I might
> have this wish I wish tonight."
> *I wish I were home.*

How many times in my childhood fantasies did I wish on that very star to be where I am tonight? Coto's scarlet skies deepen to crimson; the firey sun lowers into the palms to be extinguished. I've never felt so utterly alone. Lost in melancholy, I stand there gazing and longing for the golden sunsets of home.

CHAPTER SIX
SOUND ADVICE AND HIND SIGHT

December 26th, the day after Christmas, the family were saying their goodbyes to return to San Jose by bus. Roberto handed his father some money from who knows where and needed a little extra to round it out. He should have told me privately I was also to endorse my fifty dollar check to Don Vicente, who was very embarrassed.

Days later, during the Christmas *temporada* (a periodic two-week reprieve from rainfall during the rainy season), Roberto called from the backyard, "Mary Sue, bring the camera!" He stood there posing with his rifle and holding a four-foot iguana by the tail. "The tail's got lots of meat. Let's cook it for dinner!"

"Not in my skillet!" I'd blurted out without thinking. I should have been picking myself off the floor. Instead, he slung the dead iguana way out into the tall grass. It was confusing knowing when I could be assertive even in a "cute" way.

During that same *temporada,* I heard an engine sputter out back then a crash. Behind the restaurant and through a narrow strip of forest was an opening onto the airfield I hadn't seen before, even from the

height of our back bedroom window. I followed the others running through the trees and up the other side of a gully to a small plane on the runway. "It's Milet!" someone screamed as astonished whispers raced through the crowd. Lelo had mentioned Milet, who was friends with everyone and lived in Golfito with his wife and five kids. Except for his legs squeezed into a space barely big enough for one, he wasn't banged up or bleeding at all. What must have killed him, though, was a sharp piece of chrome window trim that pierced his temple. Noticing I was the only woman there, I retreated to the other side of the gully with doñas holding their babies and maids, their aprons fluttering in the light morning breeze.

It was late March and springtime in Tulsa. Except for the extreme mugginess that morning, Coto's falling leaves made it look more like autumn. Strolling through the Zone, I passed that bachelor VIP's bedroom window and wished to be inside where it was cool, not knowing what dry, cool air felt like anymore. It wasn't a lack of creature comforts that had me so blue or the overcast skies that made life in general seem so dreary. More and more, I questioned my decision to stay married to a violent man. Ahead, the walk was covered with leaves from a tree they called, "Shower of Gold." Dull on one side, shiny on the other, round quarter-size leaves seemed to sparkle like real gold as they fluttered to the ground. *If they were only real, I could buy a ticket home.* But home was about to come to me.

The letter Roberto brought me from the hangar that day had great news. My sister Linda was coming in June for a six-week visit! With five years of high school and college Spanish, she wouldn't have the trouble communicating like I did.

I was busy around the house one morning, when a vendor came by. *Why do they wear long sleeves here in such muggy weather?* I thought as I went to the door. Though his shirt was cotton and the sleeves were rolled up, he had to be hot, especially with that itchy strap of an old burlap bag across his chest. He whipped off his stained brown fedora as I approached, silvery gray hair showing no sign of sweat. I spoke to him confidently in Spanish through the locked outer-screen of the porch door. *"Sí?"*

"Bueños dias, Doña. Perdón la molestia, but I'm walking from Ecuador to Mexico selling things," he said in Spanish.

It wasn't my "pet" word, "molest" that got my attention but the part about walking from Ecuador. Beneath his trouser cuffs, his feet were as wide as they were long and undoubtedly callused as thick as an elephant's. He'd never worn shoes. *"Bueno?"* I nodded, waiting before opening the screen to see what he had.

Setting his hat on the top step, he stood erect and fished inside his bag. The morning shade on the staircase made it hard to tell what the round shiny object was: a ceramic bust of an Indian? *Those look like real eyelashes!* I marveled as I stared at the object. *These artisans are so clever!* I bent down for a better look and noticed twine at the mouth and eyes where they'd been sewn shut. Eyes wide, my jaw dropped!

"*Señora, mil perdones* (a thousand pardons). I've offended you!" he said, stuffing the shrunken head back in the bag. " perhaps something else more to your liking." I couldn't move if I'd wanted! He held up another shrunken head with yellowish hair! My hand went to my throat! I couldn't buy somebody's head, no matter what the hair color! A blondish one? *What's this guy doing, procuring heads from disgruntled clients en route to Mexico?* With impeccable manners, I politely declined.

My sister's coming visit was the only thing that could take my mind off the terrible sight of those heads, that stayed with me for days. Chris and I flew to San Jose to escort Linda back to Coto, taking the "long way" by motorcar to Golfito, then a C-46 and the long drive from El Coco International into San Jose. I took the time to get Chris photographed and added to my passport. I'd already registered him with the embassy as an American citizen when he was two months old. On

the embassy entry table were invitations to the annual Fourth of July picnic at the Ambassador's country home. I took one in case Linda wanted to go.

After lunch and Chris' nap, it was back to El Coco to get Linda, who looked so grown-up and sophisticated in her miniskirt and wedge sandals. Of course, she couldn't believe the baby in my arms! "How beautiful he is!" she kept repeating. And he was! Perfect strangers would stop me on the street to tell me so. Speeding toward town, I filled her in on gringo etiquette while showing her the points of interest.

"See the bushes under those tall trees?"

"Uh-huh."

"They're coffee trees."

Her answer sounded bored. I think she was just tired.

"Best shade-grown coffee in the world! See those fence posts?"

"You mean the saplings?"

"They weren't always trees."

"What were they?"

"Fence posts."

"What?" she perked up.

"Volcanic ash enriches soil so that posts sprout roots and grow."

"You're kidding!"

"No! When I first got here, the Irazú had just erupted and there were piles of ash everywhere. It sifted inside homes, caved in roofs and put a serious spike in broom sales. Some sharp entrepreneurs cleaned up in more ways than one!"

Linda's eyebrows went up. "As fertile as ash is down here, you'd think they'd bag and sell it!"

"Exactly! Only they don't think like that here. By the way, you mustn't use the word, 'down,' here. It implies we think of Costa Rica as inferior. And use the word 'nationals,' not 'natives.' They don't like that either."

"Uh, okay," Linda said, in a long sigh, not liking to be told how to speak or act.

Roberto's family was sweet to my sister, who understood everything they said right off the bat but couldn't answer back. Five years of Spanish had left her with correct grammar and a sizable vocabulary, but had not taught her how to actually speak. My own linguistic abilities impressed and frustrated her as she had always been the smarter one.

After supper, she got out some gifts: American makeup! Crest toothpaste! American chocolate! And tons of baby things that must have taken her months to save up for. She didn't know how much these goodies from home and her coming all this way meant to me!

The next morning, Linda began melting the moment we arrived in Golfito. By the time we carried her luggage down to the dock to catch the motorcar, the heat and humidity had her fit to be tied. "I understand why toddlers and babies wear knit snow caps in San Jose, where it's cool," she railed. "But why down, uh, I mean, here in a damn jungle?" I was surprised! She rarely used profanity.

Maybe because of the cool sea breezes. But if you think this is hot, wait till we get to Coto!"

At our apartment in Coto, the only sleeping accommodation I could offer her was the tiny loveseat with the easy chair to one side for extra leg room. Linda was sweet about it.

After lunch the next day, Roberto napped and Linda filled me in on the latest fashion and music. "You'll never guess what the most popular rock and roll instrument is right now!" she said in excited anticipation of my answer.

"Guitar?"

"Nope, the organ."

"You mean as in church?"

"Yeah, only the music's better!"

"Guess who's the most popular country/western singer?"

"Can't imagine."

"Dean Martin."

"You're kidding!"

"Nope!"

(There was one more. Don't tell me I'm forgetting all this!)

"Remember the Twiggy look?" Linda continued.

"Yeah."

"Well, white lipstick and dark eye shadow are out!"

"What's in?"

"All natural. And remember the miniskirt?"

"The ones where you bend over and they can see all the way to Chattanooga?" I quipped. "Made me want to take up sewing," I added. "You couldn't buy a decent length skirt anywhere!"

"Well, now there's the Maxi that goes to the ankle," she laughed. "And this fall we'll have the Middy."

Middy? Maxi? What ever happened to plain old skirts?

"You've got to hear the latest song!" she squealed, getting more excited than we usually do in our rather stoic family. "I'm Henry the Eighth I am," she sang. "Henry the Eighth I am, I am. Later, it goes, 'Second verse, same as the first.' And it goes on and on." She stood there waiting for my reaction.

I gave her a blank stare. *What kind of song is that?*

"Everybody loves it!" she added, trying to connect. "Oh well, you're a better singer than I am!" She jumped to her feet. "How about the latest dances? This is the Pony," she said, hopping in place. She changed to swimming motions. "Here's the Swim," she said, wriggling like a worm on a hook. "And the Mashed Potato," she said, shuffling her feet as if putting out cigarettes.

Didn't couples dance together anymore? Surely these "dances" would go the way of the Limbo and the Twist, like the scandalous one in the early eighteen hundreds Aunt Mozy told me about. It was so "dirty," it was the Lombada of its day. A man would take a lady in his arms, hold her close and whirl her around the ballroom floor in a public display so shocking it was vehemently denounced from every pulpit in England and finally banned. After all, the "lady" might not be the man's wife! For years, the prim and proper British kept to dances like the Minuet, while the rest of Europe reveled in the exhilarating and forbidden dance they called the "Waltz."

The "dance" we had when I was about fifteen was called the dirty bop. I only saw it danced once in the girl's bathroom at the skating rink by what were called "trashy" girls. It was so suggestive it was never danced on the actual dance floor.

The dances Linda had just shown me weren't dirty, they just lacked a certain grace. I'd only been gone from home for eighteen months and now the world was upside down. Was nothing at home the same?

Everything was sure the same in Coto. Linda was single and used to more activity. To break the boredom, Margarita and I took her around the Zone one day after lunch to sample the more exotic tropical fruit. The one that made the biggest impression was a giant pod Margarita cut down with her machete and pried open like a clam. The outside was a dull grayish green and the inside a bright apple green. Widely spaced inside the two-foot long pod, about the size of a small machete, was

oval fruit the size of large grapes that were stark white and covered with a cotton candylike fuzz. Margarita said they were safe to eat. They tasted like white grapes. I only saw it once and have forgotten the name.

"On 51, we had a cashew tree growing right outside our backdoor," I bragged to Linda as we walked to the next tree. "The nut grows from the bottom of what looks like a small pear."

"You must have been in heaven roasting those," Linda grinned.

"Nope," I said, shaking my head. "The maid said they have to be factory processed or they're poison."

"Dang!" Linda sympathized.

It was on that walk that Margarita said she knew an artisan who could make Linda some ashtrays and mugs from bamboo to take back as souvenir gifts for the family. He took Linda and me to a nearby grove to select the bamboo she wanted. Linda, afraid to venture into the tall grass, stayed by the truck. I knew how scared she was. I'd been that way. The day we moved to 51, a small lizard zipped between my feet. I nearly jumped out of my skin thinking it was one of "Lelo's snakes!" Linda shook her head in amazement as I followed the man to the grove like I'd been born and bred in Coto. He was a local and had his machete, so I was safe.

Another afternoon, we took Chris for a dip while Roberto napped. Linda had never cared much for Roberto but kept it to herself. Today, she'd know why.

Linda was a modern, All American girl, but not given to wanton exhibitionism or a reckless disregard of propriety. Among her swimsuits was a modest white two-piece; a mariner style with thin red stripes and navy trim. The bottom was a brief that covered her navel with wide straps and a large embroidered blue anchor covering the cleavage.

ALL THE WAY HOME

I hardly swam anymore with the baby and all, and as usual, threw on some shorts and a top over my suit for the short walk to the pool. Linda wore her suit with a long beach towel slung over one shoulder. We'd been in the water for less than a half hour, when Margarita ran toward us yelling and waving. "Run, Doña! You and your sister must leave at once!"

"Why?" I asked, looking up in surprise.

"Don Roberto is coming with his gun," she said out of breath. "Someone phoned and said your sister was walking through the Zone..." she turned to my sister, "a thousand pardons ma'am, 'half naked!'"

"Darn!" I crinkled my brow and pursed my lips.

Linda wasn't one to go into hysterics. She'd listened to what Margarita had to say and now wanted some answers. "What's going on, Mary Sue?"

"I don't know, but here he comes."

The scowl etching Roberto's brow could be seen a half a block away. Face dark red with fury, his eyes never left mine as he marched across the park adjacent to the pool, the German Luger rising and falling as his hands swung hard with his long, determined stride. Linda hit the panic button!

"Holy shit! Is this for real?"

"Don't worry, Linda, it's okay."

"Okay? That maniac's got a cannon!"

"Shhh! Lower your eyes and don't make a fuss!"

"Are you nuts?" Linda shouted in a whisper. "I will not lower my eyes and I plan to make one hell of a fuss!"

"Shhhh! He'll hear you!"

"Let him!" she muttered. Tucking the towel tightly around her waist, she clenched her fists for a fight, while I held Chris close.

"What the hell do you think you're doing letting her walk here half naked?" Roberto demanded.

My fuming sister jumped between us. "I believe *this* is called a swim suit."

"Sorry Linda, but people don't walk to the pool in their suits."

Linda gave me a dirty look. "No one told *me!*"

"Sorry, I didn't know either," I sheepishly said.

"Look Linda," Roberto warned, "people are sensitive here. Don't do it again, okay?" His tone went angry again, pointing his finger at me. "You! Home!"

Margarita had disappeared. Walking far behind him, so we could talk, Linda trembled more from rage than fear. "Does he do this often?" Linda asked. A long silence followed. This was the last thing I'd wanted to happen. "You don't have to stay, you know. Get out before something terrible happens."

"For better or worse, till death do us part," I said.

"Funny you should mention death! Wake up, you don't have to live like this!"

Growing up together under these same tumultuous conditions, violence had been as normal as apple pie. It's funny how the same heat that softens candle wax also turns clay hard as stone. I'd turned out compliant, while my sister was a fighter who often defended me.

I should have left him and gone home with her. She tried to get me to, until the minute she boarded for home weeks later. "You don't have to take his crap! Leave this sawed-off despot! Come with me! I'll help you."

ALL THE WAY HOME

Jump out of the frying pan and into the fire? Not me! That kind of desperation would be like a man putting his family in a rickety boat and rowing through open sea toward freedom's shore. At that time, staying where I was didn't seem as dangerous as facing the unknown. Besides, Linda couldn't help me. She still had a year or so left to graduate.

After the bathing suit incident, she'd fire angry looks across the room when Roberto acted up that said, *Leave him, I'll help you!* His temper tantrum on the drive to San Jose should have been the coup de grace of our marriage.

Just before Linda's departure, our helicopter company lost its contract with United Fruit. Roberto was broke, so I gave him the four thousand colones I'd saved for Chris' reclining stroller. After all, a married couple is a team. Right?

The company was selling all household items. I would really miss the rocking chair, which was only five dollars, but we did well to get clothes, stereo, lamps and kitchenware in the trunk. The rest went in the backseat with Linda's bags, leaving her barely enough room to squeeze in behind Roberto.

Up since dawn packing *La Uva,* he'd been hurrying us all morning. He didn't want us reaching the top of that foggy mountain after dark, its roads sometimes slick. About nine, he shooed us out the door without giving me one last look through the house. We were barely on the way when I realized, "Honey, we have to go back. I left Chris' bottles in the fridge."

"You brainless humanoid!" he shouted.

"They had to stay cool as long as possible!"

"*Pendeja! Bruta! Estúpida!*" His shouts were murderous.

Linda burned one of her looks into the back of my thick skull. At ten months old, Chris didn't know many words, but understood tone and looked scared to death! Begrudgingly, Roberto went back.

I'd hoped to show Linda the pink fields, but it was the wrong season. Roberto hurried to reach San Jose before sundown. Next morning, he went to find a new job, leaving Linda and me to enjoy our last two days together in peace. On Linda's last-minute souvenir list was a short machete in a fringed leather sheath like the men in Coto wore. Peeking in the window of a nearby hardware store, Linda saw something given prominence in many stores she'd been meaning to ask about. "I had no idea JFK was so popular, here," she commented, pointing to the portrait.

"Jackie's everywhere, too," I said hurriedly. "Listen, if the clerk knows we're American, he'll charge double."

"But we look American."

"Swiss and Germans immigrated here after World War II. The clerk won't know the difference if we don't speak English. On second thought with your thick American accent, keep quiet and don't question anything I do."

"Good morning," the clerk said in Spanish. "How may I help you?"

Though my Spanish was good, I used only words and phrases I could pronounce perfectly. "Good morning, sir. I'd like a short machete and leather sheath."

"Yes, ma'am," he said, rushing to the back.

"I might get one, too," I whispered to Linda in English.

The clerk ran back. Linda nonchalantly glanced at the one he'd brought, smiled at me and nodded.

"How much?" I asked.

"Sixteen *colones*, ma'am."

ALL THE WAY HOME

To an American tourist, a dollar fifty was some bargain! I knew I could do better. "Sixteen? That's for two, right?"

"Do you want to ruin me? Take two and it's twelve each."

Fidgeting with her purse clasp all the while, Linda was opening it to pay when I elbowed her in the ribs. "Twelve?" I asked, turning to go. "They're not worth seven!"

Linda's eyes bugged and her jaw dropped. It was the rudest thing she'd ever heard me say!

I was outside the door when the clerk caught up. "Ma'am, nine colones, and not a centimo less!"

"She's become one of them!" Linda wrote family members from college weeks later.

I took Linda sightseeing at the only two places Roberto had taken me to see: a stone fort (now a museum) in the middle of town with high walls that had been shot up in some revolution, and *Ojo de Agua,* a popular hot springs outside town. We didn't take our suits. San Jose is much too cold for swimming. Best of all was the annual Forth of July picnic at the American Ambassador's. I thought my dress with the navy pleated skirt, white top and red scarf would be appropriate.

Walking up the steep drive from the front gate, we passed an ox cart of laughing children. The first thing that struck me was how it was strange to hear children playing in English. We were handed programs inviting us to continuous servings of hot dogs, Cokes, beer, ice cream, cotton candy and peanuts. It was almost like being home. I thought I'd died and gone to heaven!

I'd heard that the ambassador's home resembled Ashley Wilkes' Southern mansion, Twelve Oaks, in "Gone With the Wind." But with its lovely portico, hanging lamp on long chains over the front door and rounded balcony above, I thought it looked more like a smaller version of the White House.

Costa Rica's large mansion near the zoo, where balls and official receptions were held was called *La Casa Amarilla* (The Yellow House).

After Chris' oxcart ride, we watched activities you'd see at any picnic back home. We were so busy eating, we never got to the wheelbarrow races, horseshoe tournaments, softball games and pie eating contest. The flag ceremony and singing of *The Star Spangled Banner* brought tears to my eyes. Until now, I'd never really thought much about patriotism.

You should have seen Chris' look of wonder and amazement when a guy walked by on stilts dressed like Uncle Sam who stood about twelve feet tall! Then the Costa Rican Guardia Civil (Civil Guard) Band played *Stars and Stripes Forever,* ending with a flag march by the children. Without Roberto there, I felt free to laugh. This, alone, should have been a major clue to leave him. He'd said many times sadness was his destiny. When we flew back to the States two months later, you'd think I would have stayed there. I wish now that I had. But hindsight is always twenty-twenty. Worse than being a regular Pollyanna was my sense of wanderlust! When Roberto suggested we drive back to San Jose, it sounded like the adventure of a lifetime! When I was younger and Aunt Mozy was pushing me to read novels, I told her I didn't want to read about somebody else's adventure. I wanted to have one of my own! Well, here it was. How stupid would it be to miss what was over the hill and around the next bend?

Chris was just over a year old when we flew to the States, Linda having left Costa Rica somewhere between the middle and last of July. We stayed with Daddy and Vivian in Tulsa through October and November. Unable to legally work, Roberto soon grew tired of idle days and cold weather. With the last of the money he earned in Coto and never mentioned to me, he bought a used fullsized station wagon in mint

condition. What an adventure this would be! I'd keep a journal! This ill-conceived trip nearly cost us our lives several times over.

Folding the back seats down, we loaded the crib mattress behind the front seat for Chris to play, sleep and be changed on, with small boxes of cloth diapers, clothes and toys at each end. In back, over the spare tire, went the crib frame, springs, luggage and a box of nice clothing Vivian was sending Doña Lydia and Andreina. The stuffed shaggy dog I'd named Miss Clark, and another large blue one buffered Chris from all the luggage and boxes in back. Stopping to buy canned sausages, bread, chips and cookies, off we went as if on a weekend jaunt to the lake.

Roberto got mean just south of Dallas. I was driving and ready to turn around, when he straightened up. Red flags go up to warn people of danger, if they'll just listen. So, Roberto was right. I was a *bruta!* I had a chance to go back home and didn't do it. If I could have reached around to kick myself in the pants, this would have been a perfect time.

According to my old passport, we crossed the U.S./Mexico border at Laredo, Texas, on December 4th, 1965. A border guard's stern warning sent up more red flags. "Good afternoon Señor; Señora. Enjoy your stay in Mexico. Stop for no one! No matter who or what you see and how much they plead. And beware of large groups of men."

Stateside roads had been a breeze. But as there were no road signs across the border, we stopped to ask a patrol officer for directions in our big, shiny American car.

"Yes, this is the road to Monterey and Mexico City," the officer said. "Before you go, sir, I have five children," he said, sticking an open hand into the car. "A little something in the spirit of Christmas?"

"We're kind of short," Roberto said. "Maybe this will help."

The officer's look said it all. *Only twenty dollars?* (Which made how many hundreds of pesos?)

Down the road, Roberto grumbled, "They expect a tip for everything down here!" Did I hear him say, *"down?"* And I'd been so careful! "If I just had my gun, I'd still have that twenty! We'd better map out our route every morning before leaving our hotel."

I'd driven all that first day. Chris and Roberto slept as I navigated hairpin curves through the mountains north of Monterey with city lights nowhere in sight. I'd only passed two northbound cars. Because I could see car lights miles ahead, I upped my speed. I could hardly stay awake. Monterey had to be close. Getting desperate to find a hotel, I sped up until we were nearly flying!

I don't recall reaching our destination, only that there were oxcarts passing from the opposite direction, each pulled by two oxen as tall as our car. Staring at the road ahead, I saw it led through a giant ribcage. Trying to focus, I sat in wide-eyed amazement before the bleached bones of the prehistoric beast. Lights blinked all around, but I kept my eyes on the bones. Someone tapped my shoulder and I jumped. "Where are we?" asked Roberto. Instantly, the bones became a silver painted girder bridge and the blinking lights, neon signs. It was the outskirts of Monterey. The dash clock said two a.m. Roberto got us to a hotel. Otherwise, I'd still be driving!

At dawn, Roberto was rested and dragged us to breakfast so we could be on the road. "I'll drive, you sleep," he said. I never could sleep in a moving car. Besides, I had a one-year-old to change and care for.

I looked around. There were no fences; cows, pigs and donkeys were running loose. I shuddered at the chances I'd taken the night before, my judgment impaired by fatigue.

South of Monterey, the terrain was flat and the road as straight as an arrow. By one o'clock, we'd gone seven hours with no sign of civilization: no towns, gas stations or cars in either direction. Not even smoke from a distant wood stove curling skyward.

ALL THE WAY HOME

The two-lane road was high as a levy. We were wondering if we were still on the right road, when two cowboys on horseback came out of the tall grass and climbed onto the highway. A huge longhorn resisted their rope and gave them considerable trouble as they attempted to cross. Roberto slowed, then stopped. Lunging toward the car, the longhorn bloodied her nose on the window next to our sleeping baby. (We didn't know she'd punctured the back tire.) Roberto reacted like any Latino. He jumped out, shook his fist and yelled, "Where's your *jefe* (boss/chief)?"

"I'm sorry, sir," the cowboy said, struggling at the rope. "Our boss is behind us with the *bolsa* to pay any damages."

After waiting a while, we realized we'd been suckered and drove on. Thank heavens the road was back on level ground, because our tire went flat and we had to pull over. I helped unload the back then took Chris and stepped to one side for Roberto to get to the jack and spare tire. He had the crowbar in hand, when a pickup going the opposite direction pulled up with four Mexican men and two older teens. Attached to their belts were short machetes and large holstered revolvers.

Most Latinos don't smile at strangers, so it's hard to "read" them. Roberto readied himself, flinched the crowbar then glanced apologetically my way. "This may be it."

Die? My baby, too? I'd only wanted adventure! I moved back to give him room to swing then went up front to get Chris as far away as possible. The teens followed. Holding Chris tight, I prayed they wouldn't hurt him. As I starred at them, they spoke and stunned me more than if they'd attacked. "Do you like the Beatles?"

I gulped nervously and said, "Yes." Then they raved about a song out several weeks in the States but new to Mexico. It seemed the Beatles had a hit out every month. "If you like that," I said, "you should hear their newest!" For the life of me, I can't remember the name of either one, only that in late 1965, these were two of their best.

The four older men changed our tire and loaded our belongings in what must have taken less than ten minutes then wished us well and sped away. Even though theirs was the only vehicle we'd seen in hours, Roberto looked before pulling out. And it's a good thing he did! A surprised look swept his face and confusion crinkled his brow. He stopped, leaned into the mirror then turned to get a better look. Walking up behind us was a man all in white pushing an ice cream cart. A Mexican Good Humor Man? We looked at each other as if asking where did he come from? After we bought two ice cream bars, the man disappeared back into the tall grass. Roberto checked his mirror again and we drove away laughing!

It took four hours to drive through Mexico City, not counting the hour to get our passports stamped at the Guatemalan Embassy; the country we'd be entering next. Nearing the edge of town, Chris looked sick, so we stopped. I told the doctor Chris had had watery stools all morning. He sold us two amber bottles of medicine. I opened the smaller one first.

With the water I'd brought gone and no bottled water as we know it today, I gave Chris the only "safe" bottled fluid available—soda pop. I didn't know then that some diseases and illnesses thrive on sugar and that pop and juices are loaded with it. I wish I'd remembered grandmother's stories about coming to Oklahoma in a covered wagon and how they'd kept silver bars in the barrel to keep the water pure and drinkable. The medicine was working, but we still had to stop occasionally so I could hand wash diapers at service stations. Roberto rigged a nylon clothes line around the back windows so they'd dry.

We had an early breakfast at a picturesque sidewalk café in the lovely southern Mexican town of Oaxaca (Wah-HOCK-ah), the last real stop until Guatemala City. We were on the road all day. By nightfall, there was still no sign of a town. Gaunt, his eyes sunken, Chris lay there staring. He'd been lethargic all day and now with the back of my hand

against his forehead, he felt feverish. I turned on the overhead and looked for the spoon.

"Hey, turn off that light! I can hardly see as it is!"

"It's time for Chris' medicine." I'd tossed the empty smaller bottle hours ago. The larger one would be harder to handle. "Stop, so I don't spill it." I was poised to pour the precious liquid into the spoon, when I spied something floating near the top. Holding the bottle up to the dim overhead, I couldn't believe my eyes!

"What's wrong? What is it?" Roberto asked, straining to see.

"A roach!" I threw the bottle out the window. "Chris needs a doctor."

We'd traveled for hours on a two-lane road that paralleled a super highway under construction. Roberto drove to the top of the entrance ramp. (The new highway was much higher than the two-lane we were on, like a levy.) It was dark up there and the road still hadn't been paved. We had to find a doctor, so we took a chance.

We were only on this road a minute or two, when we saw a light in the distance. We got back down on the two-lane and followed the light to a small village in a clearing set on a hill, where half a dozen or so small cinder block houses faced a large concrete slab on three sides. At one end, high on a pole, was the light that had guided us there.

It was well after midnight. In skies streaked with white, the waxing moon played peek-a-boo in and out of the low-hanging clouds. Not one dog barked. It was eerily quiet, except for the barely audible scratching of dry leaves as they cart-wheeled across the slab that formed the village plaza. If not for the beat-up cars and pickups, I'd have sworn the place was deserted. *Where is everyone?* I wondered. Roberto turned the car around to drive away.

"Where are you going? We can call a doctor from here."

"There's no phone lines."

"Go knock on a door. There must be parents who know what to do for a sick child."

"No one will help us here."

"How do you know? Don't you see…?"

"Yes, I *see*… the barrel of a gun pointing out that window! Look, I'd do anything for Chris, but these *campesinos* believe in evil spirits. And we drive in after midnight in a black car!"

"It's not the Banshee's coach! We're not here to claim their souls!"

"They may think so. They probably have legends where devils roam the countryside at night, disguised as people, killing and stealing souls like *la yegua y el callejón de las puñaladas* (the mare and the alley of the stabbings) in Costa Rica." The legend was that inebreated men, on the way home from bars near a certain alley in San Jose, would see a beautiful woman walking ahead of them and try to catch up. When she turned, they saw she had the head of a mare. "We can't take a chance," Roberto added.

"But you can't just…. "

"Look, I'm unarmed!" He stopped at the two-lane to look for the ramp back onto the highway.

"You'd shoot it out with the baby in the car?"

"If I have to!" He turned and shot daggers at me, then pulled onto the two-lane in the direction we'd been going.

"God's punishing us!" I cried. "We should've stopped!"

"For that baby pig I ran over this morning? They'd have shot us!"

"No, that three-car wreck we passed at dusk. Those people were waving us down, begging us to stop."

"What if they were bandits? You heard the border guard!"

"That was real blood! I begged you to stop and now…?"

"Shut up!" he yelled, speeding up. "Where's the entrance to that super highway? It's got to be around here, somewhere!"

Dump trucks parked along the road had narrowed the road, forcing us to slow down to pass the graders, bulldozers and steamrollers parked in and around the gaping space of the yet to be built underpass. If we hadn't exited the highway for the two lane when we did, and had instead followed that light to the village, we'd have plunged headlong into the massive machinery.

Car trouble had us limping into Guatemala City. Roberto's dad had friends there that we were able to stay with. They were hospitable, despite a rude remark I made. The mother was extremely proud of her oldest son going into the priesthood. "What a waste of a life!" I carelessly said. I was sorry afterward, but couldn't take it back. It was there in Guatemala City that I first suspected I was again in a family way.

The last night of our trip was spent in Nicaragua. Walking through downtown Managua, we came upon a quaint restaurant with a cute adobe wall around a patio for outside dining. The weather perfect. Our table was at the shoulder-high wall facing a major intersection where five wide avenues converged.

Chris' tummy was better and he enjoyed a little something, too. We were nearly finished eating, when sirens split the air. A passing Willis Jeep led the convoy with a large machine gun mounted on the hood pointed forward. Another jeep filled with armed soldiers was followed by a dark sedan. A fourth jeep brought up the rear with a mounted machine gun protecting the rear.

Grabbing Chris, I dove behind the wall and hunkered down! Ending almost before it began, I eased up and peeked over. "Who was that?"

Without a glance, Roberto paused before shoveling in the next bite. "Probably, Somoza," he answered, as though giving me the time of day.

"Is he President or something?"

"Dictator."

I gave a disapproving look.

"They're not evil! They may rule with an iron hand, but they also provide political stability by appeasing peasants with bigger and better social handouts, even if their promises don't always come through. 'Tell a lie long enough and the people will believe it.'" Roberto had just quoted Adolf Hitler. "Uneducated peasants are undisciplined, unable to govern themselves. They need to be kept reined-in or chaos would rule. Dictators are more closely compared to benevolent fathers, who must sometimes do harsh things for the good of their children. They elect him again and again, with a little help from stuffed ballot boxes. Once a bad one gets in, the only ways to get rid of them are assassinations and coups."

"But the 'children,' as you call them, live in squalor and the 'father' in a palace!" I objected.

"He must live well, so he can make important decisions for the people, keeping their best interests in mind."

Yeah; the very back of his mind!

Those with brains and money get visas to any country that will take them. Those who stay are spoon-fed propaganda like patriotic songs in public schools, catchy tunes on radio and TV about how good life is there, despite the fact you can't buy meat, eggs or milk. (Protein intake is limited. The physically strong can revolt.) Decent, hard-working people keep trusting leaders, who the minute they get elected, open Swiss bank accounts for the millions they siphon off aid packages (mainly from the U.S.) and retire millionaires!

The good people of those countries, disillusioned by years of empty promises, search for honest representation only to get more government

corruption. Presidential candidates promise change but once elected, become despots bringing new oppressive laws. (I hate to be cynical, but it sounds like politics as usual in the U.S. and all around the world!)

I couldn't believe it! I was back where soldiers roamed the streets with machine guns. Whatever happened from here on, I had done it to myself. Linda had warned me. Why didn't I listen? I knew how it was there. Was I nuts? I'd had my adventure; I'd seen what was over the next hill and around the bend and now I was back! Too late to think about that now. I'd think about it tomorrow. Surely, Roberto would be different this time. (Ya' think?)

CHAPTER SEVEN

DIFFERENT? DREAM ON, HONEY!

By noon the next day, December 15, 1965, according to my passport, we were in Liberia, Costa Rica. I also entered in my journal that this was horse and cattle country and it smelled like home. It took us seventeen days to drive from Tulsa to San Jose, including the two-day stop-over in Guatemala City for repairs.

We got to his parent's apartment about four that afternoon. San Jose's streets were clear of piles of volcanic ash, but the overpowering smell from that winery across from the Presidential Palace, as sickeningly sweet as ever, was causing some nausea and I couldn't get inside fast enough!

Roberto's sister, Sandra, played with Chris, who they still called *Crisanto,* while the adults talked. Doña Lydia was delighted to hear there might be another grandchild. Don Vicente had filmed TV commercials that helped get the new president elected. So because of the family's new political connections, everyone had good jobs. Even Roberto was offered second in command of the Presidential Guard with the rank of major and would sleep half the week at the barracks. He later bragged

that his favorite "duty" was rounding up prostitutes. He couldn't explain what *that* had to do with palace security.

The pay was good, yet we couldn't afford a place of our own or things for the new baby. Of course, Roberto always had money for new guns: two shotguns (twelve and sixteen gauge), a Thompson machine gun (the same Tommy guns gangsters used in the 1930's), an English Sten gun (with the wire butt), a forty-five automatic and three thirty-eight revolvers. I remember the calibers from having them pointed at me and wanting to know which one would take me out.

Daddy always said, "You don't need a gun to kill someone." I lost count of the times Roberto straddled me while I was expecting the second baby, pinned my arms with his knees and choked me into unconsciousness. He also jabbed at my tummy with a screwdriver and later, pointed a gun at me from across the room and shouted, "Bang, bang, bang, bang, bang! You're dead!" My tummy turned hard as a basketball. After that, it only took his mean looks to get that result. He didn't seem to care that the baby's oxygen was cut off when he choked me (not to mention my own)!

The next purchase on Roberto's wish list was a bazooka. He even spoke of owning a tank! (Was he planning a revolution?) Those next months, when I wasn't dodging his blows, I was worrying about how to keep from getting shot.

Roberto kept a large camouflage box under our bed that not only held hundreds of rounds for all those guns, but four hand grenades as well. I was so busy staying alive during the day, I forgot I was sleeping on a powder keg at night!

But danger didn't stop there. It's no exaggeration to say that the simple act of taking a shower was a death-defying feat! Attached to the showerhead was a sealed metal device the size of a round cake pan, used for heating water. Screwed to the tile wall was a small two-pronged switch with a white porcelain handle that resembled, a small version of

an electric chair switch. Now, here's the "good part." You get in and turn on the water. Standing there in a puddle, you take firm hold of the porcelain switch and flip it up until it touches a metal plate, its two ominously frayed black wires connected to the "cake pan." Green sparks shoot in all directions. Heated water splashes into the pan with a terrible racket that alone could scare you into cardiac arrest! If the water pressure is low, the neighbors are washing clothes downstairs. You shout, *Agua!* so they stop long enough for you to finish bathing. Roberto said it was dangerous to have the switch on with no water running through. I was too afraid to ask why.

Then there were the bugs! Giant roaches with a six-inch wingspan would fly up and down the long hallway and invariably into your hair. Late one night in the kitchen, I heard a strange crunching I traced to a small wooden box next to the stove, where Doña Lydia kept potatoes. I shuddered to see the stubby heads of several huge roaches buried in spuds just gnawing away. Other flying menaces were the mosquitoes. Without *Luna Tigre,* our screenless windows left us mercilessly chewed to death. "Tiger Moon" was a coil-shaped incense burned at night that stank to high heaven but kept the mosquitoes away.

Speaking of chewing, even though Roberto's parent's finances had improved, they bickered every day. To give them some privacy and get Chris some fresh air, I'd take him to the park to play with children his age.

Roberto had bought a stroller that didn't recline or have shocks against the rough, uneven stone sidewalks built in the 1500's. This was fine on the way to the park, but it was the bumpy ride home with Chris slumped over asleep that made me mad. To think, I'd saved four thousand colones twice to buy a nice reclining stroller! I consoled myself that at least I had this one to get our laundry to *La Lavanderia Sixaola* (Sixaola Laundry-"Sixaola" being the name of a local river). Roberto's *Tia* (Aunt) Soledad owned it with her siblings. They drycleaned free for

the entire family, and were kind enough to do regular washing and ironing for me, because I was expecting.

But Roberto never had time to drop the week's dirty clothes at *Sixaola* on his way to work. So rain or shine, with my big belly, I'd carry Chris and wheel our huge bundle the three or four blocks then go on to the park or back home. The minute Doña Rosa, the stout woman in charge of the enormous washing machines saw me trudge in, she'd shake her head, stop what she was doing and rush over to help.

I was unhappy those months before the new baby came, not because of struggling with laundry, or a stroller that didn't recline, all the bugs, or even the Frankensteinian plumbing. These would have been insignificant if I'd had a man who loved me and showed it. The only "emotional connection" I had with him was fear. (He said fear was the strongest of all the emotions, even love.) We had nothing in common but a beautiful son and a baby on the way. He only came "home" to grab a hot meal and pick-up clean clothes then resume his own interests.

It was hardly an ideal time to welcome another child.

Exhausted, emotionally drained and ever fearful, I did the only thing I knew: I "escaped" into music. I didn't know if the songs the American rock and roll station played were new, but they were good and the lyrics lively, which energized me. That summer of '66, Mick Jagger's lamentation, "I Don't Get No Satisfaction" certainly represented Roberto's sentiments, while Nancy Sinatra's, "These Boots Are Made For Walkin'," expressed my own. Walter Brennan's "Dutchman's Gold" spoke to my western roots and John Wayne's "America, Why I Love Her," tugged at my patriotic soul in a day when love of God and country were daily maligned as corny and passé. Still, I was divided between the States and the friends and family I'd grown to love in Costa Rica when they played the Sandpiper's wistful rendition of "Guantanamera," even if the soloist sang like my mother-in-law. Doña Lydia sounded a lot like

Libertad Lamarque, the Argentine tango singer who became a famous movie star in Mexico.

Our marriage was over. His indifference and brutality had driven out any romantic notion I'd ever had of him.

It wasn't a good time to have a child. Besides how could I love another baby, when Chris was so smart, beautiful and perfect? People were still stopping me on the street to admire and ask about him.

Thursday, July 28th, 1966, I woke up in labor. Lucky I was ready to leave for the clinic when Roberto was picked up for work or I'd have had to walk. The jeep was a bumpy ride, even in the front seat. Dropping me in front of the clinic, Roberto didn't even look back as they drove away. I walked myself to the front desk to check in, my determination to leave him set in stone. My doctor was trained in the States, spoke perfect English and was even married to a Tulsa girl.

A nurse wheeled in a plastic bassinette lined with linen trimmed in blue and set it nearby against a wall.

"Bring me a pink one!" I said, about to be divorced and wanting a girl.

"No, Señora, you're having a boy."

The blue one stayed.

It only took one look at the new baby for me to understand that not only did I have enough love for two, but loved them just the same. But the joy of birth was mantled in mourning. With the cutting of the umbilical went my last emotional ties to Roberto. Those three days in the clinic, I mourned the demise of a relationship that never quite was. Postpartum depression wasn't recognized in those days. I cried me a river, emptying two large boxes of tissue, then I was through. Roberto was indignant that I didn't respond to him intimately. I couldn't. Not anymore.

ALL THE WAY HOME

It wasn't the best time to bring a child into the world, but I was glad little David Michael had arrived. I'd planned to name him after Don Vicente, but after the way Roberto had been treating me, I picked a name I liked. When I got back home, Don Beh would rock David back and forth and weep. I supposed it was because the baby looked exactly like him. I regretted not naming him after his grandfather.

A couple of weeks later, I started asking Roberto again to go home, which generated considerable tension. (So, what else was new?) If I was a burr under Roberto's saddle, why not let me go? His answer was to disappear.

Those last few weeks in Costa Rica, I did one thing Doña Lydia never forgave me for, no, two. Aunt Mozy liked trivia and used to tell me little things like "if you scrape a tomato with a sharp knife, the skin will peel right off" and "if you fry a potato in grease that's been overheated and gotten smokey, the potato will absorb the smokey taste that would have gone into the next food you fry." She called it, "purifying the grease." When I told Doña Lydia I knew how to "purify her grease," so she could use it a second time, (she was out of oil) she took it as an insult. Doña Lydia was already unhappy anyway. Her frustration affected everyone, even her pet bird.

La Gata (cat) had sense enough to stay out of her way. *El Perico* (parakeet) had clipped wings and couldn't leave its perch on the back patio. The pretty blue parakeet's screeching always got on Doña Lydia's nerves. I'd seen everyone but Roberto dunk that poor bird in water to shut it up. If especially obnoxious, they'd let it float a moment before returning it to its perch. That's probably what made it try and bite everyone. I was afraid of that bird.

One morning, Sandra had left for school, Don Beh was out filming somewhere, Roberto had stayed over at the barracks, Doña Lydia and Andreina had gone to mass at the crack of dawn and the babies and I were home alone. With two babies, I was short on diapers and went out to the patio to wash some by hand. *El Perico* in its perpetual bad mood and perched within inches of my ear, soon made my desperation to escape its piercing screeches overcome my fear of being nipped. I grabbed it, dunked it and returned it to its perch like I'd seen the others do. It screeched again almost immediately. Impossible to ignore the deafening sound, I dunked it again, returned it to its perch and resumed washing. Continuing its shrill shrieks, I put it in the water to float a moment. Just then, the front door buzzer sounded through a connection over the *pila* (sink). Jumping like a child caught with her hand in the cookie jar, I ran to answer the door. It was Roberto's driver, there to pick up a forgotten uniform shirt. By the time I returned to the patio only a minute later, the poor *perico* had drowned. Doña Lydia was furious and didn't let me explain.

"*Puta condenada!*" (damned whore) she shouted. "I'm going to my sister's. Andreina, bring *la Gata* before that *macha* (female foreigner) kills her, too!"

That evening, poor Gilberto got the brunt of her wrath. Not "good enough" to come in, he courted Andreina on the front steps with the door open. Doña Lydia had her hopes set on Andreina, who was highly intelligent and had studied French for years, to study medicine in Paris. (Doña Lydia had wanted to be a doctor.) Everything was going as Doña Lydia planned, until Andreina met this "ne'er-do-well, this nothing, Gilberto!" (Andreina, who I had at first thought to be unfriendly, was simply highly focused and intelligent.)

Gilberto left about nine. The door was barely locked, when there came a loud scuffle at the street entry door. Celebrating high graduates had pushed a friend into the enclosed staircase, shut the door and were now holding it. I doubt the youth knew how loud he was being as he yelled and banged to be let out. Roberto tore open the front door, both hands gripping the German Luger he held stiff-armed at the boy. "Freeze!"

"Sorry, Mister; my friends pushed me in and won't let me out. My family's waiting at home for my graduation party."

"You're not going anywhere!"

Roberto had his Presidential Guard buddies arrest the kid and jail him.

Next day, the buzzer sounded. I opened the door and Lelo rushed in visibly shaken. "Can't stay," he hurriedly said in Spanish. "*La bolsa's* waiting in the car with the kids. *Viejo* (old man)," he turned to Roberto as Doña Lydia and Don Beh came into the room, "I have bad news," he continued in Spanish. "Jim Green's chopper was shot down in Guatemala... *y lo mataron a machetazos!*"

"Jim, killed?" I interrupted. "Who did it and how?"

"Bandits," Lelo said. "He was hacked to death by machete."

"My God!" I lived with a would-be terrorist, but this was the most barbaric thing I'd ever heard!

"Shirley had their household stuff packed and was on her way there," Lelo added.

This tragedy rekindled my urgency to go home. Roberto was at the breakfast table, smartly dressed in his uniform, waiting for his ride. Doña Lydia was eating and Chris was in his highchair. Knowing the subject was delicate, I was being very diplomatic. He suddenly jumped up and hustled me to our room. When the door slammed, David stirred slightly in his bassinet, then went back to sleep. Roberto took his gun from the wardrobe, cocked it, shoved me against the wall and put it to my face. "Get this through your thick skull, *bruta*. Keep on with this and the only place you'll go is to the cemetery!"

I couldn't move.

"Good, you're afraid! Hate's what makes the world go around."

He put the gun away, punched me in the arm and went outside to wait for his ride. He probably wished he still had our black station wagon to do the "guy thing" and get out of there faster. But he had totaled it hitting a cow right after we'd driven all that way from Tulsa to Costa Rica.

Humiliated, crushed and scared out of my wits, I had no idea how I'd get through the rest of the day. On top of that, Doña Lydia made some snotty remark as she and Andreina left for mass. I wanted to hurt her back! We all do dumb things. Guess it was just my turn. I should have counted to ten.

I cleaned breakfast off of Chris and put him in his crib with a bottle of juice and some toys. David was still asleep. I slipped into the master bedroom, grabbed the clothes Vivian had sent Doña Lydia then marched to my room, threw them on the bed and sat there fuming! It only took a moment to realize how childish and petty this was. I'd just picked the clothes up to take them back, when the front door opened. It was Doña Lydia and Andreina back to change and leave again. Andreina called to her mother in the other room. "Mamá, where's the black skirt Maria brought me?" My heart sank. "It's there," she answered. "I saw it this morning."

I backed into my room and stood by the door I'd left ajar.

"Where?"

Doña Lydia went to the bedroom. "It's between…. That's funny. It's not here."

"Neither is that sweater that goes with it," Andreina said.

She shooed her daughter away and sorted through the closet. "None of it is here," said Doña Lydia. "That miserable…! Let's get out of here! I can't stand that damned *macha* (foreigner)!"

I deserved that!

ALL THE WAY HOME

With things rapidly deteriorating between his mother and me, Roberto was forced to act. Truth was, our leaving was probably more due to his lover. Yes, I knew about her. Months later, she was expecting his child and wrote me a letter.

The few days it took me to pack and for him to get the tickets, I was singing, "Take me back to Tulsa, I'm too young to marry!" As I boarded our flight, I swore it would be a cold day in hell before I'd ever go back to him!

CHAPTER EIGHT

SAFE IN TULSA?

Aunt Mozy got us a garage apartment until I could find a job and pay for a divorce. Just because it only cost thirty dollars a month, didn't mean the apartment was a dump. In 1966, you could rent a modest house for sixty dollars. A month later, on a cold and rainy night, there came a knock at the door. "Roberto! What are you doing here?"

"I had to come. Aren't you going to ask me in?"

"It's late."

"Have you filed, yet?"

"No."

"Then we're still married."

I froze in the doorway.

"Look, I was spraying cotton in Nicaragua, when something terrible happened to a four-year old girl. Her parents, field hands, were begging me to chopper her to the hospital when their daughter began vomiting worms, inhaled them and choked. When she died, her eyes were fixed on me. I had to see my boys."

I couldn't let Roberto back into our lives, now or ever!

"You can't turn me out. It's cold and wet out. I'll sleep on the couch. Please? Just for tonight."

That night turned into a week and so on. He wasn't mean like before (there are different levels of meanness), when he sweetly "suggested" I shouldn't see girl friends or visit Aunt Gladys and Uncle Frank, who lived a block away, anymore. Soon, I wasn't to phone people or receive calls. Without a Green Card, all he could get was menial work. He'd call all day to say how much he missed me. I was so naive. He was checking up on me! Men like Roberto like controlling women, body and soul.

Chris was big enough to swing and liked to run through fall leaves, so I took the kids to the park a lot. On rainy days, we'd read stories, finger paint or model clay dinosaurs and creepy, crawly stuff that boys like. Roberto never played with the children or even talked to them. I missed talking to adults. Then I was where he wanted me: barefoot and pregnant.

We knew a couple we occasionally visited who'd escaped from Cuba six years earlier. Their three kids were born in the States. The wife said this time I would have a girl. When I indeed had my girl, she was tiny and delicate with the longest fingers, perfect for a concert pianist!

Roberto called the family in Costa Rica to tell them the good news.

"So Maria," said Don Beh, "what names did you pick?"

"I never thought I'd have a girl, and we only picked boy's names. We liked William, James Edward and Phillip Edward."

"Like the English kings, Maria!"

I'd never thought of it that way. "In the hospital, I picked Linda Michelle, after my sister and the new Beatle's song."

"A beautiful name, Maria!"

"Tell Andreina I'm sorry I haven't written," I quickly added before we had to hang up. "I've never been much of a letter writer. Tell her the wedding pictures were wonderful and that I liked the one of Gilberto, his mother and the President's wife walking into the church. What an honor that the President and his wife could attend!"

Michelle was about five months old when Roberto got a job flying. We lived in a Chicago suburb. Six months later, back in Tulsa for Christmas, we stayed with Linda a month then moved to a tiny house near the airport. Roberto, still without a Green Card, hated his handyman job. One morning, he'd already had breakfast and was putting off going to work. The kids were seated waiting for breakfast, while he paced the floor. I was serving bacon with a long serving fork, when Roberto rushed me and stopped at the kitchen table between us.

"Do you know what they made me do, yesterday?" he railed. "Clean a toilet! A trained pilot! I should be flying!" I was hurt for him, but could do nothing. "Look at me when I talk to you!" Fist clenched, he started around the table. I'd never hurt anyone, but wasn't about to let him hurt me or upset the kids! Inadvertently, I flinched the fork in my hand. He looked afraid. One more step and I'd have put it through his craw! Backing away, he turned and left.

Over the sink was a shelf where I'd put the fifteen-inch image Dona Lydia had sent me of Fray Escoba holding his broom: her saint of the hopeless. With dried tear drops on one cheek (probably splashed-on dish water), it was comforting to know someone knew and cared.

"If I only had a good job," Roberto apologized that night.

Roberto couldn't be reasoned with (and I thought men were the reasonable and logical ones). More and more, I knew we had little in common. (Fine time to figure that one out!) Still, for months I tried to help him get his Green Card, writing senators and 14 congressmen, while holding down my new office job. The cost of day care was killing me! Three kids at thirty dollars a week? Since I now used the car, Roberto said I should keep it filled. Self serve gasoline was new. I missed the men who ran out like on the Texaco TV commercials: one

to check oil, a second to check tires, a third to clean windshields and a fourth to fill the tank. I hated it! Women weren't supposed to pump gas! And on the little I earned, if gasoline went any higher than twenty-five cents a gallon, paying four dollars to fill up our compact wagon would break us!

That summer of '69, I had to call the police a couple of times. Like his hero, Ralph Cramdon, Roberto threatened to "send me to the moon," only the Apollo 11 Astronauts got there first.

When his Green Card arrived, Roberto found work as a civilian helicopter flight trainer for the Army in Texas. It paid so well, we could buy a house! "Everyone in Mineral Wells lives in mobile homes," he said. "Well, nearly everyone. We can select ours from here in Tulsa."

I picked the popular American Colonial style, which came completely furnished. The sofa was cream with earth tone greens and golds and a touch of russet. There were two green wingback chairs, green drapes covering a picture window and dimmer lights in "vaulted" ceiling beams with amber covers that looked like old world stained glass. The home had a bath and three quarters and two bedrooms complete with satin bedspreads and even pillows. There was a nook at the backdoor for a washer and dryer. No more laundry mats! Twenty-five dollar a month payments got us a Sears washer and dryer in bronze to match all our new kitchen appliances. Dishwashers were fairly new and not standard then.

Here we were with a new home, a compact station wagon, a swing set and a beagle puppy named Barbie. Roberto even bought me some new dresses, the first since David was born.

"May I help you, Ma'am?" the Sears saleslady said.

"Dresses, please," I said.

"What size, Ma'am?"

I stood there a moment, tears welling in my eyes. Roberto caught up with me in lingerie and spun me around. "What's wrong with you? Are you crazy?"

I couldn't tell him that I was twenty-five and didn't know what size I was. Mama always bought my clothes. She even ordered my meals at restaurants. I apologized to the saleslady with, "Are you crazy?" still ringing in my ears. Maybe I was.

Roberto found a small trailer park in Mineral Wells and arranged to have our mobile home delivered there. In back was a spooky barn full of spider webs. The owners, named Casebeer, lived in an adjoining farmhouse.

Neighbors warned of copperheads, corals, rattlesnakes and cottonmouth water moccasins, so Chris only went out when David and Michelle could, which was never without me. They also said to watch out for scorpions that sometimes got in houses. Then there were the tarantulas that would come out of their holes in the yard at dusk that Roberto blew to smithereens with a rifle. The boys loved it! Michelle cried, but Roberto couldn't be dissuaded.

During that next year, Roberto bought four rifles: two 30/30 carbines like Mexicans carried in their revolution, a Browning and one other. Roberto and Mr. Casebeer would often target practice out back. His friends, Rudy and Alberto, liked target practice, too. Rudy's wife, Pat, and I would talk in the house.

Chris loved learning and was excited about kindergarten. En route to school every morning, choppers would fly over our car like formations of dragonflies. Roberto had always buzzed our house in Coto but couldn't now. He liked working at Ft. Walters. Military discipline suited him.

When Roberto first mentioned the Casebeers, I heard "cases of beer" and thought he'd rented near a bar. The Casebeers were teetotalers, who had Sunday church services in their home. Mr. Casebeer even bought a three-octave chord organ and beginners music books, so his wife could accompany the singing, but she never caught on. We only went to their service once. Roberto didn't like it.

The only other time I got him to church was after he showed up in Tulsa that rainy night. It was stewardship week, so the sermon was on tithes and offerings and how giving blessed the giver. Not once was God or Jesus mentioned. "All you Protestants are going to hell!" Roberto fumed as we walked home.

Guess he didn't mind church music, because he bought me the Casebeer's organ, music books and all! During the kid's naptime, I'd escape chores for an hour into music like Aunt Mozy taught me.

I loved playing the organ, but my greatest pleasure was the children. After school, we'd sometimes stop for a Dairy Queen or browse toy stores. After supper, we'd play on the swing set. Rainy afternoons or cold winter evenings, we'd play children's records in their room and at bedtime, I'd read them stories.

Roberto was glued to the evening news reports about the war in Vietnam. I didn't like the kids seeing all that. I'd voted for Nixon the year before, because he promised to end the war. It was rumored that de-escalation was coming. Little did I know how much an end to the war would change our lives.

The fall of '69 came and went with few ugly incidents in our beautiful mobile home. For Christmas, Roberto picked an electric train set for Chris. After Chris unwrapped it and Roberto assembled everything, Chris wasn't allowed to play with it unsupervised. Instead, Chris played with the doctor's kit and The Invisible Man I'd picked. I was still directing him toward medicine.

David was more into his racecar set and remote stegosaurus that could roar and walk across the room. He loved maneuvering it to fight

Chris' tyrannosaurus! Michelle got dolls and plastic pots, pans and spoons she could "cook" with. Their stockings had the usual candy, fruit, nuts, coloring books and crayons. We spared no expense.

After Christmas, I had the strangest dream. (Dreams this vivid often came true.) I assumed I was in Italy, because of the Italian being spoken. There were marble floors and a fountain in front of a modern building at an intersection, where five streets met. That and nothing more.

Around March, Roberto became angry and abusive and would try and make up with gifts. He knew I'd always wanted a horse. But I'd outgrown girlish dreams. All I wanted now was a husband who loved me, was a good father to my kids, and a peaceful home. That Saturday, he drove us around looking for "horse for sale" signs then stopped for lunch at a country diner. "Mr. Casebeer said we could use that old barn out back," Roberto said, looking over the menu. "Now, all we need is a horse!" He looked up. "You never said what color!"

He didn't notice my lack of interest. The jukebox suddenly blared the first three notes of a song I immediately recognized. With the kids there, I was glad it was spelled out as Tammy Wynette mournfully crooned, "Our D-I-V-O-R-C-E becomes final, today...." I'd been thinking about it. But how could I support the kids and me with a high school education and no marketable skills? (Fine time to worry about *that!*)

Chris graduated from Peter Pan Kindergarten in an afternoon ceremony. It was a shame Roberto couldn't be there. The kids and I had more fun when that sour puss wasn't around, anyway!

When we bought our mobile home in cooler Tulsa, we hadn't anticipated Texas summers, and tried to save some by not adding air-conditioning. Lying on the floor in front of fans and sweating profusely, I noticed that Michelle's wispy bangs were bone dry. I reached over to touch her. She was burning up! Doc Singleton had his nurse emerse Michelle in his utility sink and spoon her this new red liquid called, Tylenol. She screamed and begged me to get her out! I cried with her. My

heart was breaking. Her lips and nails were blue nearly the whole time she was up to her neck in ice water reeking of alcohol. We finally got her out. Her temperature had hit 106.8°. Doc said it was a close call.

I bought a kiddy pool and popcicles, so the kids would stay cool the rest of the summer. One day, Roberto noticed a neighbor boy over to swim had scribbled on the siding by the front door. Instead of telling me so I could clean it off, he bulldozed me into a corner and stomped me into the floor with his heavy flight boots.

I'd had it and flew to Tulsa! Mom was traveling, so I went to Aunt Mozy's. If only I'd had some bruises or a black eye. They thought Roberto was too cute to be mean. Now it was, "You made your bed, now you have to lie in it." Roberto drove to Tulsa a week later. Without my family to help me, I was forced to go back with him.

De-escalation! It was summer of 1970. The general public didn't know it yet, but the war in Vietnam was over. Civilians at Ft. Walters found out when a hundred pilots and four hundred mechanics were pink-slipped. Five hundred wives frantically raced to get the few jobs existing in tiny Mineral Wells. With the few weeks experience I had as a nurses aid, I applied at the new seventy-bed Palo Pinto Hospital. I was happy to get the three to eleven shift, which would give me more daylight hours at home with the kids. We cashed Roberto's last check for some uniforms and white shoes.

"Report" was a thirty-minute meeting before shifts to update oncoming staff on a patient's progress or lack thereof. I discretely copied the strange symbols from Westbrook, the young head nurse sitting next to me. After a couple of days, it was like I'd done it for years. I loved my work and would look up illnesses in my medical books to be of more help to patients.

I was off that first weekend and back on Monday. Mr. Waverly was first on my list. Upon entering his room filled with family, I was startled

by a loud hiccup. Some glanced over and shook their heads, while others stayed in an attitude of prayer or read.

The next hiccup sent his pressure soaring. I tried several times but couldn't get a reading. A man stood watching. "My name is Doug. My father's been like this for days. Doc says they've done everything they can."

I fingered the alcohol packets in my pocket, wondering if I should? My hand shot from my pocket to the clipboard. Who did I think I was, TV's Dr. Kildare? I left as quietly as I came only to stop halfway down the hall. If this were my father, I'd want to at least know there was a non-invasive procedure that was completely harmless, no matter how crazy it sounded! I slipped back into the room. If they said no, at least I'd have followed my conscience. "Mr. Waverly?" I asked.

"Mr. Waverly's my father. I'm Doug."

"Doug, there's something that might help your dad."

Except for caps, aides dressed like nurses at Palo Pinto. Thinking I'd forgotten mine, the family stepped closer to hear.

"These are alcohol-filled cotton pads," I said, holding them out for all to see. "With your permission, I'll tear off a piece and place it on his forehead."

"What for?" an older man asked.

"To stop the hiccups," I said, knowing it sounded crazy.

"Will it hurt him?" asked Doug.

"No, sir. I've used this on my own newborns."

"They've tried everything else." Doug shrugged, looking around for an objection. No one moved. "Sure, go ahead."

I'd just placed a piece on the old man's forehead, when he hiccupped as loud as ever.

"Humph!" Several said, sitting back down. The rest waited.

He hiccupped again, but not as hard, sending more back to their seats. The third was mild and then there were none. Family gathered around the old man. I took his blood pressure and quietly left, not giving it another thought until Greenway practically tackled me in the hall. "Westbrook wants you, stat! Mr. Waverly's family talked to the doctor and…."

"He's okay, isn't he?" I said in near-panic.

"Sleeping like a log. Honey, you're the talk of the floor! The doctors want to know what you did."

I'd done nothing. But this brought me to the attention of the RNs, especially Mrs. Westbrook, who began taking me on her rounds. Staff didn't use my last name, like with everyone else, as it was long and too hard to pronounce. "Mary Sue, I'm impressed with your concern for patients and how quickly you've picked up our routines. You even notice details I miss. You seem a natural for nursing. Why didn't you go to school?"

Was she trying to tell me I was smart? No nursing program would accept me. I nearly flunked high school. Daddy said I was stupid and now Roberto said the same. I didn't feel stupid at work. Had I found something I could do? Was nursing my way out?

I began taking even more interest at work. A Mr. Phillips had cancer of the nose and throat. Nothing was left but raw flesh edged in black, where the disease had eaten away half his nose. It smelled awful! He didn't know smoking would do this to him. Back then nobody did! Now, it was too late.

I was smoking two packs a day when the caution warnings on cigarette packages came out. But that wasn't why I quit. A package of cigarettes cost (I believe, fifty cents) the same as a half gallon of milk. I was basically smoking away the kid's milk. I heard it took three weeks to break any habit. It took me that long to quit.

Seeing patients and illnesses changed my way of thinking. Poor Mr. Phillips' cancer reminded me I needed a cure for the "cancer" that stank in me: romanticism.

A diabetic patient with a gangrene foot was to have her leg amputated below the knee. She begged them not to, saying her husband wouldn't love her anymore. Delirious after surgery, she tried to get home to him, climbed over the bedrail, landed on the stump and broke open the incision. Her husband never visited. This taught me how stupid I'd been, chasing a man who didn't care about me.

A three-year old boy was in to have his crossed eyes surgically straightened. After the operation, they sewed his eyes shut, covered them with cotton and gauze then splinted his arms and strapped them to his sides. Completely in the dark, he could hear Mommy and Daddy. But why didn't they help? He struggled all afternoon to get free. He was tired and wanted his blanky to stroke and his thumb to suck, so he could fall asleep.

Like that little boy, I'd been blind and needed comforting; like him, my sight was better and I was about to be set free!

My unquenchable thirst for knowledge had me reading my very basic medical reference books until two every morning. I also attended weekly seminars at the hospital. It wasn't much but was a start, and I couldn't get enough!

With amazing new energy, I balanced kids, job and housework with ease. Roberto never lifted a finger, leaving newspapers, plates and glasses for me to pick up after work. He never even put supper dishes to soak. On my days off, he could have kept the kids busy so I could deep clean, but wouldn't.

With him, it was "Me Tarzan; you Jane." With any foresight, he'd have known our marriage was headed for deep do-do. The only *foresight* he understood came just before *foreplay!* Roberto had three basic

needs to make his life complete: the jingle of money in his jeans, a hot meal and a roll in the hay!

Roberto sent resumes everywhere, while I steadily worked toward independence. Personal changes were coming as fast as those at the hospital. My first days at work, food trays had metal cutlery and glass dishes with aluminum covers to keep food warm. Now, everything was plastic and styrofoam, including water pitchers, emesis basins (to spit or vomit in), bedpans, disposable pads instead of draw sheets across the middle of the bed to keep it cleaner and throw-away hypodermics. Disposable razors were a new invention not yet sold in stores. The RNs were giving me interesting assignments. Because of all the changes, I quipped to a newborn I was taking from delivery to the nursery, "You're about the only thing left around here that *isn't* disposable!" It was 1970. The unthinkable was only a couple of years away.

Births and deaths were common there. One code blue had Westbrook grabbing my arm as she passed me in the hall in a dead run. "Come on!" she said. We rushed into the room as the woman exhaled her last breath. She was only forty-eight. This taught me I would die young if I didn't leave Roberto.

I was working ER one September afternoon, when a nine-year old boy came in with a snakebite to his calf. Severe swelling called for a fasciotomy (fay-she-otomy): an incision to avoid skin tears in cases of extreme swelling. His was to both sides of the leg: ankle to crotch and ankle to hip. Weeks later, they grafted skin from his other leg. His mother, expecting her fifth child, stayed by his side the whole time. Two days after he went home, she was back in labor.

The second snakebite happened to a six-foot-six Mexican, who'd gone on a picnic with his brother and their wives. The men, who had been drinking and come upon a large rattlesnake, cornered it and tried to catch it with their bare hands. His brother went right to the hospital, while this guy waited four hours.

Drunk as a skunk, he was thrashing about and fighting. He didn't understand English, so I was brought in to explain in Spanish that we were trying to help. When I walked in, three orderlies and two nurses were trying to hold him down for a sedative. I happened to touch his arm and was the only one speaking the instant the needle went in. "*Ya, quieto!* (Enough, be still.) *Tranquilísese* (Be tranquil/calm youself)! He looked confused and stared at the needle in his arm as though the shot made me speak Spanish. I attended his skin graft six weeks later. Bitten on the hand, his arm swelled to twice its size. The fasciotomy was from thumb to armpit. He had huge muscles and must have worked out regularly. While changing his bandages, nurses would hover over to see his exposed muscles work. Flattered by all the attention, he obliged.

A nurse, who was to begin working at Palo Pinto Hospital days later, was bitten outside her home. Since copperheads aren't as venomous as rattlers and she came in immediately, she was spared a fasciotomy. (I had to leave Coto to see snakebites!)

Because I loved my job, I felt good about myself and had more energy than I knew what to do with. Up at six to fix big breakfasts, I then cleaned, washed, worked out with TV's Jack LaLanne, got the kid's lunch, played with them, cooked supper, left it in the oven and cleaned the kitchen, bathed the kids, and was at work by three or by one on seminar day. When I got home, the table was full of dirty dishes and toys littered from one end of the house to the other. I don't know how I got everything cleaned by the weekend, when Rudy, Pat and Alberto would come over for barbeque.

One evening, twenty-one year old Alberto had one too many and began lamenting his mother's death from cancer. (He tried to find someone to save her, and was only seventeen when she died.) He threw up all over our kitchen curtains racing to the bathroom. Decent and clean-cut, you could tell the kid didn't make a habit of this. As he left for home, he apologized and never repeated the behavior.

ALL THE WAY HOME

Rudy, a natural stand-up comic, had been at it for two hours, when I got home from work one night. Instead of changing out of my uniform, I sat down to enjoy the fun. I couldn't help but notice Alberto's intense stares. He couldn't have been flirting. He was just a baby!

The hospital's floor-to-ceiling corridor windows reflected almost like mirrors at night, and I paused to stare more in astonishment than to admire myself. I wasn't skinny anymore. I actually had a figure and looked good! Was this what Alberto had seen?

Roberto began to get replies from the resumes he'd sent all around the world. Among the replies was one from Columbia, South America, and another from Rhodesia, Africa. "Look what they pay on this one from Afghanistan!" he shouted. "John's already inquired. They want pilots to spray in the desert."

"For locusts?"

"No, just a gas."

"For what?"

"Well, it's odorless, invisible, and hovers in canyons."

"Hovers?"

"Yeah. When nomad caravans go through it they, well, you know...."

"No, I don't know. Get sick?"

He looked down and didn't answer.

"What? They die?"

He continued to evade my stare.

"Whole families *and* their animals?" I said, astonished.

"Don't look at me that way!" he said. "There must be a reason."

"For killing innocent people? You're not taking that job!"

"They'll only hire somebody else!"

"Let 'em!"

"They're all backward over there!" Roberto argued. "Where do you think slavery originated? Those countries are full of thieves and drug runners! It's probably a crime-fighting measure!"

"Probably? Probably? It's genocide! That could be you and *your* family unknowingly walking into those canyons!"

His expression fell. He'd never thought of it that way.

While we were discussing this and his insufferable attitude of late, Chris kept interrupting. "We're hungry, Mama." Lecturing Roberto had robbed the kids of their early breakfast. When Roberto noticed Chris lingering too long inside the fridge, he jumped up to see. Chris had been sticking a finger in the chocolate meringue pie "tasting" it and had eaten quite a bit. Roberto shoved the rest in Chris' face.

Out of work for weeks now and desperate, he and three other pilots decided to drive around the Gulf Coast and apply as shuttle pilots to offshore rigs. I would need a sitter for a few days. Answering my ad was a tall, plain woman who brought along a ninety-seven pound Bible and tape albums of the Old and New Testament. She wore a dove *and* a cross and was one of those "silent witnesses," who never say what they believe or why. As long as she did her job that was fine with me.

A whole week with no fighting, no fear and no frayed nerves, only uninterrupted peace! I thought I'd died and gone to heaven! And that woman not only took excellent care of the kids but washed dishes and picked-up toys at night. This was better than I thought it would be! I found myself singing Marilyn McCoo's new hit all week.

> "One less bell to answer.
> One less egg to fry.
> One less man to pick up after....
> Oh the laughter!" (Made this line up myself!)

Then he came back. It was too late. I'd seen the "Promised Land" and wanted a divorce. He went to pieces.

"Why? What have I done?" he cried. "I know! You put the horns on me while I was gone, didn't you?"

Why was it always *that* with men?

"No, it's just best we go our separate ways."

"And the kids?"

"You don't even know they're around!"

"And you and me?"

"There is no 'you and me.'"

For six and a half years, the one who'd ruled with an iron fist, used violence to enforce his will, believed hate was stronger than love, bragged that no female would ever rule over him, that he'd never cry over any woman, now cried like a baby. Then anger took over. "You can't leave me! You can't take my children!"

"You left *us* years ago."

"I didn't know. I'll change. I promise!"

"Sorry."

"But where will I go? What will I do?"

He didn't know, but he'd just quoted Scarlett O'Hara from *Gone With the Wind*. My first impulse was to smart off with Rhett Butler's reply, "Frankly my dear, I don't give a damn," but knew it would go over like a lead balloon. I was about to tell him he could stay until he found a job. "Don't *preocoop*..."

"You mean.... "

"No, I don't mean...." He thought I was taking him back. My tone was hard as I told him I wouldn't just throw him out.

"Then there's no chance?"

"Nope."

Weeks passed as he tried to wear me down by talking me out of it when I got home from work. I'd sleep a few hours then get up with the kids. Hours later, when he finally got up, he'd start in on me again. Only this time, he would *not* change my mind. I'd had it! I was through!

A friend was going to Dallas' Neiman Marcus to buy herself a wig, which were popular at work, so I went along. It was a much needed break after all those weeks of badgering. A wig would make it faster and easier for me to get ready for work. We were back in time for our three o'clock shift. Roberto didn't like my new short blonde wig at all, so I wore it to work. The nurses thought it was sensational! One flirty old doctor did a double take and asked a nurse who I was. Little me turning heads? *Moi?* This was new and I loved it! Here I was with three beautiful children, a job I loved, offered a promotion with higher pay, nursing school in my near future and now attractive? A good life had just gotten grrrreat!

It was the last week in October when I bought the wig. Roberto still hadn't found a job. It was seminar day and he needed the car that day and took me to work. I got out and stuck my head in the back door. Chris and David were playing way in the back of the wagon, so I blew them a kiss. I then gave Michelle a peck on the cheek, tousled her hair and brushed off the seat. "Shell, you got crumbs all over the place, again! Here," I said, handing her the vanilla wafer, "you dropped one. Bye, kids. See 'ya tomorrow mornin!"

Roberto, who'd begged me not to leave him all morning, was leisurely stretched across the front passenger seat. "Sure you won't change your mind?"

"I'm sure," I said with the sobriety of a judge.

"Then I guess *this* is goodbye."

ALL THE WAY HOME

Red flags went up by the dozens as our white station wagon pulled away. Chris and David stared at me in a strange way out the back window, their faces pressed against the glass. I wanted to run stop them, then thought what my reliable, duty-bound mother would say, "You're imagining things! Get inside and do your job!" And she'd be right! I couldn't let scare tactics affect me if I expected to get do well at work and study, too. Pursing my lips, I turned and walked into the building. He'd be waiting at home to argue tonight. All day, I had no peace. Something was up! Meanwhile, in Mexico City...

———————

"Mr. DeBenedictis," said the customs agent in Spanish, "These children aren't on your passport. Are they yours?"

"Of course," Roberto said to the man he viewed as an insect.

"I can't allow you to board your flight to Costa Rica."

Roberto dipped down to cut the glare on the nametag then read it aloud. "Mr... Gomez. What kind of passport do I have?"

"Diplomatic," he answered respectively.

"I'm a Costa Rican Consul on a diplomatic mission. Hinder me and I'll have your job!"

There was no Tulsa consulate. This was one of those Don Vicente government connection deals. Roberto had no official or even personal letters from Costa Rica. Only a special passport in case he ever got in trouble.

Mr. Gomez had a family and couldn't afford to lose his job. With a broad sweep of his arm, he stood aside. "Consul, your party may board."

———————

MARY SUZANNE LOPEZ

My shift seemed to last forever. We had no phone (Roberto didn't like them), so I called neighbors and the Casebeers to check on my family, but no one was home. I hitched a ride home with Greenway, who talked all the way. By now, I imagined the worst. Beneath cloudy October skies, faint shadows of gnarled Texas oaks stretched across our huge community yard, and an owl hooted from the old barn. Roberto forgot to turn on the porch light. I felt my way up the front steps, fished for the keyhole and opened the door. The living room was messy, but somehow different, like when you move. "Oh my God, no!" I ran to the kids' room. Their closet was wide open and empty.

I had to find a phone! I raced down the country road toward town, hoping to be stopped. *Cops are like husbands,* I thought. *You can't find 'em when you need 'em!* "The police station must be around here, somewhere," I grumbled aloud as I flew down Main Street. "There it is!" I swerved into a parking space and dashed inside.

An officer sauntered by with a stack of folders. I ran to the officer behind the desk. "My children have been kidnapped!" He was finishing an entry on his clipboard. "Sir, I need help!"

In a drawl slow as molasses, the cowboy in uniform pulled out a pencil and touched it to his tongue. "Hold on there, ma'am. Let's jest start frum the beginnin', here. First uv all, yur full name."

"Mary Suzanne DeBenedictis."

Noting that, he touched the pencil to his tongue again and poised over the page. "Yur ad-dress."

"My husband's kidnapped my kids!"

He rubbed the stubble on his chin. "Yur husband, huh? Well, that's a whole 'nuther deal," he drawled. "Ain't nary a thing we kin do 'bout that."

"About what?" I said, taken aback.

"Yur husband's got as much right to them thar young'uns as you do. Beggin' yur pardon, ma'am, but he kin take 'em clear on tah hell, if'n he's a mind tah, an' thar ain't a sight a body kin do 'bout it."

"That thar might be whar he's done headed to," I muttered under my breath.

"Beggin' yur pardon, ma'am?"

"Nothing, sir."

"Jest whare is it 'ya think he's ran off to?" he added.

I breathed in deepy. "I...," and exhaled "...don't know. Africa... the Middle East? Maybe I need the FBI."

The officer squeezed his beer belly out from behind the desk, pushed himself up from the squeaky, wooden executive chair and waddled to an adjacent office with me on his heels. "Take a seat thar, ma'am an' I'll git someone who kin hep you a mite better."

I argued with the FBI for a solid hour on the phone. "A father's got a right to take his kids where he wants." I left to find a phone to call Costa Rica. "No Maria, we haven't heard from him," said Don Beh with concern and sympathy in his voice.

It was pushing three a.m. when I got home. Half-stumbling to the kids' room, I fell across the boys' double bed, buried my face in their pillows and tried to catch their scent. At dawn, I got up and wandered around the house sobbing, finally slumping into a wingback chair, stared at the first rays of morning shining amber through the cream sheers. When the sun was high enough to hit my eyes, I went in my room, collapsed across the bed and tried to escape into music. Though I knew the difference between fairytales and reality, what persisted was from Disney's Cinderella. Maybe because it offered such hope.

"A dream is a wish your heart makes
when you're fast asleep

MARY SUZANNE LOPEZ

In dreams you will lose your heartaches
Whatever you wish for you keep
Have faith in your dreams and someday
your rainbow will come smiling through
No matter how your heart is grieving
if you'll keep on believing
the dreams that you wish will come true."

Asleep only a couple of hours, I awoke expecting to hear the TV blaring out Saturday morning cartoons. My babies weren't there. Were they alright? Were they hungry? (There was lots of food here.) Were they warm? San Jose could get cold. (There were plenty of blankets here at home.) Were they afraid? (I'd protect them if I were there.) I don't know how long I lay there, unable to move. I finally went out to look for a phone to call Costa Rica. "Hello?" came a familiar voice.

"Roberto? Is that you? Are the kids alright?"

"They're fine. My folks are furious! They said you were a good mother and I should never have done this to you. I'd like to make it up."

"Just give me the kids."

"Of course. They need you. I see that, now. Come get them and I'll send you all back. A great job just opened up. If I leave here, I'll miss out on it. If you need extra for your ticket, Rudy and Mr. Casebeer might buy my rifles. See if you can get a week or two off, so I can show you around. It bothers me I never did. At least let me do that, okay?"

I didn't want to be there any longer than necessary! "I haven't worked long enough to get vacation time."

"Try, okay?"

Sunday, I called Rudy and he came over with cash to pick up the rifles.

Monday morning, a bell tinkled as I opened the door to the office of T.C. Hutton, attorney. "Won't you be seated," the receptionist smiled. "He'll be with you in a moment. There's coffee and pecan sandies on the credenza."

My mind wasn't on cookies.

CHAPTER NINE

TRUTH AND CONSEQUENCES

I flipped through a magazine from the table. Why didn't I divorce him years ago! Mama's steel sense of duty had kept her in the "tender trap" for fifteen years. But back then, divorced women were shunned. Mama had no choice... no place to go. Their marriage got worse, so she played cards and went to picture shows with girlfriends twice a week, and he built model airplanes in the garage.

Was Daddy angry and distant because he had no sons? Mama said he should be glad to have two healthy daughters. He never appreciated Mama. I didn't know why. Prettier than any movie star, she was vivacious, articulate, frugal, efficient, a great cook and immaculate housekeeper, yet he physically abused her. Roberto had been abused as a child. What was Daddy's excuse?

Daddy was born into a comfortable middle class home. His father didn't seem very nurturing. Granddaddy was sick at the end, and restricted to his massive four-poster bed. People died at home then. Children were seen and not heard, so when the youngest members of the family were ushered in to say goodbye, Linda and I, even at three and five, knew not to speak. No sooner were we standing at the foot of his

bed than a grownup loudly whispered, "Get the children out! His feet are turning blue."

From outside the door, we heard weeping and wailing. "He's gone to heaven," Mama said. We were never to ask questions. Mama liked him but didn't cry, at least not in public. It wasn't hard for me not to cry. I had no memories of climbing on a doting grandfather's lap for a story or of him buying us ice cream cones or taking us to picture shows. I don't even remember his voice. He was simply the austere giant, who would stop and stare down at me through cold, steel blue eyes.

Grandmother was kind, sweet and quiet. Maybe because she was stone deaf. A hearing aid hung around her neck, the size of a pack of cigarettes. When around those she didn't like, she'd turn it off and smile a lot.

Daddy said if not for the Crash of '29, we'd have all been rich! Mom told me just before she died, "Not having money didn't keep your father from living like a millionaire!" Maybe it began with his parents, who at last had enough to spoil their last child. His older siblings were made to toe the mark, but this one they would enjoy. So, Kirk's happy, carefree childhood was filled with the advantages not given the first three children. Growing up, little Kirk wasn't made to do household chores. As a teen, his dad offered him work at Hoover Built Homes making twenty-five cents a day, good wages during the Great Depression. Kirk didn't like hot, sweaty work. With his people skills, intelligence, good looks, beautiful speaking voice and gift of Blarney, he belonged in a coat and tie! As it was, Kirk kept banker's hours, bent every rule and learned to make excuses. Sometimes, he didn't even show up at work sites. His father couldn't be harsh. Kirk was still a boy. "Let him enjoy his youth!" he said. "He'll grow up soon enough."

Rumblings of war in Europe began to appear on newsreels at picture shows. Was the Army Air Corps the greener pastures Kirk longed for? He could fly for commercial airlines now flying all around the world.

His dad sent him to Spartan School of Aeronautics in Tulsa, where he met Josilee (Mom). Her big sister, Mozelle, knew exactly what he was and sent Jo to visit relatives in California. Discovering the date of her return, Kirk intercepted Jo's train in Texas, where July 21st, 1941, they were married by a justice of the peace.

Josilee lived above reproach, and like most women of her day waited two years to have a baby. This was done so people couldn't say a woman had been forced to marry, because she was in a family way. Wanton behavior was so dishonoring to a family and shameful to the girl, it was rare. Even men were looked down on then, though women took the usual brunt.

Couples didn't have children until they could afford them. (Imagine that!) Daddy wanted a boy, so the names John and Phillip were considered. I came along and Daddy went off to war hoping for a boy the next time. Linda Jo, born with Daddy's blue eyes, was named for the pop song, "Linda," and "Jo" after Mama, and Aunt Mozy's husband Joe, who "walked the floor" for her. Linda was conceived like most babies of that time, while Daddy was home on furlough.

Grandmother happily spoiled me, teaching me one of my first words, "cream," her word for ice cream. Barefooted, I once stepped onto her hot floor furnace and froze. Daddy yanked me off, but not before the bottoms of my feet looked like grilled steaks. "Some cream!" Grandmother cried, running for the burn ointment. Thinking she was getting me ice cream, my tears stopped and I shouted, "i keem, i keem!" It was the cutest thing she'd ever heard! The ice cream stopped the pain faster than the ointment.

Mama didn't think the next word I learned was "cute" at all! She must have thought the vulgar word she often used would go right over my head until the day I pouted, stomped my little foot and cried, "Oh, sit!" She finally figured out the naughty expletive, she cleaned up her act.

ALL THE WAY HOME

I didn't hear words like that again until I was sixteen and my stepfather's niece used everything from "sit" to the infamous "F" word. All this from a fourteen year-old, who's folks had her on the front pew of the Broadway Baptist Church every time the doors were open!

Mama worked in a Tulsa war plant while Daddy was overseas. To economize, she moved in with Aunt Mozy and Uncle Joe. Linda and I stayed with an older couple during the week and came home on weekends. Mama paid bills, bought war bonds and put the rest in the bank. She saved enough to buy an old jalopy I called the "fudgsicle," because of it's dull brown exterior. When Daddy came home from the war, Mama's thriftiness had them a paid for car and over a thousand dollars in the bank to help restart their lives. This was quite a nest egg in a day when a burger, fries and Coke cost a quarter and a new house was around ten thousand.

Granddaddy planned to leave his business to his sons. Recognizing the opportunity, industrious Mama tried motivating Daddy by involving herself in the business. When Daddy's brother, Glen, blocked Daddy's getting paychecks he didn't earn, Daddy sought greener pastures.

With part of the money Mama saved, they made a down payment on a new house Granddaddy built us at cost (nine thousand). Daddy used the rest for a down payment on a dark gray, four-door Cadillac. Unless you were the Good Humor Man, Jo couldn't expect him to impress the "right" people driving all over town in a fudgsicle!

With post-war business booming, Daddy could have been one of the GI's climbing the executive ladder who would eventually command top dollar. He talked a lot, but accomplished nothing.

Instead of aggressively following leads and closing sales, he'd go home at lunchtime, and as Mama put it, "play" in the garage. He'd go clock out, then after supper, "play" until bedtime.

MARY SUZANNE LOPEZ

The detached garage was Daddy's domain where he built his model bi-planes, English Spitfires, Japanese Zeros and German Messerschmitts to hang from the garage ceiling. He even had a B-29 Super Fortress Bomber with a six-foot wingspan. The ones he put gas engines in and painted bright yellow, he'd dogfight on weekends at a nearby field with other ex-pilots who were also model airplane enthusiasts. I was to hold the plane until Daddy could run out, grab the lines and take-off. But I didn't like loud engines that sprayed gas on me or watching small planes fly endless circles around a hot dusty field, so I opted out when I could.

Also in the garage was a ping-pong table. Mama didn't play anymore, Daddy could beat me and I could beat Linda. So, Daddy set up the train set he gave me for Christmas, complete with countryside scenes and elaborate miniature towns I wasn't to touch unless unsupervised.

In the back of the garage was a paper target over a bale of hay. Daddy's forty pound bow was too much for an eleven year old, so he got me a twenty-five pounder. When he told me I was a natural, I practiced for the attention. When hitting the bull's eye every time got boring, I used different shooting positions. Impressing Daddy was all that mattered.

One day, he came in the garage and shut the door. I thought I'd done something wrong.

"Ten hut!" he shouted like a drill sergeant.

I snapped to, thinking I was in trouble like when I gave wrong answers to math problems during homework sessions and he knocked me backward in my chair.

"I've been watching you, soldier. Good shooting!"

I raised my head and smiled, my green eyes sparkling.

"Can that smile, soldier! You're not at ease!"

"Yes, sir!" I shouted back and stared straight ahead.

"Know what this is?" he said, pulling something from a bag.

"A rifle, sir!" I said, quickly glancing down then straight ahead, again.

"I can't hear you," he sing-songed like TV's Sgt. Bilko, leaning forward, hand to ear.

"A rifle, sir!" I shouted.

"And a gun is not a what?"

"... a toy!"

"I can't hear you!" he sing-songed.

"A gun is not a toy, sir!"

"As a woman, you'll never go to war and will only use guns for hunting or self-defense. But listen-up, soldier! If ever cornered by some jerk who wants to hurt you or yours, don't be a hero and try and wing him. Aim for the torso and put him down! Got that mister?"

"Yes, sir."

War was a defining point in Daddy's life. In his rough way, he was imparting important lessons the only way he knew how.

"One more thing," his voice grew softer, throwing me off. "Kids had guns when I was young. They carried rifles to and from school everyday to participate in gun clubs. There, they taught us that guns weren't alive; they couldn't think, couldn't reason and damn sure couldn't fire themselves! It takes a finger to pull that trigger, mister, and I'd better never hear of you ever shooting someone out of anger, vengeance or malice. Owning guns is a privilege of freedom. And with that freedom comes responsibility. Never abuse it."

"No, sir!"

"Now, let's fire this baby."

It was only a pellet rifle, but hot stuff to me! He had a German Luger I wasn't allowed to touch unless he was there, and I obeyed. He'd taken me into the world of adults and his trust was important to me. His methods weren't tender but that was his way. Both my parents were big on discipline that came in two flavors: Mom's English stand-offish/stiff upper-lip kind or Daddy's military rigor and German no-nonsense.

Linda and I were to stand at attention while he barked commands then shout back, "Yes, sir!" or "No, sir!" If we didn't answer loud enough (and we never did), he'd get in our faces until we got it right. What I hated worse than that was how he'd take his hand, and cup the back of our necks. Years after leaving home, I couldn't stand being touched there.

In between the military moving Daddy to different cities, life was mainly weekly target practice, model airplane meets on weekends, military drills all the time and answering to the name of John till I was in third grade. (If I had to be called a boy's name, why not Edward, which I liked?) In many ways, I was the boy he had wanted. And since fathers can be rough on sons, I might have died more than once at his hands if not for luck.

We were stationed in Alexandria, Louisiana, and living in off-base housing when I saw "The Thing," with James Arness. The scientist in the film didn't want the creature harmed but wanted to communicate, even reason with it. Even a child knows you can't reason with a monster! Why the creature didn't jump off the wired ramp and run away during the electrocution scene was beyond me. From then on, I was afraid the creature would pop out from under my bed and I was scared to death of electricity! The movie wasn't even in color! But I was more afraid of Daddy than any movie!

Our home in Louisana, once a duplex, now a joined single dwelling, was surrounded by old Southern mansions long past their glory days. Our parents slept in one side and we the other. Our side had a large screened-in porch and a second bedroom Mom converted to a parlor, where we'd listen to radio programs every evening. In 1950, there was no TV.

ALL THE WAY HOME

Mama, who kept her hardwood floors to a mirror shine, said when Daddy was overseas and she was lonely or afraid for him, she'd pray and scrub or polish floors. (I think she got that idea from one of her favorite movies, "I Remember Mama" with Irene Dunne.) She must have prayed a lot after the war, too, because her floors were always perfect.

With no air-conditioning in muggy Louisiana, we took frequent baths. Afterwards, we'd listen to the radio while Mama plaited my hair into French braids. Linda's hair was short.

One evening, Mama had to go to the PX. Up until then, we'd never been left alone. "We won't be long," she said then warned. "Don't open the door and don't go outside, hear?"

"Yes, ma'am."

It was still light enough to play outside. Girls didn't wear shorts much in the 1950's and still played in dresses. Mama always looked nice and dressed us in pretty dresses Grandmother Hoover made (she made all our clothes), polished shoes and put big ribbons in our hair. I couldn't find any play things. That day my selection wasn't so much out of carelessness but to try and please Mama; to show her I knew how to dress well, too: light blue dresses with white pinafores Mama had just starched and ironed, white anklets (thin socks to Mama) and white sandals. Standing Linda next to me, I looked us both up and down in the mirror. We looked nice. Mama would approve.

The screened-in porch floor painted pale blue sparkled with raindrops that dazzled my eyes. I never noticed all the puddles in the yard and street as I ran for the newly bought bicycles leaning against the house. That they were faded, scratched and second hand didn't matter. They were new to us! (Mine was a boy's.) The game was to run down the steps, grab our bikes, ride past the big tree and into the street before the oversized screen door slowly banged shut. We won! We raced down streets smelling of fresh rain. Around corners we flew and in and out of driveways, the spray from puddles cooling our backs.

Knowing we were to be in before dark, we turned down our block, glided into our yard and parked beside the house exactly like Daddy had taught us. It wasn't until we were on the porch that we noticed our mud drenched anklets and sandals. We dutifully removed them, so as not to track mud over Mama's nice floors, and placed them neatly in a row. Our wilted pinafores were mud-spattered, along with Linda's white-blonde hair and pink scalp. This should be no problem. I'd watched Mama plenty of times.

A small box of Ivory Snow that Mama used for bubblebaths sat behind the ball and claw tub that sat high off the floor. Linda got in, while I sprinkled flakes like I'd seen Mama do. Mama never let me have the water high. But then, she wasn't there. Sprinkling more flakes atop hilly mounds of bubbles filling the tub turned them to snow-capped mountains sparkling in the stark light of the naked bulb over the medicine chest. My imagination took me to the North Pole, where I would save the day and destroy the Thing, and all without electricity! Sliding the empty flake box under the tub, I slipped into the warm, delicious water, stared at the shimmering light dancing off the bubbles and chased adventure in far-away places.

The bubbles eventually went down the drain, but the mud I had to get with a towel! (All towels were white then.) The grouted floor was even harder. Wrapping clothing and used towels in a clean one, I stuffed it all in the hamper. Mama would never notice. After all, you just dump laundry in the washer and it comes out clean, right?

When our folks returned, we were innocently listening to the radio in wet hair and underwear the way they left us. Mama went to the kitchen to put away groceries and Daddy sat to catch the last of the program. Daddy was slow to notice things, but not Mama. Taking toothpowder to our bathroom, she spotted muddy streaks across her white ceramic floor. Something told her to check the back porch, where she found spattered anklets neatly stuffed in mud-caked sandals. Her next hunch was the hamper. The jig was up! We were blissfully unaware of impending wrath when she slipped into the room to whisper in Daddy's ear. "You know what" was about to hit the fan!

Mama stood back up and Daddy's eyes narrowed. Grabbing us by the back of our necks, he pushed us to the floor and went to get the razor strap. Though we cried and pleaded, rules had been broken and it was time to pay. The strap came down on our bare legs and buttocks. Whack!

"Your mother told you not to go outside. Will you ever disobey a direct order again?"

"No, we promise!"

Whack!

"I can't hear you!"

Whack!

"No, no, we promise! We promise!"

Whack!

"Will you muddy the house like this again?"

Whack!

"No, please!"

"I can't hear you!" he sing-songed.

Whack!

"We won't! We won't!"

Whack!

"I still can't hear you!"

Whack! Whack!

"No, sir!"

Whack!

"We're sorry, sir! We're sorry!"

Whack!

"You'll never do it again?"

"No! We promise!"

Whack!

"Please, sir, we're sorry!"

Whack!

"Not half… "

Whack!

"… as sorry… "

Whack!

"… as you're… "

Whack!

"… going to be!"

Whack! Whack! Whack! Whack! Whack!

When he finally stopped, one thing was clear: obedience was *not* an option! Afterwards, we got no hugs or tender explanations about the the dangerous thing we'd done. We had simply disobeyed. And that was "unacceptable, soldier!" Feeling alone and unloved, I'd cocooned myself in music and movies with happy endings, when I learned another important lesson: not paying attention had the same consequence as disobedience.

On a family picnic to the lake, Daddy took all the kids for a ride in his motorboat. I was seated at the bow as we glided into shore. As a skinny, not-so-strong ten-year old, I knew better than to move or even

think without permission. How was I to know he expected me to jump out and hold the boat steady for the rest? He'd never told me to do so before. Without "orders from headquarters," I stayed safe in my own little world. Wind in my hair, I was dreaming of adventure in far-away places, when without warning, Daddy broke the paddle over my head. From then on, I anticipated his unspoken orders.

A month before my thirteenth birthday, I begged Mama to go horsebackriding, which had given me a new dimension of freedom and adventure. I usually rode Danny, a small pinto who reared a lot, because of his tender mouth. The stable hands had told me to be careful, so I did. Obedience, remember?

Danny and I were both trained to be obedient, but Danny was already being ridden that day, so they brought me Tony, a four-year old bay gelding who pranced in place, his shoulder muscles rippling. When I stepped forward to mount, he pawed the ground, his wild eyes filled with the youthful exuberance that possessed us both. Standing beside him, I reached for the reins and saddle horn. His ears flattened. Though far from being an expert, riding Danny had given me a certain mastery and confidence, leaving Tony unsure of his new rider.

The stable, originally built out in the country, was now surrounded by suburbs with two-lane streets running parallel to the tree-lined bridle path. The cool, crisp air of that overcast February day had both horse and rider feeling frisky. He tugged at the reins, wanting to go faster. Danny stopped on a dime. I'd have to test Tony. I cantered him, thrilling to the strength of the powerful muscles beneath me. Dying to see how he took turns, I leaned into his neck. Soon, his long, black mane was flowing beside my golden tresses. Having flown around the turn, I pulled back on the reins to walk him the rest of the way. But the bit was in his teeth. Tony was in charge now!

"Whoa," I yelled, gripping the horn, standing in the saddle and tugging the reins. Whoosh, whoosh, whoosh, low-hanging branches

brushed the top of my head! Diving into Tony's neck to miss them was all the encouragement he needed for a dead run.

That first turn was at street-level; the second at the bottom of a steep slope up to the street and coming up fast! Standing in the stirrups and pulling the reins accomplished nothing. Thinking it better to walk to the stable than be carried back in pieces, I kicked my boots from the stirrups to grab the next branch. Tony slowed and appeared to be stopping, so back went my boots as my salvation brushed by. Then everything went black.

When I came to, a crowd had gathered. The wind knocked out of me, I was barely able to talk. "Where's Tony? What happened to my horse?"

An old cowboy crouching beside me held my hand. Aunt Mozy would have thought his grammar atrocious. "I saw it all," he said in a soothing voice. "Yur horse run up the slope all spooked like the devil hissef wus after 'im! Iron shoes ain't made fer concrete, 'ya know. Sparks wus a flyin,' and he slid around tryin' ta keep frum fallin'."

"Is he all right?" I asked.

"I'd say he is. He run back ta the stable."

They won't let me ride here, anymore, I thought. "Help me up, sir. I have to tell them that...."

"Whoa there li'l filly! Lay on back down there now. They done called you a ambalance."

"I'm okay. I...."

"You're not okay, honey. See that?" He pointed upward. "Horse and saddle went under them telephone guy wires slick as a whistle. You hit purdy hard. Won't surprise me none if'n you're all bruised 'crossed yur middle."

Couldn't do any worse than a razor strap, I thought. Gripping the cowboy's hand, I tried to pull myself on up.

"Stop her!" a woman called from the crowd.

"Her hand!" another whispered, echoed by others.

I raised it to see, then lowered it back in the dirt. I'd busted it up pretty bad. An officer came and knelt by the cowboy, while another directed traffic for the ambulance as it inched around parked cars and through crowd-choked streets. Half dazed, I didn't hear the officer ask my name. I could only wonder what Daddy would say and what he would do? Above the noise and confusion around me, like that of a battlefield, came Daddy's voice. "Rank and serial number, mister! A soldier makes it through by keeping his head."

"Little girl?" the officer asked. "What's your name?"

"Uh, Mary Sue Hoover, sir."

Attendants made their way through the crowd with a stretcher.

"Can you give us your address, honey?" the officer asked.

"805 N.W. 49th Street, sir," I said slowly and distinctly like I'd been taught. *"You're pioneer stock,"* came Aunt Mozy's voice. *"Just put one foot in front of the other,"* came Mama's.

"Here in the city?" asked the officer.

I can't hear you! Daddy sing-songed.

"Oklahoma City, sir."

"Do you know your phone number?" the officer asked.

I STILL CAN'T HEAR YOU...!

"Yes, sir!" I all but shouted. "Victor 6-6336, sir!"

"We must get her to the hospital," the ambulance attendant interrupted.

As they got me onto the stretcher, I heard that officer ask the other, "Did you get her information?"

"Yeah. I've never seen such a calm and compliant child in an emergency. Her folks should know what a trooper she is."

Good! Daddy will be proud of me!

Days later, I awoke to a white blur, my heavily bandaged hand propped against a pillow. A young nurse, her short hair bouncing as she walked, said with an animated expression and dimpled smile, "I'm Miss Clark. How do you feel?"

I was groggy. "Where's Mama?"

"She must have gone for a bite. Want some ice cream?"

"Cream" wouldn't take away the hurt this time. I wanted to smile at my little joke, but could only groan.

"I'll get something for pain, Sugar."

Miss Clark gave me a pill then sat with me until Mama came back, who worried how they would pay for all this. Fed up with Kirk's excuses, she'd starve rather than stay another minute! She flitted about the room, admiring the flowers, straightening covers and fluffing pillows.

Miss Clark was loving and reassuring. After two operations and weeks in the hospital, it was hard to leave her. "I'll never see you again, will I?" I asked sadly.

"Friends aren't separated by distance," she said, reaching down to kiss my forehead. "I'll always be with you in spirit."

"Miss Clark?"

"Yes, Shug."

"Could you hand me my stuffed animal?"

"The one you hated, because the school friends who sent it didn't really care about you? Got a name for this shaggy dog?"

"I'm going to call her, Miss Clark."

"I'm not sure I know how to take that!" she giggled then slipped from the room and out of my life.

Barely thirteen, arm in a cast to my elbow, Mickey Mouse Club Mouseketeers came to perform at the fairgrounds in Oklahoma City. They were everything I wanted to be. Since we moved so much while I was growing up, I'd no sooner find a friend than I'd lose them. The Mouseketeers were "friends" I'd never lose. I liked the Bible verses at the end of shows. I began jotting them down, then took minutes of the whole show. My family ridiculed me, saying I was too old for Mickey Mouse. But I'd finally found a place I fit in with kids like me. I belonged. I was happy. I knew it was make believe. But it was all I had, and I stubbornly clung to it.

Another attraction at the fairgrounds was to be the tall, dark and dreamy Keith Larson, who starred as an Indian chief on my favorite TV show, "Brave Eagle." Spending so much time alone, I'd written stories about a girl my age with my height and looks and....Okay, it was me! I hoped my stories would take me all the way to California, where I'd star on his show, be adored by all and live happily ever after.

Daddy was the local talent they'd picked to announce some of the events. I wanted him to take me but he wouldn't. I was disappointed, but didn't make a fuss. Obedience, remember?

I'd no sooner been dropped off at school and left homeroom than I was called to the office. It was Daddy, lying about a dental appointment. Once outside, he said we'd have to run by the house and change before going to the fairgrounds.

At home, off came my poodle skirt and five petticoats replaced by blue jeans, popularized by Marlon Brando and James Dean. I wore them rolled up with saddle oxfords and one of Daddy's long tail shirts.

Daddy didn't mention that certain VIP's would be backstage with Mr. Larson and he expected us to look like young ladies, not silly beboppers. He knocked on the door. "Come in," I said, fumbling with my shoelaces, because of the bulky cast still on my arm.

He rushed across the room, cuffed me on the back of my neck and shoved me into the wall. Lifting me by my ears, cheeks, and hair to his height of 6'2", he slammed my head against the wall again and again then dropped me. I crumpled to the floor.

Hearing the scuffle from the bedroom we shared, Linda averted my fate by quickly changing into a dress. When the "fireworks" were over for Daddy, they were supposed to be over for everyone. We were to smile and act happy, so we did. Obedience, remember?

Speaking of fireworks, when I was about eleven, part of our Tulsa family drove to Oklahoma City to spend Christmas with us. Aunt Mozy's opinion of Daddy, whom she politely tolerated, went a notch lower. Looking for something to eat, I spied a quart of fresh strawberries, rare in the winter months of the 40's and 50's.

"Uh-uh-uh," Daddy wagged his finger, "those are for me."

Aunt Mozy was incensed! How could he refuse his own child? Maybe that prompted her next move. I'd say it was planned all along.

I was sitting on the foot of Mama's bed stroking our cat, Myrtle, and watching Mama nestle silk flowers in her crown of beautiful red curls, when I heard Daddy coming down the hall. Aunt Mozy unwrapped a shiny object from her purse and laid it on the wool blanket next to Myrtle. (She didn't care for cats, and less now, because Daddy did.) I'd never seen anything so revolting! You could almost smell the pungent odor rising from the moist-looking mound of rubber poop! My hand shot to my mouth to keep from laughing.

In rare form, Daddy circulated from room to room in his red plaid flannel shirt spreading Christmas cheer. Family cats were sacred cows, so I wasn't worried about Myrtle when I moved away. The "Christmas Pudding" was about to hit the fan!

Daddy was always saying stuff like, "I'm having so much fun it should be illegal!" Aunt Mozy let him have his laugh then pointed at the foot of the bed. "Speaking of illegal," she said, "is that what I think it is?"

Purring, Myrtle looked up, waiting for Daddy to make his usual fuss over her as he leaned in for a better look. Before we could tell him it was a joke, he back handed poor Myrtle, who went flying into the hall! Meooow!

Aunt Mozy took a tissue and picked up the do-do. Turning it upside-down, she exclaimed sober as a judge, "My goodness!"

Was it worms? "What?" Kirk was almost afraid to ask.

"Call 'Ripley's, Believe It or Not!'" she said. Increasing the suspense, while masterfully maintaining a poker face for the punch line.

"What?" he repeated.

Daddy's nemesis held the oily do-do up closer. "Something I can't quite...."

"What is it?" said Daddy.

"Why something's written here," she paused.

"Huh?" Daddy said with a queer look.

"It says, 'Made in Japan.' What a cat!" she exclaimed.

Neither felt the worst for not speaking to each other again that Christmas. Linda and I spent Christmas Eve comforting Myrtle, who tried to climb the walls every time Daddy walked in.

Daddy didn't mistreat his cats. He loved them. Sometimes, I wished I could be a cat so he'd love me too. In my jammies and ready for bed once, I climbed onto his lap. He hardly noticed, engrossed in a TV show about a cat being chased by dogs and eventually mauled. I threw

my arms around Daddy and cried. I felt deceitful, but got the attention I craved.

Linda already knew this and used it to her advantage. Two sisters reared in the same home and ending up so differently. When she didn't measure up, she blew it off, where it cut me to the quick. She effortlessly glided through life, while I invariably stumbled. She took slights with a grain of salt, where I was openly devastated. Knowing perfection was as unrealistic as it was unattainable, Linda invested her time and energy in study, while I threw myself into a quest for the Holy Grail (love). Two sisters looking for truth and heading for different consequences.

CHAPTER TEN
STORM OF THE SOUL

I left the attorney's office with the child custody and divorce papers I needed to rescue my children from Costa Rica. Getting those papers was easier than I thought. Backing out of my parking spot, I spied Shell's vanilla wafer on the back seat and remembered her face when I scolded her for getting crumbs on the seat. Tears began to well. *I can't think about this, now, I'll go crazy!* I went home to pack.

To save room, I left my hairdryer and curlers and took the ready-to-wear blonde wig, which flipped up on one side for that Doris Day look. I left other things just to take my old favorite, "Handel's Messiah" plus the mail order old-time Gospel album that finally came on Saturday. I had no way to play them at home and hoped Roberto had his stereo set up at his parents.

Taking perishables to neighbors, one offered to care for Barbie, our tan and white beagle puppy. I ran back for her bag of food, which was more than enough for the two weeks I'd be gone. Knowing Sandrita loved chocolate chip cookies, I packed my bag of chocolate morsels. Costa Rican brown sugar, or *tapa dulce,* isn't sweet enough and doesn't measure the same as American. I'd seen *tapa dulce* being unloaded once: unwrapped rock-hard bricks of it, thrown from an open farm truck,

unloaded without gloves and stacked on the mercado floor. Reason enough to take packaged brown sugar from my own kitchen!

After laying out my clothes for the trip, I tidied the house, grabbed a bite and hit the hay, setting the alarm for five a.m. Mr. Casebeer was to drive me to the shuttle for Love Field in Dallas. It was the least he felt he could do since he'd inadvertently helped Roberto leave the States days before. Both the Casebeers apologized. How were they to know Roberto was lying?

I lay staring at the ceiling. Were the kids okay? Were they scared of their new surroundings? I got up and rummaged through their toys for something soft and cuddly to take to comfort them until we could get back home.

The next morning, with only about an hour's sleep, I was running into doors, bumping into furniture and stumbling over luggage. I couldn't wait to board the plane and sleep! Mr. Casebeer loaded my luggage while I locked the door and felt my way down the steps, blinded by the sun's glare.

Finally aboard my flight and desperate for sleep, a baby in back screamed all the way to Mexico City. When I asked why the long wait on the ground there, the stewardess said, "Minor engine problems."

To pass the time, I flipped through travel magazines of couples playing in frothy surfs, beautiful women sipping umbrella drinks under palms, and tan, well-built men running along ribbons of white sugary beaches beside turquoise waters that blended into azure skies. I wasn't impressed anymore.

While that baby whimpered itself to sleep, I thought about the mean things Roberto had done; about Chicago and how I'd stood there and let him punch me. I saw myself crumple to the floor and felt him kicking me again and again. The baby in back suddenly screamed. My eyes flew open! *Where are my children?* I thought. Blinking hard then squinting, I

looked down at the armrests I was gripping. Oh yes, an airplane. I was on my way to get the kids.

Sitting on that runway for more than three hours, I was finally nodding off to the cozy warmth inside the cabin, when the sudden roar of engines thrust my heart into my throat! I felt the same as I did when my impish little sister and I were on the very top of a Ferris wheel and she began rocking our seat like crazy. Or when I rode the rollercoaster and heard the chain's click-click, click-click, click-click pulling us ever upward toward the certainty of the plunge. Like the wail of a banshee, jet engines screemed impending doom. Numbed by stumbling fatigue, eyes squeezed shut, I groped for the armrests.

Had the children been this afraid to fly? Was Roberto being good to them? Or lashing out in anger? I feared flying but was anxious to reach them! Yet, in all my guarded eagerness, I was no hero. Nonconfrontational by nature, I was about to challenge Roberto on his own turf. Who did I think I was, John Wayne leading a cavalry troop? It was only me, buckled in like a convict waiting for the warden to throw the switch! Me, who stayed off ladders, headed for the wild blue yonder! Me, white-knuckling armrests in a heightened state of fear! Me, sitting on a gazillion gallons of high-octane jet fuel about to be launched off another runway in a streak of fire!

Outside the small round window, the ground crew pulled wooden stops away from the plane's tires. It jerked forward to taxi. Next stop, Costa Rica! But before we got too used to actually being in the air, we found ourselves in Tegucigalpa, Honduras, for more repairs.

We pulled up to the terminal and the engines were switched off. I was warm and left my sweater on my seat. Passengers quietly grumbled as we inched our way up the aisle, down the air stair and across the tarmac. On the horizon, lightning sent fiery traces dancing from cloud to cloud, followed by muted thunder.

Repairs would take some time, and supper was on Pan Am. We ascended stairs to an open-air section of the restaurant that ran nearly the length of the small terminal. Umbrellas furled for the night, the soft glow of patio candles cast kaleidoscope patterns on tables down the triple-tiered terrace. Crisp edges of tablecloths, fluttering in the light breeze, were secured by inverted plates, glasses and cutlery wrapped in paper napkins.

I headed for the top far end, tired and wishing to be left alone. To avoid eye contact with other passengers, I stared at the flickering candle, which only made me drowsier. Someone sat down near me, laying his overcoat on the chair between us. He politely tried to engage me in conversation but I declined, citing a sizable loss of sleep. Apologizing for the intrusion, he sat back to look over the scanty menu.

My burning eyes were shut for who knows how long, when I felt Roberto standing there ready to punch me. I jerked to avoid the blow and nearly fell out of my chair. I pretended something was wrong with my chair and decided I'd better stay awake. Maybe that guy still wanted to talk. Sizing him up, I saw he was nicely dressed, graying temples giving him the refined air of a diplomat and distinguished look of a judge. I'd stared too long. I looked away, rubbing the cold from my upper arms.

The wind had picked up, bringing the smell of fresh rain. I was cold, but was nodding off anyway, when something was draped around my shoulders. I looked up. It was the man next to me.

"No thank you," I said in Spanish, declining his coat.

Latin men misinterpret such innocent situations as flaming come-ons, so I'd have to act like a tough Latina. After all, when in Rome....

"Take it, *Doñita*, you're freezing," he answered in Spanish.

"No, *Señor*, I can't."

"Why not?" he asked with a friendly but puzzled look.

"You might need it," I said, half asleep, thinking of no better excuse. "You might get...."

"Cold?" he interrupted. "I have my suit jacket, *Doñita!*"

Doñita? Fresh! I turned and glared! His smile was humble. I softened. He *had* said, *Señora,* recognizing me as a married woman. Maybe I'd misjudged him. *Ticos* put "ito" and "ita" at the end of everything. That's what makes them *Ticos!*

"*Gracias, Señor. Muy amable,*" I smiled, stumbling with a language I never expected to use again, hoping I'd said, "Thank you, sir, you're very kind."

"Ahh, *bollitas (bo-yeet-tahas)*!" He laughed at my rusty Spanish accent, pretending to be happy at a basket of hot bread being placed on the table. "Want one, *Doña?*"

I hadn't had *bollitas* since I left Costa Rica with my two boys over three years ago. I cupped the football-shaped bread in my hands to enjoy its warmth. Bread never tasted so good!

The middle-aged couple at our table began introductions; a doctor and his wife returning home to Costa Rica after some New York shows, great shopping and a visit to her sister in Kansas or somewhere. Two young salesmen were next, traveling Central America to show a new line of elegantly fashioned jewelry from fine Mexican silver. The lady next to them was interesting. Her name, *Santos* (saint), suited the petite, silver-haired widow on her way to spend Christmas with her daughter and family in Costa Rica.

Next to her was an empty chair. (The man had moved next to me.) His last name was Fuentes or fountains (how pretty!), a Costa Rican plantation owner returning from business in the U.S. Not divulging my last name in case someone there knew Roberto, I borrowed the title of a

popular daytime soap and introduced myself as, "*'Simplemente María,'* (just Maria,) on my way to a family reunion."

Soon, chummy laughter blended in amidst the soft clatter of cutlery on stoneware. Irresistible aromas promised our orders would come soon. But as Murphy's Law would have it, they came just as Pan Am gave its boarding call. Hardly begun, much anticipated meals were reluctantly abandoned, leaving those like me quickly eating before scurrying away. I wrapped *bollitos* in napkins and put them in my purse to go with coffee on the next runway we were stuck on. Stuffing the last one with chicken, I hurried down the steps to return the coat.

"Keep it for now, *Doñita*. It's cold and we might have to wait in line while they check us off the passenger list."

High on the terraces, waiters collected tips and tossed out half-eaten dinners, some still warm. I wasn't the only one wishing I'd stayed up there eating.

Shivering on the tarmac, I wasn't so eager to give up the coat. We boarded and I slid into my seat, hoping to keep it until I warmed up. *Señor Fuentes* sat next to me. How could I object? I would come to wish I'd never accepted his coat.

A stewardess passed out blankets and pillows. He tucked his pillow behind his head, laid the blanket across his lap, turned to me and smiled. I no longer distrusted Don Julio, but was at ease in his formality and quiet reserve.

"We might make it to Costa Rica tonight, after all, Don Julio!"

"Please, just Julio."

I knew I mustn't. We began to taxi. Giving me a nod of assurance, he smiled down in a fatherly way. I acknowledged him, then scrunched down and pulled the coat's collar around my face to a hint of some

wonderful men's fragrance. Daddy wore Old Spice. He was supposed to protect me, love me. So was Roberto.

I finally yielded to what should have been peaceful repose, the drone of engines muffling my restless moans of terrors past, yet ever present. Thinking of Roberto wasn't exactly conducive to sweet dreams, but dream I did. A dream so vivid, so real, I could swear I was there. And for a while, I was.

———————

Chicago was cold and we had no sweaters. It was dark. The kids were hungry and begging to go in. Roberto had been angry and threatened me, so I ran. I couldn't go to neighbors for help. He said he'd kill me if I ever did!

Reluctantly, I signaled my shivering boys, four and a half and three, who raced upstairs and burst into the kitchen, laughing and playfully shoving each other, happy to be indoors. I held eight-month old Michelle close, carefully listening as I mounted the narrow staircase. Pausing in the shadows of the small, screened-in porch, I peered in at the red glow of a cigarette. Roberto waited in the kitchen, that by day was a cheery yellow, but was now drenched in darkness. Reaching up, he turned on the light and called out Michelle's pet names. "*Pollita* (baby chick). Come to Daddy, *mí reina* (my queen)."

Squirming out of my arms, she crawled to her daddy as fast as she could. He scooped her up and bathed her in hugs and kisses. Still glaring daggers at me, he set her down. With the kids around, sweetness dripped from his lips like honey. "*Pollita,* go see what the boys are doing." Michelle basked in his fake smile. "Run on *mí reina*. Daddy's going to be busy a while," he said, his eyes never leaving mine. As she hurried to join her brothers, he patted her diapered bottom. She giggled then scampered away on all fours. How could she know Mommy was in trouble?

He respected courage in others. Maybe if he saw it in me. Scared spitless, I timidly offered an uneasy smile. His eyes, piercing and menacing, he calmly closed the door Michelle had just crawled through and walked toward me. I wanted to bolt, but couldn't leave the kids. Surely, he wouldn't hurt them. If he'd only talk! "Roberto, I...."

He pointed his arm ramrod straight. "You; shut up!"

"But...."

"Down on your knees," he commanded, his finger too near my nose for comfort. I edged toward the backdoor. "Crawl to me and beg my forgiveness!" he ordered in a guttural growl.

"Forgiveness? For what?" What was I going to do? The kids! I couldn't think!

"For disturbing the peace of my home, open disobedience then running away. You'll take your punishment like a man."

He reared back to punch me! "Never!" I shouted and wheeled around to run. Down the stairs I flew. There was a blow to my back and I stumbled on the narrow staircase. My left hand went to the wall and my right flailed the darkness for the handrail. If I could brace myself between the rail and the wall, I could prevent a tumble or at least slow my fall. Grabbing the rail in the nick of time, I caught myself as I tumbled into the pitch-blackness. *God, help me!*

A light flashed! I turned and it was gone. I was sitting, but didn't remember hitting the ground. Was I knocked out? How long? Where was Roberto? Did he have his gun? The wall was so cold. I did a double-take then stared. It didn't feel like wood siding, but was smooth like glass. There came a series of bumps then everything suddenly dipped. I clutched the rail and braced myself against the wall. A blow hit my back! The light flashed as I turned, expecting Roberto's raised hand but instead saw the back of an upholstered chair. A chair? It suddenly dipped! Through the glass wall, I saw lightning streak across the sky. Sky? Glass

wall? Wait a minute! Just before this, I was at the top of a staircase and fell. No, I was pushed! If not for this rail…. It looked so different now. It *felt* different. *How did this blanket get here?* The rail moved away from me; a man next to me winced in pain. *Señor Fuentes?* I couldn't let go of his leg fast enough! What must he think?

"I'm sorry, Don Julio! Did I hurt you?"

"Don't *preocoop, Señora,*" he said, patting the offending hand. This weather could scare anyone! Hey, you said you'd call me plain Julio!"

"No, Don Julio, I…."

"Now you're making me feel old!" he said, mimicking a tottering old man. Bending forward, he leaned on an imaginary cane. "Well, if I'm *un viejito,* (a little old man) then you're *una viejita!*" he said, smacking "toothless" lips together.

I burst into laughter! It wasn't that funny. It was *how* he said it with the exaggerated mannerisms. Still, I kept my distance. "Think we're any closer to San Jose?" I asked, changing the subject.

"Who knows?" he said, checking his watch. "We might be dealing with a strong head wind. Hurricane weather, you know."

I sighed and turned away. How I longed to stretch out on a real bed. An announcement came over the intercom: "Ladies and gentlemen, due to inclement weather over San Jose, our flight has been diverted to Panama…." After all the previous delays, a crescendo of concerted sighs rose, peppered with a few choice words. Irked voices went back to a disgruntled hush, while the stewardess finished her sentence "… with complimentary rooms for the night. Free transportation will be provided to several hotels near the airport. Pan Am wishes to apologize for any inconvenience and promises that special care will be taken toward the comfort of each of our valued passengers. We should arrive around one a.m. Thank you for your continued patience." The Spanish version brought groans from those who hadn't understood the first. "*Damas y*

caballeros, lamentamos informarles que.... " When she finished, begrudgingly appeased passengers resumed what they were doing.

I wish I'd gotten more rest before this trip. Lightning flashed as we dipped and rolled in the terrible storm. Fat chance I'd sleep now!

At least this wasn't one of Coto's dinky mail planes! If we had to set *this* baby down.... Wait! There were no runways down there; no grassy fields, only thick, raw jungle with two hundred foot trees jutting into the sky.

Trying not to think of being shish-kabobed was like trying not to think of a certain color ... let's say, "pink." I shifted my weight in the seat. Don Beh once said that when planes went down, jungle quickly grew over crash sights and the wreckage was never found, even fully equipped military transports during World War II, en route to ships in the Panama Canal. Young soldiers aboard would not die in battle but in a fiery crash somewhere in the jungle wilderness of Central America. Pink, pink, pink, pink, pink! Was there no other color?

Don Julio was gazing past me outside the window. I could return his kindness by getting his mind off the storm. That way, time would pass more quickly for us both. We talked about everything and nothing at all; our likes and dislikes, things we'd done and what we'd like to do; places we'd been and those we had yet to see; the coffee business and his plans to expand; his children and mine and the darling things they'd said and done.

Laughter revitalized and energized us so much we were almost disappointed to finally land in Panama. But my emotional high soon ended and fatigue returned with a vengeance! After endless delays to retrieve luggage and tedious lines through customs, exhausted passengers filtered through the dark lobby, their echoing footsteps the only sound breaking the silence of night.

ALL THE WAY HOME

Where were the shuttles to the hotels they had promised? After thirteen hours scrunched in coach, it was hard to be this close and still have to wait for a bed. Most passengers, who took earlier hardships gracefully, were now past their limit of patience. Resigned complacency had turned to fuming agitation!

Airport staff mercifully came from nowhere to organize an orderly exodus. Eyes glazed over, passengers stood by as though abandoning ship as cabs were hurriedly loaded and launched. Single men gave their seats to the elderly and women with small children, but there was never enough room for me and my things. My legs had turned numb from the knees down, so I slipped in through the lobby door and sat down. That straight-back wooden chair turned out to be a bed of nails! But nothing was more urgent than getting off my feet, even with my spine against all that ornate carving. I secured my things by stretching my legs over my luggage and folding my arms over my purse. I had only meant to rest my eyes, but sank into much-needed sleep.

My eyes flew open to the sensation of movement! *I don't recognize these streets! Where am I? How did I get here? Who are the men on either side of me?* Their faces were distorted by passing shadows and flickering streetlights. The big guy dozed, arms folded; the triple chin that rested on his chest sported a gangster-like five o'clock shadow. I imagined the worst. To escape, I'd have to act tough. Squaring my shoulders, I swallowed hard, tapped his shoulder and promptly lost my nerve. "Sir," I meekly said, "where are we going?"

Opening one eye, he looked down at me and inhaled. In a breathy reply like a wind blowing through a mighty cave, he spoke in a gravelly, Bronx accent. "Relax a little, it's just a short ride."

In one movie I had heard a gangster say to his victim, "Relax Shorty, we're going for a little ride." I lunged for the door handle! The other man caught my wrists in mid-air. My blood ran cold! Shaking them, he loudly whispered, *"Tranquilita!"*

What did he say? I kept struggling and pulling.

"*Tranquilisese!*" he repeated louder.

I had to get away!

He squeezed my wrists until they hurt. "*Pero, por favor!*"

Por favor? That meant "please." I stopped struggling to think about the other word, *tanquilisese*. Be still? Was he kidding? "Let me go!" I shouted.

He shook my wrists harder. "*Pero, calmase!*"

"I won't be calm!" I shouted in English. "Let me go!"

"*Doña Maria, soy yo,*" he said in Spanish then switched to English. "It's me! *Doñita*, it's Don Julio!"

I stopped resisting and he released his grip, reassuring me in his deep, soothing voice. "Tranquil. Be calm. It's all right. You're in a taxi. We're on the way to our hotel. We'll be there any minute."

The gentle giant, backed into the corner, his hands up to protect his face, realized it was over and his horrified look melted back to complacency. Giving me a contemptuous look, he closed his eyes and refolded tree limb-size arms across his portly girth.

The cab turned onto the hotel grounds. Don Julio released my wrists, placed my hands in my lap and gently patted them. I let him. Would I insult him on top of everything else?

Down the long drive, I studied him as the glow of hotel street lamps softly ebbed and flowed across his face. I had no romantic interest. I needed a man like I needed a bad rash! His kindness and gentleness was almost Christlike. If only Roberto was like this. If only he weren't so bitter and volatile. If only we could have turned things around in time. As I stepped from the cab, regrets and rose-colored conjecture

blew away in balmy breezes, banished in the fragrant perfection of a tropical night.

The hotel looked like an Old California Spanish Mission. Through immense, hand-carved doors, guests passed into a virtual paradise. The men got the luggage and rushed past, never noticing the beauty all around us.

Inside, I was awestruck at columned archways that framed the long verandas, of bushy palms in hand-painted ceramic pots, of bamboo and rattan patio groupings on gleaming floors of red terracotta. The hotel desk, tucked in a nook, was also in the open air. Honeycombing the lush array of exotic foliage and dim footlights were polished flagstone paths wide enough for arm-in-arm strolls. Benches and small candlelit tables were nestled in secluded settings with special lighting that reached up into the palms.

The occasional muffled squawks of a parrot could be heard. I edged up the Japanese bridge overlooking a lighted pond, to watch as gold fish swam in and out of water lilies. From there, I could see a free-form swimming pool, a flagstone footbridge across its middle. On either side were small, flagstone islands with palm trees and flowers.

Spots of aqua hues from underwater pool lights beneath the water's glassy smooth surface added magic to the reflection of the refreshment kiosk's palm roof against a starry night. The sound of rustling palms drew my gaze to the millions of diamond-like stars flung against the indigo velvet of a moonless sky.

Lost in a delight of the senses, I barely heard Don Julio call me from across the courtyard. I hurried to the desk, intending to return later.

"It's beautiful here, isn't it?" Don Julio commented.

"Something good came of this trip, after all," I responded positively.

"Right!" he laughed. "You're next to check in." He had bellboys ready by the time I had my key. I liked being taken care of in such a gentlemanly way. This time, I was first to smile at him in thanks.

On the way to our rooms, Don Julio began acting silly. If he was as tired as me, he was probably running on fumes! It wasn't fatigue that made me lower my guard. I now trusted him and didn't hear him call me, *mi* (my) *doñita*, a forbidden familiarity. It sounds archaic, but words considered innocuous in the States should be avoided by women alone in foreign countries. I knew better and should have corrected him.

"Don Julio," I began my goodbyes, "in case I don't get a chance tomorrow, I want you to know I've enjoyed knowing you and I thank you for everything," I smiled, offering a hand of friendship.

"*Hasta entonces... mi Mariquita.*" He stood gazing at me then shook my hand, slipping something into my palm.

What did he mean, "Until then my little María?" I thought.

"Goodnight," I said over my shoulder, as I headed down the hall. Once in my room, I looked to see what he'd given me. Strange; a business card?

The bellboy turned on the air and drew the drapes; I tipped him and he left. On my way out to the garden, I noticed there was writing on the back of the business card I'd thrown on the bed. "Meet me at the pool in ten minutes for a drink." So much for "Christlike" behavior! I sat down and picked up the phone. "Operator, I'd like a wake-up call for five forty-five. And no calls to my room, please. Thank you."

With only about three hours sleep, morning came a little earlier than I'd have liked. But I was alert. How could I not be? This was the day I'd waited for... prayed for. By lunchtime, I'd be with my kids! We'd go home and forget all this. I'd already decided not to gloat. I had my divorce and child custody papers and could afford to be civil a few days.

I got to the airport early. We would fly to Costa Rica on a Panamanian turbo jet. It was about time someone grounded that other one!

It seemed they no sooner picked up our breakfast trays than we were banking over San Jose. Spreading for miles, were clusters of dark orange flowers that dotted the flat-topped trees, welcoming me to a place I thought I'd never see again.

Clearing customs, I hailed a cab that sped down narrow roads past old coffee plantations. Nothing had changed: coffee trees still looked like bushes, the faint smell of volcanic ash still lingered on the cool mountain air, fence posts still grew into trees that lined the road, and Roberto was still a jerk!

I had to think more positively for the kid's sake, so I imagined holding them. For a fleeting moment, I could feel their cool cheeks against mine and smell their sweet breath.

The cab pulled up to the address Roberto gave me. The cabbie got my bags, while I went to knock. The door slowly creaked open. Who was it? My eyes adjusted to the apartment's dark interior. A shaft of light shone on hair the color of light brown sugar. "Shell!" I cried. Chris and David came over by their sister and stared up at me, blinded by the outside glare. Gaunt and pale, their sunken eyes not only lacked expression but curiosity. Didn't they recognize me?

I jostled their hair and bent down to gather them in my arms. They were as unresponsive as rag dolls. I squeezed them harder. They gasped and whimpered. I backed off so they could see me.

"Mommy, you cut your hair," Chris said.

"It's a different color!" David added.

Michelle was still trying to decide if it was really me. The boys grabbed me around the waist and brought her with them into a big group hug.

Roberto and his family came from inside and stood quietly.

David pulled back and looked up. "What took you so long?"

Chris immediately followed with, "Waiting was so hard!"

Michelle quietly sobbed.

I was once more at the mercy of a man with a troubled soul. Michelle's soft weeping echoed down the long hallway as we huddled together. My legs gave way, my knees crashing on the threshold of that house. And kneeling there in the shadowy doorway of hell, we clung to each other and cried.

CHAPTER ELEVEN
A BITTER VINTAGE

Not yet three, Michelle had already learned to tattle. "Mommy, guess what!"

I wiped my tears and answered in an overly animated way. "What, honey?"

She paused and looked at her brother. "Know what David did?"

"Don't listen, Mama," he said. "It's a lie!"

"Is not!"

"Is too!"

"Is not!"

"Is too!"

"It's not nice to shout and call people liars, David," I half scolded. "Now, say you're sorry."

"But Mama, she always gets us in trouble."

"I do not!" Michelle said looking up at me, her eyes filling with tears.

"You do!" David taunted, sticking out his tongue. "You're a tattletale!"

"Mommy, make him stop!" she wailed.

"Liar, liar, pants on fire!" he teased. "Michelle is just a big fat liar!"

"Enough, David!" The five-year old pouted and Michelle flung herself in my arms. "It's okay, baby. Don't cry."

"On the plane," she sobbed, "I was scared."

"Of what, honey?"

"David crying. He cried all the way here. Mommy, where is here?"

"We're at your grandparent's."

"Can we go home, now?" she sniffled.

David's head hung in shame, having been exposed as a crybaby.

"David, can you keep a secret?" I asked.

"Uh-huh." A big tear spilled down his chubby round cheeks, now flushed red.

"I cried on the plane, too."

"You did?" David perked up.

"Sure did!"

He paused, then angrily smeared away his tears with the back of his hand.

"You're supposed to cry. You're a mommy!"

"Daddies cry, too," I softly said.

"They do?" His eyes were wide with surprise.

A nervous foot-shuffling came from those waiting at the door behind the children. It had to be Roberto and Don Vicente, uneasy at what I'd said. I was uneasy myself, "explaining" men, when I hadn't figured them out myself! I continued, saying what seemed logical.

"Real men sometimes cry when they're sad." I emphasized the word "real" to rub Roberto's nose in his own machismo. "But real men also know when to stop crying."

"They do?" David said, crinkling his brow.

In over my head, I wished I'd never begun this!

"Men have something special inside that makes them want to protect those they love by being brave and choosing not to cry."

"How can you choose not to cry when you're sad?" he said, sounding confused.

"What happens to your hiccups when Mommy surprises you with a loud noise?"

"The hiccups stop?"

"Exactly! When you suddenly left home and all that was familiar to you, it surprised you so much, you stopped being brave, but only for a while. Right?"

"I... I guess so," he stammered.

"You see? You weren't crying. You were grieving and...."

"What's grieving?" he interrupted.

"That's when you're really sad like when you lose someone or something very dear. It's different from plain old crying."

"It is?" he asked, confused.

"Yes! Even 'real men' grieve. Then they stop and choose to be happy, so loved ones can lean on their strength until they're strong again, too. That's how I know you were grieving. Why, you're from pioneer stock! Pioneers acted brave when they were scared, happy when they were sad and helped others when they didn't feel like it. Do you know how they could tell if you were one of them? By how happy you were! That showed who the real men were. Which one of you boys is the real man?"

"I am!" the boys said in unison.

"Me, too!" squealed Michelle.

"You can't be a man!" David rebuffed. "You're a girl! Bet I can be happier than you!" he challenged his brother.

"Bet you can't!" Chris countered.

"Okay guys!" I said. Pandemonium was about to break out.

"Wait, Mama," Chris interrupted, "you grieve when you lose someone or something you love?"

"Yes like your home, friends, swing set and…"

"… my dolly!" Michelle exclaimed.

"My race car set and remote dinosaur!" David added.

"And Barbie?" Chris asked with deep concern.

"Your puppy's fine," I said. "The Conyers are taking care of her. How about helping me off this cold floor?" I groaned. "We have the rest of the day to catch up. Come on, help me up."

"When *will* we see Barbie and home, again?" Chris asked. "I wanna go home real bad."

"Badly, honey."

"Badly."

"Yeah, when do we go home?" asked David.

"We'll be home before you know it," I smiled.

Leaving me on the floor, the kids ran inside and marched around the living room challenging each other on who could be the happiest.

"Here, let me," Roberto said.

In guarded contempt, I reached up and he pulled me to my feet with ease.

Roberto's family stepped up for the customary hug and peck on the cheek. Don Beh, embarrassed that I'd been dragged all this way, worried how to feed us all, but concealed it in his genuine happiness to see me.

"*Bienvenidos,* Maria!" he said, hugging me. "Welcome!" he repeated in English, his green eyes sparkling.

I hugged him back. "Don Vicente! Good to see you!"

Doña Lydia could barely hide her contempt. Her eyes held no joy as she touched her cheek to mine, loudly smacked the air and welcomed me with a toothy grin. "*Hola* (hi), Maria!" It was clear she didn't like me being there any more than I wanted to be. Oblivious to it all, Roberto and his dad stood there smiling like ambassadors at the signing of a peace treaty.

"Good to see you!" she said. "Don't you look nice? I must look awful. But I've been cooking over a hot stove all morning. I'm all greasy, so I won't hug you. Lunch is ready. You can wash if you like. The bathroom is down the hall, last door on the right. Roberto, take her luggage to the room."

Waiting her turn, Sandra threw her arms around me. "*Tia!*"

"Sandrita!" I laughed, hugging her tight, "You've grown!"

"I'm seventeen. I complete my *bachillerato* this year."

Costa Rican students didn't skate through school like in the States. They *earn* their diploma, and have eleven years to do it, not twelve. In the eighth grade, they choose literature or science and concentrate on that. Senior finals are taken from students' notes those last five years. Seniors get out the last six weeks to study and quiz each other at friends' homes, cafés and libraries.

Shooting for top honors, Sandra was hitting the books hard. I told her how proud I was of her then told the kids in English. "Tia Sandra is graduating from high school and...."

"Please don't have them call me 'aunt,'" she interrupted in Spanish. "*'Tia'* is old-fashioned and makes me sound so old! Have them call me by my first name like Mamá's sister, Carmen."

I bristled. I'd have been slapped into next Sunday if I'd tried this when I was her age! But since we'd be gone in a few days, I let it go and gave her a big hug.

Lunch was tasty, what there was of it. My seconds went to the kids. I could eat when I got home. Better enjoy Roberto's family. This was the last time I'd ever see them.

The tense afternoon I'd anticipated turned out nice. Everyone confined conversation to comfortable recollections. Excited that I was there, the kids had a hard time falling asleep that night.

Sandra now bunked with her mother in the master bedroom, which they graciously offered to us. It was spacious with mirrored sliding closet doors on an entire wall. There were wooden hangers in the closet they had cleared for us, and some shelves, too. The room had a wrought iron mirror and glass-top vanity in white with a gathered skirt, cushioned stool and bedspread to match.

A glass door opened onto a patio with no furniture. Its high stucco walls were dingy and gray with volcanic ash. On the half-brick designed floor were several pots with dead plants. The picture window made the patio seem more like part of the bedroom. How pretty it would look with a table, chairs and some flowers.

Paralleling that window were joined twin beds. Doña Lydia had made Japanese lantern lamps for the nightstands from narrow strands of rope woven in and out of metal frames, one gold, the other turquoise to match her spread. Hardwood floors, indented by high heels, were black with ash and wax build up.

In a far corner was Roberto's cot. I'd be sleeping across the double bed with the kids. Using a dining room chair for my long legs left me with knee pain. But I'd be home soon.

The kids were asleep by ten, when Roberto suggested we take a walk, I thought it was to discuss the trip home. He avoided that subject until four in the morning. I quit from exhaustion, believing it would be eventually resolved as he'd promised.

The next day, realities like not having hot water set in, making me wish for the "Frankensteinian" shower in his parents' old apartment. Heating water in enormous pots took an hour and a half on their dilapidated electric stove, so I'd feed the kids and wash their clothes while we waited. Doña Lydia, up since five, had hers nearly dry. Washing by hand would be fun for a few days. The "fun" soon wore off. Chores took longer. By the time I fed the kids, washed, made beds, picked up our room, got everyone bathed, dressed and cleaned the bathroom, it was lunchtime and I was ready to collapse! Thank the Good Lord for *siesta*; a fine old custom!

Roberto left every morning, returned for lunch then left again. I assumed he was planning our trip home. Days later, he returned as I was tucking in the children. "Let's go for a walk," he grinned. "I've got some important news."

We walked until the wee hours, talking about everything but going home. "You know, Costa Rica is a beautiful country," he said. "People are friendly. Food and housing is cheap. Maybe you should stay."

"I can't! We'll lose our house and car! Chris has already missed too much school, and my classes start soon." I was fed up with abuse, meaningless apologies and walking on eggshells!

For two weeks, I rose early, did my chores, took the children to the park, read to them and attended to their needs, while he disappeared most of the day, only showing up to walk me over hell's half acre to talk my dang ear off! He tried to wear me down, but I wouldn't budge! One evening, his charm was crassly shed in a last-ditch effort to stampede me into compliance, finally ending with, "You're not leaving! I'll bury you here!"

Then the phone call.

"It's for you," Roberto frowned, handing me the receiver.

"Hello?"

"Mary Sue? It's Aunt Mozy. Can you talk?"

Roberto stood there listening.

"How are you, honey?" she asked.

"Okay... I guess."

"Good! Long distance is expensive. You need to know about your house."

"The house?" I asked, afraid to take it any further.

"The Casebeers, who think you're not coming back, called the loan company that financed your mobile home and they called me for this month's payment or they'll repossess. Mr. Casebeer wants his money, too."

"Repossess?" I gasped. "Everything we own is in there!"

"No payment," she said without emotion, "and you lose it."

"But I was offered a promotion with more pay before I left. After nursing school, I'll make even more! I can make payments, easy, if I can just get home!"

"Easily."

"Huh?"

"I can *easily* make payments."

ALL THE WAY HOME

Was she correcting my grammar? Then the unpardonable: I asked for money. Having lived through the Great Depression, she hoarded food and saved everything else: string, rubber bands and especially money. She'd skip Coke breaks at work with friends and put that nickel in the bank. She had accounts in three different banks that I knew of.

"Can't you make the payments this month?" I pleaded.

There was a long silence.

"Aunt Mozy, they're about to haul away everything we own!" There came a soft clearing of a throat and a silent eternity. "Aunt Mozy, are you still there?"

"Yes," she sighed.

"Then how about it?" I prodded.

"How about what?" she evaded.

"The lot rental and house payment," I sighed impatiently, "till I can get back home. The lot's thirty, the house a hundred nineteen, utilities around thirty, which comes to a hundred seventy-nine. Oh, and a twenty-five dollar payment to Sears on the washer and dryer. That's just over two hundred. Won't you help us?"

"Honey, you know I don't have that kind of money."

I was stunned! *That kind of money? She can write a check for a car, even a house! Surely, she doesn't mean it!* "Aunt Mozy, you can't mean it!"

If silence were golden, I'd have had enough for tickets around the world! "Aunt Mozy, let's try something else. Send the tickets, then I'll be home where I can work and start paying you right away." Roberto grabbed the phone.

"Look Mozelle, Mary Sue is my wife and these are my kids. I have a chance at a good job here. We can have a good life, if she'll give it half a chance."

"Aunt Mozy," I shouted, "he's keeping us against our will!"

Jerking the receiver up, he held it like a club. My arms flew around my head against the impending blow! Muffled chatter spewed from the receiver, words I couldn't make out. It stopped and the receiver was once more against his ear. He was royally ticked but under control as he handed me the phone. I was sure she'd read him the riot act. And nobody could do that like my Aunt Mozy! She probably told him if he didn't send us home right away, she'd come down there and ring his fool neck! "Hi, Aunt Mozy! I'm half packed. When do the tickets get here?"

"I'm not sending any."

"But...."

"Mary Sue, I told you I don't have that kind of money. It's invested." There was a long silence. "I'm sorry, honey," she said, tenderly. "Do the best you can for now."

"But you don't understand!" I stuttered, pausing to see if Roberto was nearby. He was, with daggers that would have given Vlad the Impaler serious pause. Aunt Mozy broke the silence.

"What's wrong? Can't talk?"

"Right," I answered nonchalantly, forcing a pathetic little laugh to throw Roberto off.

"You must remain calm, dear. Do you understand?"

"Yes." I didn't need advice to lay low. I needed to get out of there!

In a fit of paranoia, he grabbed the phone! "Look Mozelle, I don't know what you two are planning, but this is where it stops! She's *NOT* taking my kids! *She* can leave, but the kids are Costa Rican citizens and

are staying where they belong!" He hurled the receiver at me, narrowly missing my head. "Say your goodbyes and hang up!" he commanded, storming from the room.

Cupping my hand over the phone, I spoke as clearly and loudly as I dared into the antiquated 1940's receiver, hoping she'd hear and he wouldn't. "Aunt Mozy, we're in danger!" I waited for her reply. "Aunt Mozy, can you hear me? You're our only hope. Please! He's threatened to kill me!" My voice began to break up.

"Mary Sue, get a hold of yourself! You'll scare the kids!"

"I'm in complete control of myself and the kids are clear in the other room." Maybe if she knew there wasn't enough to eat. "Aunt Mozy, we're hungry! There's not enough food!"

"I can't believe he'd let his family go hungry!" she said, then paused. "If things are that bad, I'll send you a ticket tomorrow morning."

"What about the kids?"

"Sorry."

"I can't just leave them!"

"Men don't cope well with kids. In several months, he won't be able to send them back fast enough!"

"If I leave, I'll never see them again."

"Then divorce him down there!"

"Women have no rights, here. In a divorce, the man gets the house, the car and the kids and the paternal grandmother rears them. Roberto's family has political clout and can fix it where I can't get back in the country. I tell you he's crazy and liable to do anything!"

"You said his folks like you. Can't they talk some sense into him?"

"His dad doesn't like this but won't interfere in what he considers none of his business."

MARY SUZANNE LOPEZ

"And his mother?"

"She hates me!"

"Now, Mary Sue...."

"She does! She'd have me committed if she thought she could get away with it."

"That can't be true! You don't do that to family."

"I'm not *her* family. She thinks I stole her son from her!"

"I thought I told you to hang up that phone in there!" Roberto hollered from the next room.

Aunt Mozy heard and spoke quickly. "This call isn't cheap! Things will work out. Give them time. Stiff upper lip. You're pioneer stock. I'll try and call when you're alone and things aren't so hectic. Bye, now." The phone clicked.

"Don't hang up!" I softly pleaded, frantically tapping the receiver button. "Please, I need you!" I slumped in the chair, face in my hands.

Mozelle was still holding the receiver in Tulsa and turned to her new husband, Gordon. "We're going to Mineral Wells for her stuff."

"Is she okay?"

"She couldn't talk. They're having problems. It'll blow over. These things always do. I'll call her at Christmas."

Roberto swaggered back into the living room. "Hung up on you, huh? Dumped you cold, did she? You deserve to be dumped!" he smirked, moving slowly toward me. "You're nothing and always will be. Have you looked in a mirror lately? No man would keep a woman like you."

Before I knew it, he was in my face, crumpling my blouse in his fists and ramming me against the wall.

"Look at you," he said, pressing in nose on nose. "You're skinny, ugly and stupid. The best thing about you is that you've got me!" Roughing me up, he pretended to hit me, so I ducked. "Coward! I should beat the crap out of you right now!" He pretended to deck me. My hands shot up to protect my face. Grabbing my wrists in mid-air, he slammed them beside my head and leaned into me, his breath hot and foul. "I own you!" he taunted. "You're mine!" Pushing off me, he mimicked how he thought women and *maricones* (gays) talked, using a limp wrist. "He's *crazy*, Aunt Mozy! He's liable to do *anything!*" He took my wrists again, leaned into me and hissed like a snake. "Why, he might even *kill* me!"

The corners of his mouth curled upward then into a child's pout. Slinging my hands from his, he pushed away and I could breathe again.

"I won't kill you today," he taunted with a crooked smirk. "There's something — shall we say — better." The smirk broadened to a grin. He was going to deck me. I braced myself! "Something *rather* shocking," he mused. "The city asylum has some nice shock treatments. I hear it cures what ails but leaves you with one hell of a headache!"

My jaw dropped and my face went white. *He knows how scared I am of electricity!*

Delighted by my reaction, he mimicked me in falsetto. "Aunt Mozy, his mother *hates* me! She'd have me put away for good if she thought she could get away with it!" Using his own voice, he added, "And with all our connections, that shouldn't be hard. So keep on and I'll see what we can 'cook' up for you." He paused for effect then said with an evil chuckle, "Maybe what's 'cookin' will be you! And if that doesn't work, we'll try a frontal lobotomy!"

"No doctor would do that just because you tell him!"

"Wanna bet your life on it? Husbands used to be able to order hysterectomies to 'remove' their wives hysteria even in the U.S. of A. Try stealing my kids and see what happens!" Then he smiled almost civilly. By the way, minor children can't leave here without written permission from the father, who must sign before the the Child Welfare Office or *La Oficina del Patronato*." He got in my face. "Without this document to present at the airport, you'll be arrested on the spot and automatically given a stiff prison sentence. And our jails are nothing like the 'country clubs' you call prisons in the States, more like medieval dungeons." His expression softened and his brow crinkled. "Why do you keep fighting me? To hell with you!" he shouted as he stomped out and slammed the door.

He spent the next week trying to convince me how happy we could be if I'd just give it another "shot." (He had such a way with words!) "Besides, he said, you'll be a baroness, someday." *Yeah, if I live long enough!* I wanted to reply, only he might have accommodated me.

Roberto had gone to extraordinary lengths to bring us to Costa Rica, then never stayed home. I suspected he had a lover. In a constant rage, he majored on minors, thinking every fixable situation was a crisis. He blew tiny setbacks out of proportion and couldn't adjust to much of anything. He thought "modify" was a word you used in reference to engines, not his character. Was he really that incapable of growth and change? Even the seasons changed.

So much had taken place the year before, in 1969: the premier flight of the Boeing 747, the first test flight of the supersonic Concorde and an Apollo mission to outer space. A political rising star met his Chappaquiddick and Hurricane Camille slammed into three Gulf states. We saw the last issue of the Saturday Evening Post and a doubling of the presidential salary effective upon the inauguration of President Nixon.

In May, Hamburger Hill was taken in one of the bloodiest battles of the war. That same month, Dwight D. Eisenhower succumbed to lifelong heart trouble and was laid to rest in Abilene, Kansas. In December, a heart attack would claim the life of Ho Chi Minh, in Hanoi. In Houston,

ALL THE WAY HOME

Texas, research ushered in the historical first implantation of a stopgap artificial heart.

In Paris, France's beloved World War II hero, Charles de Gaulle, would surprise many by suddenly resigning the presidency. In the United Kingdom, there was much anticipation at the coming investiture of the promising young Prince Charles as their new Prince of Wales.

But, the most astonishing change came on a hot July Sunday. The world watched the precision landing of the Apollo 11 lunar module, the Eagle, as it gracefully set down in the powdery dust of the Sea of Tranquility. An American astronaut took man's first steps on its silvery gray surface, inspiring millions of kids to dream of space travel.

From a moon shot to a partial eclipse, from a messy war in Asia to my own private war, the world was changing. As 1970 dawned, dramatic changes were absent both on the world scene and in our lives as Roberto vehemently resisted the very changes that would have resulted in his own happiness. (Go figure!)

If it's true, what I've heard said, that a plant is judged by the fruit it bears, comparing Roberto's behavior to fruit, I'd have to say it was grapes. He had crushed so many hopes with his wrath, rooted in self-loathing, and it had finally fermented to an acrid vintage. But he wasn't counting on a day of reckoning, when he'd be forced to drink of his own bitter cup.

The year was 1970... and that's the way it was.

CHAPTER TWELVE

THE COWARD'S WAY OUT

Three weeks later at lunch I realized it was Thanksgiving Day. To keep the kids from forgetting the traditional holidays of home, I decided to take the last of my money and buy a hen we could roast on Sunday. The kids were too young to know Thanksgiving is on a Thursday. Giving Doña Lydia a day off KP would also be a nice gesture. If we were going to live under the same roof for a while, we might as well get along.

"Everybody, I have a wonderful idea!" I announced with Pollyanna enthusiasm in Spanish. "Let's have a Thanksgiving Day feast!" The children looked up when I repeated it in English. "Don Beh, Doña Lydia, do you know what Thanksgiving is?" I asked in Spanish.

"An American holiday, no?" he said in broken English.

Doña Lydia kept eating and never looked up.

Sandrita struggled to pronounce the long, foreign word. "Que es este (what is this)... uhmm... Tahnksgeeveen?"

ALL THE WAY HOME

Already understanding some Spanish, Chris laughed and said in English. "It's a day when you eat so much, you get more stuffed than the turkey was!"

"Nuh-uh!" David said, elbowing Chris. "It's when you watch a stupid parade on TV all morning then waste the rest of the day eating and washing dishes, when we could be playing outside!"

"Better let me explain!" I laughed, half-scolding. I spoke first Spanish then English. "The first Thanksgiving is about some…" and turning to Roberto, I asked, "How do you say Pilgrims?"

"*Peregrinos.*"

"Thank you. *Peregrinos,* who were forced to leave England then Holland for the New World to escape religious persecution. Unprepared for the hardships they found, many died that first winter. Next Spring, the Indians taught them how to plant corn, pick edible berries and find the locations of the best fishing and hunting."

Everyone seemed to enjoy the story but Doña Lydia. Maybe she was just tired.

"A couple of years later, things were going so well, people wanted to have a special day of thanks to God. Each Pilgrim and Indian family brought to the table of friendship, vegetables from the bountiful fields and turkey, deer, fruits, nuts and berries from the vast untapped forests.

"While the children played together, Indians shared their dances with drum and flute to the Great Spirit and Pilgrims sang hymns praising the goodness of God, both giving thanks in their own way. History books say these two peoples lived in peace and harmony together for fifty years, until the arrival of greedy unregenerate Europeans looking for gold.

"Today, Americans all around the world still invite family and friends to join them in giving thanks for… " I paused and looked at

Roberto, "...*freedom* to live how and *where* we choose." I ignored Roberto's stern look. "And that's why we celebrate Thanksgiving."

"*Ay, tia, que linda historia*" (Oh, aunt, what a pretty story), Sandrita sighed all starry eyed!

"Gracias," I smiled. "Let's celebrate Thanksgiving right here in Costa Rica!" I said a little too dramatically. "We can relive history and have a great meal at the same time!"

Doña Lydia looked up, her face flushed with rage. "A *great meal?* What do you think I serve here everyday, pig tripe?"

We stared at her in shock then everyone's eyes turned to me. "No, Doña, you serve wonderful meals everyday. I don't know how you do it!"

"I'll tell you, *macha* (female foreigner), by getting up early, finishing late and working my butt off all day long. Nobody knows all I do," she screamed, springing to her feet, pointing in my face and sputtering, "least of all, you! You hardly lift a finger here!"

My jaw already hanging open, dropped to my lap. It was true that I didn't help with the general housework, because she and Sandra finished before I could get the kids bathed and fed. She wouldn't let me cook, but I helped clean up. She didn't have to do our laundry or pick up our mess, and I had nothing to be ashamed of!

She muttered something, grabbed her plate and glass and disappeared into the kitchen to stand at the sink and eat.

Roberto, who usually took her part, stared at me as if to say, "Leave me out of this!" and left.

The library was Sandrita's escape. She got her books and left. The kids went to play, leaving me with their grandfather.

"Don Beh, I don't know what to say, except, I'm sorry. I had no idea this would cause such trouble."

"Don't worry Maria," he consoled, "she won't stay mad for long. She blows off steam then goes back to her old self."

That was hardly promising! Don Beh tried to help, but I don't think his heart was in it. "I like it, Maria," he smiled. "I've never had a Thanksgiving dinner. But I'm curious."

"About the dinner?" I asked, looking up.

"No, about the Indians giving thanks to the Pilgrim's God."

"They didn't. That's the beauty of America. As long as we don't hurt others, we're free to worship how we please."

"You Americans are very religious, no?" he asked.

"Most still are," I said, "even with all the hippies, free love, drugs and rock and roll."

When I was growing up, my family was traditional, but we didn't go to church, much. Still, I felt that somewhere out there, God *must* exist.

"Maria, are you listening?"

"I'm sorry, Don Beh, what did you say?"

"Does God exist? Do you think He's real?"

"Yes," I quickly answered, not wanting to offend my host.

"How do you know?" he said. "Nobody's seen Him."

"Maybe we see Him in your majestic mountains and matchless tropical sunsets; in the dawning of new days or the beauty and fragrance of blossoms; in the raw force of a storm and the gentle touch of a friend."

By the weekend, I'd smoothed things out with Doña Lydia.

Saturday, I took the kids to *El Parque Japonés* (the Japanese Park), in the next block to play with other children in its gardens and around the lovely arched bridge, where we fed bread crusts to fish, ducks and swans in the pond. On the way home, I bought them some square-shaped *copos* (snow cones) from a street vendor's cart, who shaved the ice by hand from a huge block.

The kids always seemed so hungry now, and ate most of the popcorn I bought on Sunday afternoon to feed the monkeys, ducks and otters at the zoo. We so enjoyed our weekends without Roberto; if I could get us back to the States, the whole week would be this peaceful, too. That Monday, I awoke with new resolve. Officials couldn't ignore my divorce and child custody papers. I'd visit *La Oficina del Patronato* and get us out of there!

I put on the only dress I brought, which now fit me loose, and my wedding ring so men wouldn't approach me in the streets (it fit loose, now, too). I didn't realize it, but I'd lost thirty pounds those first six weeks. (Wish it came off that easy, today!)

The birds were singing as I kissed the kids good-bye for the pleasant walk to the building that housed *La Oficina del Patronato*. Solitary footsteps echoed down the corridor, click- clack, turn back, click-clack, turn back, click-clack, turn back.

I was ushered into the Director's Office and explained my situation. He said my papers would be ready the next day to exit the country. That was easy! Why hadn't I done this before? The ever smiling director failed to mention that he'd gone to school with my mother-in-law. I wasn't out of his building before he phoned her about my visit. "Liar!" Doña Lydia screeched as I walked in the front door. "Wait till I call Roberto!"

I was reading to the kids in the living room, when he stormed in and strong-armed me through the house, above the screams of the children being corralled by his mother. He locked the door, slammed me against the wall and proceeded to make me wish I'd never been born. "*Estupida!* The Director of the *Patronato* will have this all over town! It could cost Papá his job and Mamá one she's been after and maybe even the one I've been chasing all this time. *Bruta,* everyone here knows everyone else!"

He began beating me senseless! "Never embarrass me or my family like this again, *pendeja,* or I'll have you drugged and deported and you'll never see the kids again!"

I shivered on the floor, not daring to look up.

"Damn you! Look at me when I talk to you!" he yelled, kicking me, once again.

I lifted my head. My eyelid was madly twitching.

"What's that?"

I looked down, hoping it would stop.

"Don't look away when I'm talking! What's wrong with your eye?" He yanked my chin up. The twitch turned to a flutter. "Aren't you a pretty sight? You can stop, now."

I couldn't make it stop.

"You're disgusting! Just don't repeat what you did today, if you want to live!"

He walked out and the children rushed in. I'd managed to drag myself onto the bed. Michelle snuggled close.

"Don't cry Mama," Chris pleaded. "We'll take care of you."

"Do you want me to beat him up for you?" David said.

"Don't talk like that, honey. A child must never raise a hand to his parent."

Concern written on his face, Chris asked, "But why'd he do it?"

"Did you do something bad," David said, "like when I got in the car to play, moved the gears and almost rolled over Chris?"

"No," I whispered, straining at a smile, remembering how it had scared both boys.

I'd been worried about Chris for some time, now. He'd been Roberto's second whipping boy (I was first) in the States and was developing deep insecurities. "Did I do something that got you in trouble?" he asked.

"No, baby, nothing like that," I reassured him.

"Then what?" the boys asked in unison.

"I…,I…. " I hid my face in my hands and wept. How could I burden children with something that was even too much for me? Childhood should be happy and carefree, not terror-filled chaos.

After that, I tried harder to give them as close to a "normal" life as possible: we read, played games and went on outings. Did Roberto see this as an opportunity to join our family in these pursuits or reconnect with me? No! He'd leave me to deal with things alone then reappear when he needed me physically. Like many women in these situations, I dared not rebuff his *amorous* advances. I'd been reduced to a handy convenience, intimacy to an appeasing, loathsome annoyance and "making love," as he called it, a necessary evil. "Love" had NOTHING to do with it! It was a ploy to stay alive long enough to get out of there. But you could also call it Russian roulette with all six chambers loaded. I was out of birth control!

Now in Costa Rica, you could walk into any drug store and buy anything over the counter. But birth control? Not on your life! Doña Lydia popped Valium like candy, and thought I should take it too. I wouldn't even take aspirin! I ended up getting some, thinking it would make me so out of it, Roberto would leave me alone at night.

A small family party was planned for the twenty-eighth of November, Roberto's birthday. With hors d'oeuvres made and Roberto's favorite cake baked, Sandrita and I went in the living room. Doña Lydia, who kept her mocha icing recipe secret, preferred to ice the cake, alone.

ALL THE WAY HOME

The children played, while Sandrita and I happily chatted. Don Beh walked in and handed me a letter from home. I tore into it with the giddy enthusiasm of a child on Christmas morning!

Dear Mary Sue,

We got to Mineral Wells late Friday and worked all weekend, packing your things into a U-Haul, because they were to pick up your mobile home Monday morning. We sold the swing set to the Conyers next door for ten dollars. They also bought your car.

It wasn't new, so we let them have it for thirty dollars, which we applied toward our travel expenses to Texas. Everything is stored at my house in Tulsa and here when you need them. Sears took the washer and dryer on Saturday. Oh, and the Conyers said about two weeks ago, your little dog ran onto the highway and was run over. They said there was nothing they could do and that she died peacefully. Guess that's all. Hope you're well.

Love,
Aunt Mozy

She was never celebrated for tact or mincing her words but she might have tried, seeing we'd just lost everything! Motionless, I sat with a glassy stare. *Our house gone? Where will we live? The washer and dryer? Three more payments and they were paid for! Our car; only about five years old; sold for thirty dollars? How will I get the kids to school? How will I get myself to school? Buy groceries? Get to work? Most of all, how do I tell the kids what happened to Barbie?*

All color had long since drained from my face, when Sandra touched me and softly asked, "Bad news?"

What could I say? That we'd lost everything? That the world had just crashed in on me? That because her brother dragged us down here, a sweet little dog had needlessly died? It was more of life than innocent

Sandrita was ready for. Besides, what if Roberto got his nose out of joint about my making a fuss over this and had me deported?

I couldn't let the kids see me upset, so I sat out lunch in my room and slept. When I awoke, the room was getting dark. I took my purse to the bathroom to freshen up for the party.

When I turned on the tap, the water strangely sounded like a cheering crowd in a distant stadium. Listening and staring into the mirror, my arm fell to my side and my hand struck the packet of Valium. I dumped most of them in my hand, gazed at myself in the mirror, shrugged and took them.

Doña Lydia and Sandra had left to run and buy some last minute items. The kids and I were alone in the house.

Opening one of their storybooks, the plan was to leave them positive memories. I hoped they would always be there for each other, help those less fortunate, be good, kind, honest, loyal, brave, faithful and true, appreciate classical music, read fine literature like we were about to read now and spend their lives pursuing noble goals and higher learning. In my zeal to beat a hasty retreat, it never occurred that life's lessons are lovingly taught down through the years, not in a single moment of desperation.

Flipping through the pages, I came upon a picture of a little Indian boy with big black eyes set in an adorable round face, standing by his canoe at the river's edge; a little American Indian, Little Hiawatha. I read:

> "By the shores of Gitche Gumee
> By the shining Big Sea Water
> Stood the wigwam of Nokomis
> Daughter of the Moon, Nokomis"

I began to feel woozy.

ALL THE WAY HOME

> "Many things Nokomis taught him
> Of the stars that shine in heaven
> Showed him Ishkoodah, the comet,
> Ishkoodah, with fiery tresses;
> Showed the Death Dance of the spirits,
> Warriors with their plumes and war clubs"

Death dance? War clubs? Gun, silencer? They're all the same and will kill you just as dead. Boy, am I dizzy!

> "In the frosty nights of winter;
> Showed the broad white road in heaven,
> Pathway of the ghosts, the shadows,
> Running straight across the heavens,
> Crowded with the ghosts, the shadows"

Ghosts? Shadows? Death? I'm cold and sleepy. It's harder to see the page.

> "At the door on summer evenings,
> Sat the little Hiawatha
> Heard the whispering of the pine trees,
> Heard the lapping of the waters,
> Sounds of music, words of wonder"

The cadence was steady, steadier than I was, but the words, meaningless. With blurred eyes and slurred speech, I attempted words I wouldn't have tried on a "good" day!

> "'Minne-wawa!' said the pine trees,
> 'Mudway-aushka!' said the water.
> Saw the fire fly Wah-wah-taysee"

My ability to think straight going fast, I found little to appreciate now of what I'd before pronounced to be "fine" literature. This was the most stupid thing I'd ever read!

> "Ere upon my bed I lay me,
> Ere in sleep I close my eyelids!"

I'd love to close mine, but I won't leave this unfinished! Didn't I know I was letting the rearing of my children go quite unfinished?

> "Once a warrior, very angry,
> Seized his grandmother, and threw her;
> Right against the moon he threw her;
> 'Tis her body that you see there."

Caught off guard by the poignant words, I thought of Pushy. Through a glassy stare, I slipped into euphoric confusion, repeating the haunting phrase to myself.

> "Right against the moon he threw her;
> 'Tis her body that you see there."

I stood suddenly to a huge head rush. Pausing with eyes half-open, legs wobbling, body teetering, I swayed like a drunk on a Saturday night, uttering words that were to be my last; the gushing, fuzzy-headed, slobbering, incoherent babblings of a fool.

"Children," I slurred, thick-tongued, "Mommy is tired and needs a little nap. Stay here and play, while Mommy lies down."

I turned to walk away then turned again and in an overly animated, drunken fashion, clumsily brought finger to mouth, broadly missing the mark. "Shhhhhhhhh," I hissed until I got their attention and found my lips.

"Mommy's so funny," they laughed as they watched and waited for the next thing I would say.

It sounded like roaring stockcars in the whirling room. I paused and looked around and said, "Toto, I don't think we're in Kansas anymore," and giggled to myself at a joke only drunks understand. As my mind went, slurred words and phrases trailed off. "Play quietly, now, be good little children and remember that I... remember... I forget!" I paused for the longest time. "Oh, yes that Mommy loves you very much." Turning, I staggered down the gyrating, kaleidoscope hallway. "Mommy will always love you... always... love... 'member... always...."

My troubles were nearly over only I couldn't remember what they were. I'd think about it tomorrow. Crashing onto the bed, I curled up in the fetal position I swore I'd never get caught dead in. Closing my eyes to the dizzying rotation of the room, I tried flopping over on my back, but the room spun anyway. Happily relinquishing all ties to reality, I abandoned myself to the delectable euphoria sweeping over me to "The Dance of the Sugar Plum Fairies" was playing. Tchaikovsky was never more brilliant! Tiny naked fairies from Walt Disney's "Fantasia" flitted above, joined by waltzing flowers in the psychedelic vortex that spun me around and around and downward, ever downward.

Voices echoed in the far distance, calling my name.

"Leave me alone!" I moaned. "I'm tired."

A voice shook me with increasing frenzy.

"Go away!" I mumbled.

They shook me harder.

"Leave me to my music!" But the music had stopped.

The voices pulled and tugged at me. "Do what? Walk? Where?" They pulled me upright. I sat nodding.

"Get up and walk!" they insisted.

"No!" I drunkenly batted at the air. "I hate walking! Leave me alone!" I fell over onto my side.

When I "came to" I was sitting on a gurney watching two orderlies, who made the Three Stooges look good, scurry around bumping into each other trying to get me to drink a yellow concoction that looked like pee. "Please *Señora*, drink this!" they begged, pressing the plastic gallon jug to my lips.

You don't beg in a medical emergency! This couldn't be a hospital. I'd be restrained with a tube down my throat! Able to rationalize, I knew I'd be okay and kept politely refusing the nasty looking stuff in the jug.

While waiting to be released, I overheard the new shift talking outside my door. "She can't have taken twenty Valium. She wouldn't be alive!"

Roberto didn't make a fuss at the hospital, but waited to rough me up at home. It was one of the few times Doña Lydia intervened, and I was grateful. Hearing the ruckus, the kids came running, so he switched to Spanish and spoke in a deceptive tone. "You ruined my birthday party! You ever do something that lands you in another hospital and I'll have them put you into a *cura de sueño* (sleep cure), one you'll never come out of!" (That's when a patient or his family checks him into a hospital, he's hooked up to an IV and knocked out for several days of needed sleep to avert a nervous breakdown. I understand this was also done in the States, before the use of drugs became so prevalent.)

"*Cura de sueño*? You wouldn't dare! No doctor would...."

"Wanna bet your life?" He sneered, then turned and quietly left.

With the children mesmerized in front of the tube, I went to my room to ponder what I'd nearly done. When the kids discovered me gone, they followed and cuddled around me.

"Don't cry Mama," Chris softly whispered. The other two echoed the same, ignorant of the circumstances that had brought their mother to this place. In the hissing argument that followed, Chris' voice rose

above the rest. "Let her cry!" he repeated several times. "She must be grieving. Maybe she lost something dear to her."

"Nuh-uh!" David shot back. "Mama says we're the dearest she has, and we're still here."

Hovering like researchers studying an interesting specimen, Chris whispered, "Mama, time to stop grieving."

In the dead silence that followed, I struggled to pull myself together. I was alive! I mustn't waste it. He leaned over me. "Mama, I'll bet I can be happier than you."

Wiping my nose with the back of my hand, I rolled over. "No you can't, 'cause I've got you guys to make me laugh!"

"I'm the happiest," Michelle giggled.

"No you're not!" David shouted. "I am!"

"Nuh-uh, I am!" I said, beginning another round.

"That's impossible, 'cause I am!" Chris said.

Soon, we were rolling all over the bed, tickling each other and laughing as we repeated the absurd phrase over and over.

Later, when the boys were playing elsewhere, Michelle whispered, "Mommy, was that how to be a real man?"

"What, honey?"

"Chris said you were grieving, but you stopped and were strong again."

"I hope I was, baby."

"When I'm big, will I be strong like you?"

I wasn't strong. I'd tried to take a coward's way out! "No!" I said in a tone that was dead serious.

Her adoring look of wonder vanished.

"Do you know why?" I asked.

She could only stare up at me with puppy dog eyes.

"'Cause when you grow up," I whispered, "you'll be stronger than I ever was!"

Her eyes grew large and bright with a smile that revealed two perfect rows of baby teeth. "Honest and true, Mommy?"

"Honest and true, Shelly Belle! Cross my heart and hope to… " I stopped, remembering what I'd almost done.

"…die?" Michelle finished my sentence.

"W… what?" I said, stunned back to reality.

"Cross your heart and hope to die," Michelle repeated. "Daddy said you were going to die. But you're not, are you?"

I held her close, so she wouldn't see the tears welling in my eyes. "No time soon," I sniffled, quickly adding a verbal 'knock-on-wood.' "Lord willing, honey, Lord willing!"

Look what I nearly missed. She felt so good in my arms! I tried swallowing the growing lump in my throat as waves of self-condemnation and gratitude washed over a penitent soul. Looking toward heaven, I whispered my thanks.

CHAPTER THIRTEEN

SILENT

After nearly two months living with his parents, Roberto's dream job still eluded him and we hadn't a penny to contribute toward household expenses. Days before Christmas, Roberto brought two pine branches from the mountains which I tied together into a scrawny four-foot tree.

When the kids saw it, they squealed with delight! I helped them make decorations by cutting pretty pictures and a colorful chain garland from the slick pages of magazines. Don Beh had some typing paper for lacy snowflakes. We had no string of lights, but Doña Lydia chipped in sparkly tin foil for silver bells and a top star that gave it a little light. With a white sheet around the bottom for snow, our tree was complete. The children laughed and played beneath its merry boughs, eagerly awaiting Christmas mornin' to see what Santa would bring.

Roberto's parents could afford a turkey but no presents. Roberto borrowed seventy-five dollars from Tia Soledad two days before Christmas. His folks wanted it used for the kids, so we ran to shop.

Roberto picked out two battery operated planes that taxied, stopped to flash landing lights, moved flaps, revved engines and taxied again. The military fighter was for David, and the commercial passenger jet for Chris. I think it reminded him of our flying home.

For Michelle, we bought an imported doll all the way from France, its blue eyes complementing a crisp blue and white gingham dress and white pinafore. As we left the store, I saw another doll with hair the color of light brown sugar that looked just like Michelle. To my surprise, Roberto got it, too.

With most of our money gone, we bought the rest at an open-air bazaar, where fathers had set up booths in the plaza to sell their handmade, unpainted wooden cars and trucks with wheels that rolled, for extra Christmas money. The boys, especially David, who was always making engine sounds, would love these!

In a five and dime, we found some small plastic dishes and miniature animals. Topping off our shopping spree were hard candy and fruit for stockings. As a child, I'd always received tangerines and oranges. But *Ticos* preferred more exotic (and expensive) imported fruit like apples, grapes and pears. Roberto added his own pocket change to what was left of our Christmas money for a cluster of grapes, an apple and a pear to be shared among them.

Doña Lydia had some wrapping paper for the big gifts she would iron and reuse each year which I tied with faded ribbon. Roberto hid the gifts high in our closet, next to his gun.

On Christmas Eve Day, Doña Lydia took the children to visit relatives, while I baked a special surprise. After helping Doña Lydia with preparations for the Christmas feast the next day, I sat with the children to tell the story of the First Christmas with silhouette figures I cut from newspaper of Mary, Joseph, the Baby Jesus and his bed of straw I propped against a cut-out manger. Around them we placed a shepherd, a sheep, a donkey, an ox, a camel and Three Wise Men. The Christmas Star, borrowed from our tree, I suspended by string on a bough above the manger.

I was personally amazed the figures were even recognizable! But the kids greeted each emerging character with "ooos" and "ahhs." My

hands were black with printers ink from the newsprint that ended up on the end of my nose. The children pointed and laughed hysterically.

Then it was time to reveal their gift from me: chocolate chip cookies. They couldn't believe it! "So that's what smelled so good when we got back home with grandma, today!" they squealed.

After washing off the ink, we took cookies and milk to the living room for a second telling of the story, finishing with "Silent Night." Aunt Mozy always had stories to go with her musical pieces and now, so would I. "Years ago," I began, "there was a priest in a German town, who led the music in his church. The organ broke, threatening to ruin the Christmas Eve program, so he got his guitar and sang a song he'd written for the evening mass, *Silent Night*."

To keep our American traditions fresh in their minds, I sang two of Grandmother Hoover's favorites, "Oh, Little Town of Bethlehem" and "The First Noel." I even recited, by memory, mind you, the traditional and much beloved children's poem, The Night Before Christmas, and think I got most of it right. Half-way through "Jingle Bells," David interrupted. "What's 'one horse open' mean?"

"It's one horse pulling a sleigh with no roof."

"What's a sleigh?" said Michelle.

"Dum-dum!" David chided.

"I didn't call you names when you asked me a question," I teased with a pretend scowl. "Say you're sorry."

David didn't like apologizing, but did.

"Mama," said Chris, "sing it in Spanish, like on TV."

"I'll try. *Cascabel, cascabel, linda cascabel...*" I began. Cascabel meant jingle bell, but I could also be saying, *Rattlesnake, rattlesnake, pretty rattlesnake...* (talk about lost in translation! Kind of spoils Christmas scenes of dashing through the snow, doesn't it?) The more I

sang, the more I laughed. When I told them the alternate meaning, we all rolled in the floor!

We set cookies and milk out for Santa then I swung Michelle onto my back and galloped down the hall singing, "Here Comes Santa Claus" with a Gene Autry twang as two excited little boys followed close behind. Able to remember only the verse about "jumping in bed and covering up your head," I switched to "Santa Claus is Coming to Town," about Santa knowing "if you've been bad or good, so be good for goodness sake!" Kneeling by their bed, I tucked them in and playfully warned they'd better go right to sleep, because Santa never comes when children are awake.

"Mama," David groaned, rubbing sleepy eyes, "does Santa even know we're here?"

"Yeah," Chris echoed, "we left home so fast! I forgot to write Santa a letter, and now it's too late. He won't know where we are."

"I don't think anyone does," David mournfully added.

Michelle pointed upward. "God knows."

"Then why aren't we back home by now?" Chris asked.

David squinted and his nose crinkled. "Maybe you're 'posa ask, first!"

We held hands and bowed our heads. "Lord, don't let us get separated and help us get back home. And please tell Santa where we are. Amen." Their eyes glazed over with visions of sugarplums, I turned out the light and slipped from the room.

Doña Lydia had gone to her sister's party with Sandrita and Don Beh was developing film in the maid's quarters, a small room off the kitchen he'd converted to a dark room. I arranged gifts beneath the tree, filled three of Roberto's socks with fruit and candy then got the book from the Dallas airport I'd been wanting to finish about Mother Cabrinni.

Handel's "Messiah" was playing in the background when Don Beh came in and sat down to look over his new film tech magazine.

"Music too loud?" I said, getting up to turn it down.

"No Maria," he answered kindly.

"Are you sure?" I added. "I don't mind."

"No Maria," he said, a smile creasing the lips of a face etched with care, "let it play." Gazing across the mists of time, he was once again a little boy in Florence, Italy, listening to classical music on his mother's radio. The meaning of this music changed after he and his family emigrated to Costa Rica. Classical music played on the radio here signaled a national crisis, a time when maids were sent out for extra food staples, mothers rushed to schools to find their children and men cleaned guns and bought ammo. Music of the great masters was any banana republic's ace in the hole for its calming effect in averting civil unrest during military coups. The beautiful music of his childhood now brought flashbacks of shooting in the streets, power outages, frozen bank assets, food and water depletions and guarding a safe place for his family to hide. The thought of another coup left him feeling old and drained. Doña Lydia had long since ejected him from their bedroom. Tonight he would seek comfort in the music of his childhood. "Maria, what's playing?"

"Handel's 'Messiah'," I said, looking up from my book.

"The German composer who lived in England long ago?"

"I believe so," I answered, knowing very well it was.

"What's she singing? I can't make out the words."

I knew it by heart, having sung it for years in public high school Christmas or Easter presentations.

"He shall feed His flock like a shepherd
and He shall gather the lambs with His arm
and carry them in His bosom
and gently lead those that are with young.
Come unto Him, all ye that labor
and are heavy laden and He will give you rest.
Take His yoke upon you and learn of Him
for He is meek and lowly of heart
and He will give you rest unto your souls
for His yoke is easy and His burden is light."

"It is beautiful, Maria," he smiled. "From the Bible, no?"

"Yes," I answered.

"What is 'meek?'" he asked.

"Most think it means humble, but I believe the Biblical meaning is one who is 'self-controlled.'" A far-away look overtook him. The words the soprano sang were about love, peace and security; the cry of the human heart set to music. Empty sentiments for a heart that couldn't feel anymore. He could hardly get out of bed every morning and go through another day. As he listened to the music, his demeanor changed. *Nothing but the words of poets and priest,* he thought to himself. *What do pretty words have to do with real life?* He rose from the vinyl easy chair and shuffled to the tiny bedroom his wife had assigned him.

When Roberto got home late, he liked how we'd done up the tree and not only sat down for an "Ozzie and Harriet moment," But continued it through Christmas Day. (You know, that "family thing" from the fifties that skeptics like to make so much fun of today?)

Next morning, the kids couldn't wait to open their gifts! I helped so they wouldn't tear the paper. The boy's eyes nearly popped out at the sight of the airplanes! Michelle loved the French doll but froze when she saw the other. "Mommy, she looks like me!" It was dubbed the "Shelly

Dolly" and has been ever since. They needed those toys, and played happily the rest of the day.

Christmas dinner was wonderful, and there was plenty of it! I nearly turned green with all the guacamole I scooped up with *plátano* chips! Then came roast turkey and all the trimmings, Costa Rican style. The stuffing with capers and green olives was different and deliciously similar to traditional Christmas tamales served piping hot to holiday visitors. Doña Lydia's secret to her *masa* (dough) were the pork rinds that the mill specially ground into her cornmeal.

There was no pumpkin pie with mounds of whipped cream, but Doña Lydia's chocolate cake with fluffy mocha frosting was out of this world! I made sure Don Beh got lots of hugs and pats on the back for providing such a meal. And Doña Lydia seemed pleased with the compliments I lavished on her culinary skills and untiring efforts. My stomach couldn't seem to hold as much food as before, but I still "oooed" and "ahhed" over every morsel.

After New Year's came my worst nightmare. I was expecting! Delighted, Roberto found the money for a doctor. "No baby, this time, *Señora*," the doctor announced. "Only a small case of *pseudocyesis*." It had two meanings: a woman's fear she can't conceive or a fear she'll get pregnant. I could have sworn I was! Roberto agreed to wait to have another baby and bought me some birth control pills. Surely six months worth would give me enough time to get us back home.

The doctor weighed me, and I was five pounds lighter than the day I married. *So that's the reason my dress and ring don't fit!* That thirty pound weight loss those first six weeks I was in Costa Rica would not only sap my physical strength months later, but would also affect my ability to think on my feet and to remember details during the escape attempt.

Meanwhile, Roberto's long-held beliefs about his mother's supposed infidelity agitated him more and more. He recounted how Don Beh finally got his dream job about the time he met and married Lydia Mongue. The company offered higher pay if he'd move to Panama City, Panama. Then Japan attacked Pearl Harbor. Though Costa Rica was the first country to declare war, being Costa Rican didn't exempt Italian-born Don Beh from becoming a "necessary causality of war." A wartime government couldn't gamble on workers of certain backgrounds and uncertain loyalties tinkering with airplanes or overhearing arrival and departure dates of important VIP's and high-ranking officers. Mottos were posted everywhere: "Be careful what you say," "The walls have ears," and "Loose lips sink ships." After he was let go, Don Beh often had to work out of town, leaving his wife and child alone.

It was customary for unmarried female relatives to move in with young couples, to be the wife's companion and chaperone and help with chores and small children. Carmen, who wasn't fiery and vivacious like her sister, Lydia, had the same almond-shaped eyes, black hair, cameo skin and voluptuous hour-glass figure. Cultured and elegant I assume Carmen had many suitors.

After the war, Don Beh was still after his old job with Pan Am and still working out of town, when Roberto overheard his aunt making plans on the phone to go out one evening. His mother left with her. I argued that his mother may have been her chaperone or gone on to the market. This was his mother, for crying out loud! Why not give her the benefit of the doubt? Nothing could change his mind, so I avoided discussing it further.

Years of seething resentment toward her tormented his soul and swirled in his mind like the unbridled fury of an Oklahoma twister. He was like a pressure cooker ready to blow! Soothing him when he'd let me, I tiptoed over the eggshells of a bruised memory that could neither forgive nor forget. And so bubbled the cauldron of his raging hate.

Doña Lydia wasn't evil, just difficult. If I could get him to see her in a different light, maybe he'd change.

ALL THE WAY HOME

January is a summer month in Costa Rica. Sandrita had graduated from high school among the highest in her class. Don Beh thought daughters working outside jobs was beneath his dignity, so Sandrita was home to watch the kids when I offered to help Doña Lydia with the grocery shopping.

The short bus ride put us at the *mercado central* before six a.m. I was hardly awake yet as fully alert crowds scurried past us. The *mercado* covered an entire city block with windowed ceilings three-stories high. A hazy light shining through glass panes, dusted in volcanic ash, gave merchants just enough light to show their wares. In rows of small booths that lined the narrow aisles were dried herbs for natural remedies, live monkeys and parrots, fresh meat, fish, eggs, clothing and shoes, machetes, saddles and fresh-cut flowers. The possibility of my getting lost in that labyrinth was real, so I stayed close to Doña Lydia.

The concrete slab, exposed at the scraped edges of the steps to the mercado's lower level, was inches deep in dust, crushed stems, leaves and volcanic ash that now formed the uneven, clay-like floor. Throughout the great hall, the pungent aroma of decaying vegetation mingled with that of animals, flowers, leather, potatoes and melons. I liked lingering at the corner where they ground fresh roasted coffee.

Everything sat in the open uncovered—*tamarindo* (something that looked like mashed raisins they made a sweet drink with), or halved fruit for customers to taste, chicken and seafood laid over ice—yet there were no flies, anywhere. Doña Lydia said it was because of the high ceilings. Flies came in and flew up to the third story windows of the great hall and stayed there.

During those weeks I shopped with her, she said I shouldn't speak out loud. My Spanish accent wasn't as perfect anymore and they might think I was a "rich" American and charge double. But I got to see where the best vendors, merchandise and prices were and listened and learned as Doña Lydia masterfully haggled down the prices of *plátanos* and

mangos, *chorizo*, (like Polish sausage) and ox tail, *pollo* (chicken) and *chuletas*, (pork chops) skills that would be invaluable to me later. Then our trips to the *mercado* stopped.

I needed a haircut, which was only five to ten colones (seventy-five cents to a dollar fifty, American). I chose the mod "Dutch Boy," made popular by both Doris Day and Barbara Streisand, which looked great that first day! But since I'd left my curlers and hairdryer in the States, I couldn't maintain it. What began as a yummy hour of pampering turned to weeks of self-imposed seclusion. Doña Lydia was offended I couldn't leave the house until it grew back.

If not for a relative of Don Beh's, whose visits became an oasis of warmth and acceptance, I'd have had no adult company. Tais (pronounced, Tice) had a surfer's golden tan and flaxen hair streaked with sunshine to match his youthful exuberance. He was irresistibly winsome and easy to love, but not in the way you might think. You see, Tais was gay.

Doña Lydia would sit with us a while, feigning an interest in his latest craze, like that new hair spray, something "real" men wouldn't dream of using, much less discuss in those days, then she would wink and make fun of him later. She once ridiculed the one defect in his otherwise flawless face: his eyes; one blue eye and the other green. This, along with his unconventional dress and behavior, only fanned the fires of an enigma that dogged him since he could remember. It emphasized the dichotomy of his precarious perch in a society where he could never really belong. An impressive job, extensive travel, intelligence, good looks and impeccable manners couldn't buy enough indulgences to rescue him from a life in limbo; of never quite being good enough. He helped his mother, aunt and three older sisters who reared him get wonderful jobs, but even they turned their backs.

Johnny Cash had a hit called, "A Boy Named Sue." Tais would never be seen "rolling around in the mud and the blood and the beer," but his name brought to mind a certain opera, "Thais," by the French composer, Messenet, renowned for his genius in linking human feeling with religious sentiment. "Thais" is a tragedy about a lovely courtesan, a young woman of wealth and rank who is persuaded by a monk to enter a convent. Unable to forget her, he goes where she lays dying and collapses in anguish over the physical love for her that has overcome him. Beautiful, rich and privileged, the world at her feet, Thais instead lives a lonely and miserable existence, having missed love, the thing she desired more than money, position and piety, and then dies.

Throughout his sufferings, the Tais I knew reached out to those, like me, who hurt. After only three weeks, his visits stopped and my gentle friend never returned.

Roberto had never voiced disapproval, but made sure I knew how his friends took care of guys like Tais. "*Es un condenado maricón* (damed queer)!" he sneered. "We fix Tais' kind by waiting on corners where *maricones* pass, loosening our belts, so we're ready. Pretending to admire items in the store window, we wait until he's close then one of us calls out, '*Hola mamacita*' (hi little mama), like we're one of 'them,' you know? When he turns to acknowledge, like the damn whore he is, we rip out our belts! And he'd better stay down and take it like a man. If he runs, we use the buckles and beat the crap out of him! Some of those little fagots can really run, but we catch 'em anyway! Quivering there like a dog you kick around for fun, you can hear 'em yell clear down the block, even with their arms folded over their heads and faces kissing the sidewalk!" he laughed. "Some even cry, 'Mommy'! Can you believe that?" he grimaced arrogantly.

He expected my approval. Instead, I brushed by in disgust. "Come on!" he laughed tauntingly. "You should get out more and have fun!"

He often had "fun" at another's expense. Like when Sandra went to the spare bedroom they used for storage. We were in the living room watching TV, when we heard her bloodcurdling scream! "Ayyyyy, raton!"

Roberto jumped up and ran down the long hall, but not to her aid. He sailed past to retrieve his gun from our closet. He fired volleys of deafening shots into each huge paper packing barrel. When he held up the largest of the four rats he'd killed, Sandrita ran from the room screaming. He jumped over furniture and chased her around the dining room table, dangling the limp rodent over her until his mother intervened. (He would never have done this with Don Beh there.) Exhausted, he fell on the floor laughing, trying to catch his breath then turned to me with a wistful look. "I wonder what it's like to stalk and kill human prey?"

When I wouldn't let him speak of such barbarities in front of the children, he stomped from the house in a huff. And good riddance!

A day or two later, Andreina called. Tiny Lydiana was in the emergency room. Doña Lydia rushed to the hospital. Later, she called and told us that Lydiana was dehydrated and had been put on IV medication for amoebic dysentery. Now a citywide epidemic, its favorite victims were the elderly, infirm, and small children.

We'd stayed home because of my hair, but had seen Lydiana and her parents on Sunday at lunch. When Michelle got sick, I called our pediatrician. He'd studied in the States, spoke perfect English and was even married to a Tulsa girl.

In the States, well-off people went to hospitals and the poor to clinics, the opposite of Costa Rica. We couldn't afford a clinic. Our doctor understood why we didn't want to take her to a hospital, as they were rumored to be downright dangerous. He said the closest thing to putting her on an IV was giving her a teaspoon of ginger ale every three minutes. I was to give it to her the rest of the day and to keep him informed.

ALL THE WAY HOME

Sandrita ran to buy the soda, while I bedded Michelle on the sofa so we'd be near the kitchen and I could feed the boys. For nearly eleven hours, I read them children's books, told family stories they loved and never missed a dose of ginger ale. TV came on at four with the boys' favorite, *El Hombre de Acero* (The Man of Steel), a Japanese cartoon, followed by Shell's favorite, *Topo Gigio,* an Italian puppet show, giving my voice a rest.

Just after nine, Doña Lydia walked in with good news. Lydiana was better but would remain hospitalized a few more days. Michelle was better, too. Her thirst would return the next day, followed by her appetite.

I was up the next day before the children to get all the extra dirty sheets and towels washed and on the line. (I forgot to say that Doña Lydia now had a washer for heavy wash, thank the Lord!)

It was nearly lunchtime before I had the children bathed and dressed. I was still in our bedroom fixing myself up, when the doorbell rang. Roberto, who was never home, answered and swaggered back to announce I had a visitor.

I hurried to finish, thinking it was Tais. "Who is it?"

"Alberto," Roberto answered.

"Who?"

"That guy who used to come over with Pat and Rudy to our weekend barbeques."

Mineral Wells seemed so far away and long ago.

"Not Alberto!" I whispered.

Roberto was sure he'd caught his no-good wife at last! She hadn't attended those seminars at all, but was out with Alberto!

I gazed in the vanity mirror thinking, *I can't go out there like this! I'm thin and pale and my hair is so short.* I was about to have Roberto make my excuses, when I saw the jealous look on his face. *He can't possibly think that Alberto and I…?* Knowing I'd have to present myself in this bedraggled condition to prove to Roberto that this boy meant nothing to me, made me furious!

Always a gentleman, Alberto stood as I entered the living room, but I'd expected that much. What I didn't expect was the look on his face. I knew I was thin and looked a fright, but his shocked look embarrassed me more. I looked around for my husband for support. He'd sent me in alone and was listening down the hall. Alberto and I must have talked less than five minutes, when he made his excuses and left.

I wanted to strangle Roberto, who was sitting on the bed cleaning his gun when I walked in. He looked at me, down at the gun then back to me. Was this some kind of threat? I wasn't impressed!

A week or so later I was getting ready for an appointment Roberto had made for me weeks earlier at the school of nursing in an attempt to try to get me to stay in Costa Rica. This gave me the idea for our escape. My hair was long enough to slick back with lacquer and wear the ponytail hairpiece I'd brought. It looked good. Gazing in the mirror, I imagined myself in a starched white nurses' cap.

After our interview with the Director of Nursing, Roberto left so I could attend a three-hour lecture. I could read Spanish, but was concerned about studying in another language. Finding out that a Russian was enrolled there sparked some friendly competition. Surely I could do as well as a Russian girl! The six words I didn't understand from the lecture I jotted down phonetically to look up later. Knowing I could hold my own in another language made education feasible. Now there was a question of where to find the tuition and book fee of five thousand colones. It might as well have been five million! My committing to study in Costa Rica meant to Roberto I intended to stay. So naturally, he'd give me more freedom of movement.

Saturday, his folks took the kids to the zoo so Roberto and I could have friends over. More confident of my appearance now, I was eager to make some friends. With Sandrita gone a lot and Doña Lydia angry all the time, I needed someone to talk to.

Social gatherings in Latin America are traditionally gender segregated. So, while wives caught up on "girl stuff," the guys talked about what interested them (at least what they could discuss around their wives). The duel conversations happily droned on until Roberto got out his gun and a cylinder-shaped object I'd only seen in movies. Women looked on as their men made the biggest fuss. "Gentlemen, my Walther PPK," he said, presenting the gun as if introducing a fine lady to the men's flurry of "oos" and "ahhs." "Most of you know this as the weapon James Bond uses in the 007 films."

They buzzed excitedly like bees around a queen as the gun was carefully passed to each male admirer to be stroked and petted. When the gun was back in his hands, Roberto had an even more special introduction. "And *this,* gentlemen, goes with it," he beamed, holding the metal cylinder to an even louder flurry of sighs. "My new silencer," he announced to their enthusiastic approval, "imported all the way from England," he shouted over the clamor then basked in the unashamed envy of his admirers.

He said we had no money! He never mentioned this to me.

"How do you attach it to the gun?" one friend asked.

"Easy," he answered authoritatively, holding the silencer to the end of the gun. "It screws on the end like this, only I haven't had the barrel threaded, yet." He got that mischievous look, the one I once thought so cute. Still holding the silencer against the barrel, he swung them toward me in his vocal rendition of James Bond, which under different circumstances wouldn't have been half bad. "Goldfinger," he grinned, cocking one eyebrow, the gun pointing up with the barrel resting against his cheek. A deadly silence filled the room. He looked straight at me, milking the moment for all it was worth. "Someday I'm going to shoot her," he indicated toward me. "But it's not going to be bang-bang." Pausing for effect, a James Bond grin curling the sides of his mouth upward, he swung his aim toward me. "It'll be *thuk thuk!*" He made the gun "recoil" as he pretended to fire a couple of shots.

Chills ran up my spine as the room exploded in thunderous laughter! I tried to make light of it, too. The wives thought he was such a doll, the way he smiled and winked. He played the same "joke" for months to come. My quasi-peace turned to numbed resignation. He would eventually kill me. It would be sudden and silent. Daylight or shadow, it could it be around the next street corner or waiting outside my bedroom door. Death could be only a breath away.

CHAPTER FOURTEEN

SANTA ANA

While I waited to die, life just plodded on.

Roberto had spent the better part of the week foaming at the mouth about his mother having betrayed his father. I never expected him to go off the deep end after I told him to stop the conjecture and go ask her and left him to stew in his misery.

The kids had been in bed a while. It was about ten-thirty. I'd gone to the kitchen for a drink, when I heard a shout and muffled commotion. I ran to the hall. His mother and sister had their backs to me. Roberto faced them with his gun! *"Por Dios, Roberto no lo hagas!"* Sandrita hysterically pleaded.

I came alongside her, not knowing what to do except repeat in English what she'd just said. "For God sake, Roberto, don't do it!" then adding, "What are you doing?"

"Getting answers!" he said, glaring at his mother.

"But not this way!"

"Shut up or you're next!"

A man out of control holding a gun. I was scared spitless! Doña Lydia and I had had our differences, but I couldn't complacently stand there and watch him shoot her! "Roberto, think what you're doing!"

"I said shut up!" he snapped.

Edging in front of Sandrita, I motioned to her behind my back to take her mother away. Doña Lydia wouldn't have it and stood her ground. "How 'bout a walk, honey?" I coaxed.

"Don't honey me!"

I reached up and had barely touched the barrel when he jerked the gun away. Shoving me back, he ducked under my arm, reached around my waist and took aim at his mother. Knocking the barrel upward, I screamed, "Stop it, you bastard! Are you crazy?"

Our bedroom door creaked open. David stood squinting up at us in the glare of the naked bulb. Roberto was too strong for me. I'd have to try reverse psychology. With a broad sweep of my hand, I stood aside and motioned him to go ahead. He froze, Sandra went pale and Doña Lydia aghast, finally fixed her gaze on her only son. Straightening her shoulders, she clenched her jaw and raised her chin, preparing to take the shot.

"What are you waiting for?" I said.

No one was stopping him. He hesitated.

"She's hurt you all your life!" I pressed. "Do it!"

The other two children joined their brother in the doorway and like David, sensed something terrible was about to happen. "Mommy? Daddy?"

"Go back to bed," he ordered, upset they were watching.

"First tell your kids why you're about to shoot their grandmother in cold blood!"

The hall was quiet as a tomb. Even Doña Lydia was quiet.

His hands dropped to his sides. It was over.

"*Condenada* (damned one)!" his mother pointed at me and shrieked. "You tried to get my own son to kill me! Wait till I tell the family! Out! All of you!" she screeched, flailing her arms. "Out of my house! Before Robertico met you, he was such a good boy!"

That "boy" nearly killed her!

She wouldn't listen to my pleas to stay until morning for the children's sake. The walls reverberated with her screams, as Roberto paced up and down chain smoking and I packed.

Roberto walked to Tia Solidad's, who offered us refuge at her farm. Ana Rita, Luis and little Luisana were staying there free until he finished law school. Ana Rita, who came to her mother's several times a week to wash her hair in hot water, loved the idea of having someone else to talk to out there besides the caretaker's wife. They spoke English.

"Luis has an early class tomorrow," said Ana Rita. "Are you ready to leave?"

"Sure!" Roberto lied. "Most of our stuff is already at the curb." Roberto sprinted back to his parents' apartment to help me pack, leaving his aunt and cousin to finish their goodbyes.

We sped along the narrow two-lane into the mountains, stopping for gas in the village of Santa Ana. Three-year old Luisana fussed and fidgeted on her mother's lap. I was tired and glad our three were still. As we started back up the mountain, I noticed the air was no longer cool like in San Jose, but warm like springtime in Oklahoma.

We turned down a long drive lined with pines toward the farm the family also called *Santana*. Luis pulled up to the small, ranch style house, pointed the headlights at the steps then ran to the barn to turn on the generator, their only source of power. Ana Rita and I helped sleepy children climb the steps, while Roberto got the luggage onto the veranda. The breeze that rustled treetops blew dry leaves in from the fragrant shadows. The engine cranked up at the barn and the lights came on. Beyond the French doors and a furniture grouping, moonlight poured through the picture window onto an armoire and formal dining table piled with boxes and papers. Turning left at the table, we entered a tiny, windowless room with a double bed that filled three of the four walls. A bathroom separated it from the main bedroom, which was not much bigger. "There's a flashlight on the floor by your bed," she said. "Luisana can sleep with us. Tomorrow, we'll fix up the spare room."

In the quiet of country sounds, I drifted off to the sound of Luis walking to the barn to turn off the generator, croaking frogs and the "whooshing" of pine trees.

All of a sudden it was morning and I was trying to make out the silhouette on the edge of the bed against the dim light of dawn. "Wake up," Roberto whispered, gently shaking me. "I'm going into town with Luis to corner the guy about that job."

"The one who's put you off all this time?"

"Yeah." He fingered a small box in his lap. "I was saving this for your birthday. Maybe you should have it now." He slid the intricately carved ring on the tip of his little finger and held it to the light.

"For me?" I said, sitting up on one elbow. "Beautiful!"

"Eighteen karats," he said as if gold could erase the past. "Look, I know it's been rough on you and the kids, but I...."

I sighed loudly and rolled my eyes. *Not again!*

He nervously fumbled with the empty ring box then looked up. "I *do* want you to be happy. Look, I'm lousy at this. Tell me what I should do and I'll do it. If I ever hurt you again, you can go home." He hadn't

meant to say *that*. Silence followed, then he placed the ring on my finger. It was too big.

"And the children?"

"They belong..." he choked on the words "...with their mother." He gave me a quick peck on the forehead and left.

I heard Luis' car pull away as I groped for my shoes. Once out on the chilly, sun-drenched veranda, I looked around for the kitchen and a hot cup of coffee. In the light of day, I noticed the "backyard" was flush with the veranda, except where we'd climbed the steps to the side the night before. A few feet away, surrounded by a three foot high cyclone fence, was a tiny swimming pool with patches of foam and slime floating in its green water.

I followed a gasoline smell to an open door off the veranda, where a woman was bent over an old-fashioned cook stove blindly reaching for more wood to stoke the fire. Beside the kindling box was a red, five-gallon can marked kerosene. She saw me and jumped. "*Ayyy, me asustó* (Oh, you scared me)!" she said, covering her mouth with a weather-worn hand then continuing in Spanish. "You must be one of *la doñita's* guests Luisana told us about this morning."

"Luisana?" I asked, glancing at the rising sun.

"*La doñita* sleeps a lot now that she's expecting again. Luisana knows we're up and comes over for breakfast."

"You live nearby?"

"You can't see our house from here, but its just past *la pila*, up the knoll, through those trees and across the gully." She smiled, revealing the loss of several front teeth. "*Gerardina, a sus ordenes.*" (at your service)

Her tongue-twister name sounded like it might be Geraldine.

"Hair-are-dee-nah," she repeated, amused that this foreigner couldn't pronounce something so easy. "I've lived here all my life and

used to take care of *la doñita* Ana Rita, her brother and two sisters, when they came up with their parents on weekends."

"My name is, well, I'm called Maria. My husband, Ana Rita's cousin, went into town with Luis. The children will be up soon. Is there something I can fix them for breakfast?"

After she showed me around the kitchen, I leaned over the sink and looked both ways out the large window. Citrus groves! So that's what smelled so good last night! If I do die in Costa Rica, it *certainly* won't be from scurvy!

I took my cup of java to the veranda and eased into the plush cushions of a patio chair to bask in the sun's warmth. It was now February. At Daddy's, there'd be a crackling fire in the den fireplace. Shimmering icicles, the size of broadswords, would be hanging outside the picture window and red cardinals would be squabbling over breadcrumbs on the glittering crust of snow. A pretty scene. But Daddy's was just a house, never my home. Actually, Daddy's fourth wife, Vivian, who sent a box of her nice clothes to Doña Lydia, owned it. Her brilliant mind must have suffered a relapse when she married Daddy, a man who was the life of the party and had the gift of Blarney but no money or future.

I was sixteen when Linda and I moved in with newlywed Daddy and Vivian. Mom once sent us home from a weekend visit with Daddy's favorite: a lemon meringue pie, which made Vivian insanely jealous. Too young to understand adult intrigues, I stayed in my room dreaming of tropical adventures, playing my guitar and writing mournful teenage ballads.

Though Vivian was bookkeeper for some doctors and could afford groceries, there was never anything in the fridge but butter, half gallon bottles of rosé wine and six-packs of Brown Derby dark ale. She began drinking the minute she got home then followed me from room to room, slurring and accusing me of trying to break up her marriage. I didn't know what she meant. That's when I discovered the basement with its

plush sofa and lamp; a place away from her where I could study. She would yell at me from the top of the stairs, lock the basement door and turn off the overhead. Around ten or eleven, Daddy would unlock the door and tell me to go to bed.

Linda read in the newspapers of a Judge Dorothy Young, who helped teens in difficult situations. I took a bus downtown to see her. Not knowing enough to lie about who I was and where I lived, I was then ushered into a nice office where I practiced what I would tell her. A while later, who should walk in but Daddy, acting like the Good Shepherd who'd just found his lost lamb.

He said nothing after we got home, but two months before graduation, Vivian had Daddy throw my clothes in the yard and kick me out. But for the kindness of my friend, Suzanne, and her mother Jean who lived behind us, I had no place else to go.

Daddy used to slap me for wrong answers during math homework, so I grew up thinking abuse was normal and that I was hopelessly stupid. It was years before I realized there were different kinds of intelligence, and that, yes, I *could* do algebra. Both sets of parents offered to pay for the school of my choice, but by the time I decided on nursing a year later, the offers had been withdrawn.

Mom's exciting life with her new husband was filled with banquets and travel. With his money and connections and her beauty, charm, and developing leadership talents, mother was an emerging celebrity in her lodge work, and was loving it! Aunt Mozy had divorced and was busy with her new husband. It was Uncle Joe who took me in. I was unprepared for life and living on Country Club Drive.

Used to being taken care of, I didn't have enough sense to even find a job. I'd never made a decision on my own. My folks had always told me what to do and when to do it. Prodigals like me have to learn the hard way. After eighteen months of smoking, drinking and wild parties

with Latino students from the University of Tulsa, I came to myself in the proverbial pig sty. This wasn't who I was.

I tried every church I could think of, even a Jewish synagogue, but couldn't "find" God. What I did find was a job managing a uniform shop downtown. A year later, a mutual American friend would introduce me to Roberto.

I took another sip of coffee on the veranda in Santana. Was it his good looks or eyes reflecting a boyish awkwardness that first attracted me to him? Had I seen only what I wanted, when Roberto's smile reminded me of Rock Hudson's and his little sneer seemed, pure Elvis? (Actually, he was a dead ringer for future star, Antonio Banderas!) Like Elvis, Roberto sang in a rock and roll band, and said if not for the loud music and girl's screams, they'd have found out sooner he couldn't carry a tune.

I'd only known him four months when we married. A month later, we moved my household goods to Uncle Joe's attic in preparation for our trip to Costa Rica, borrowing Uncle Joe's truck while he was home for lunch. I remember how eerie it was when we pulled out of the apartment parking lot. Lunch crowds were usually scurrying in and out of downtown restaurants. Now, only newspapers blew past a scruffy stray meandering down the middle of the street.

We were getting back late. Uncle Joe, who owned his own business, stuck to a schedule. "Sorry Unkie Joe. We'll empty the truck in a jiff."

He didn't answer but puffed on his Black Hawk cigar, his eyes riveted to the 21" TV Aunt Mozy said was the second color set sold in Tulsa. "Ladies and gentlemen," Walter Cronkite somberly said, "if you're just tuning in, President John F. Kennedy, dead at 46."

That weekend, we sat through replays of the assassination, on-the-scene reports of the linked murder of a police officer, Jack Ruby killing

ALL THE WAY HOME

Lee Harvey Oswald in the police garage, and JFK's funeral. There'd never been such coverage!

We barely had time to mourn, for immediately following the assassination was all the speculation surrounding the the first curse word to be aired on TV. It squeaked by on the same technicality used to excuse Rhett Butler telling Scarlett O'Hara off in *Gone With the Wind:* "Frankly my dear, I don't give a damn!" *Damn* was again pronounced a mild vulgarity, not a curse word. In 1963, people assumed public decency would be defended and preserved by some sort of TV Hays Commission.

In the Silent Era, motion pictures were being condemned because of nudity, immoral storylines and the scandalous behavior of their stars. The public was demanding congress place stringent regulations on the film industry. Due to ever-increasing pressure for some sort of censorship, in 1922, heads of studios appointed Will Hays to oversee all film projects. By 1930, what was known as the Hays Office had created the Motion Picture Production Code, a strict self-regulatory charter of do's and don'ts that became known as the Hays Commission. Their first principle was that "no picture shall be produced which will lower the moral standards of those who see it."

Baby-face Tony Dow, big brother in "Leave It to Beaver," was chosen to deliver the infamous "D" word in a TV tearjerker about teenage lovers who have a baby; she wants to give it up for adoption and he doesn't. (This was a time when using the word "sex" was frowned on and it was still considered shameful to have a child out of wedlock. A pregnant girl, now a bad example, was expected to drop out of school. A married girl couldn't participate in a cheerleading program to avoid her inadvertently saying or doing something inappropriate around the carnally uninitiated.) A week or two before the scheduled airing, a shocked public tuned in as both sides verbally duked it out on TV;

traditionalists warning that one curse word would invariably lead to others, countered by the intellectuals' passionate cries for free speech.

Who'd have guessed it would mushroom into such a media event? The public was on overload, having endured the British invasion of the mop-headed Fab Four, having witnessed assassination and murder on live TV, and now advisors were being sent to police a skirmish somewhere in Southeast Asia that was about to escalate into war. Is it any wonder there was so little opposition to this innocuous event of one little curse word on TV?

Shock broadcasting was becoming a suppertime norm as the three networks vied for ratings with more blood and gore from far-off Vietnam than the night before. Into our homes poured the cries of sons, brothers, and fathers as they were carried on stretchers and we now witnessed atrocities never seen by civilized people: street executions; napalm burnings; monks dousing themselves with gasoline, lighting a match and calmly sitting cross-legged in the middle of streets, burning alive before news cameras and throngs of on-lookers. The latest joke on late-night TV was, "What goes farthest on a gallon of gas? The answer: a Buddhist Monk!" Disturbing scenes of a troubled time. And the whole world was watching.

On that veranda in Santana, I wondered if the war had ended? I'd been in Costa Rica four months. Had the killing stopped? The morning was cold. Scooting my chair into the sun, I slipped both hands around my warm cup and turned to nicer thoughts. It was March, Spring at home, and tiny crocus' had already pushed through crusts of snow. If we were home, I'd be taking the kids to the park to fly kites. In May, Chris would be finishing the first grade and I, my first semester of nursing school. On March 26th, I'd be twenty-seven. Job and school opportunities back home wouldn't wait forever. In San Jose, I got my news from the English language column of *La Nación*. But papers never made it out to the farm. There was to be an Apollo shot this spring. Was it still on?

Were our troops at last going home? I wanted to go home. Too bad some soldiers couldn't swing by Costa Rica and pick the kids and me up, except I couldn't have told them where the rescue was to take place! All I knew was that Santana was in an orange grove on the side of a mountain. Were Mama there, she'd have told me to stop whining and do something useful. So, I looked for dirty clothes I in our dark bedroom to get them washed and on the line before the kids woke up.

Gerardina had gathered eggs and piled some oranges on the small table in the middle of the kitchen. "For you and the kids," she said.

"What about Ana Rita and Luisana?"

"She gets up around noon and Luisana's eaten."

When Ana Rita got up, she was surprised to see clothes on the line. "Gerardina, did you wash?"

"No Señora, it was *la macha*."

"Maria, you don't have to wash," Ana said. *La Sixaola* does our things. Leave your bundle on the veranda and Luis will bring it back tomorrow night all ironed and folded."

There IS a God! Now, I'll have more time for the kids!

We fixed a quick lunch and got busy on the spare bedroom, a maid's quarters off the kitchen that was also accessed from the veranda. By the veranda door was a tiny room with a toilet, and just outside that, a double utility *pila*. The small room had a twin bed and narrow cot and no curtains on a picture window that covered one entire wall. With no dressers or shelved closets, we'd have to live out of the suitcases I stacked between the doors to the kitchen and veranda, an exact fit with the doors open. With Roberto gone, it was peaceful. What's that old saying? "It's better to eat a crust of bread in the attic of a shack in peace than dine sumptuously in a palace filled with strife."

Ana Rita was tired and nauseated most of the time, so I cooked. There was a modern gas stove and propane bottle used for baking, and for regular cooking, an old-fashioned wood stove that took three times as long to cook food and left me smelling like I'd been to a three-alarm fire.

Ana Rita had an old-fashioned, stainless steel can opener with a black, textured poly handle that had a flat, three-inch "thorn-shaped" protrusion to make holes on top of cans and a "ripper" to remove lids. Ana Rita made her precision blows to the tops of cans look so easy. The sound of that sharp little "pickaxe" piercing soft metal sent shivers up my spine. "Guess I'd better behave around you!" I quipped.

"Why's that?" she asked.

"So you don't part my hair with that thing!"

"Oh this!" she laughed. Since I did all the cooking, I soon wielded it as well as she.

I didn't see Ana Rita except at supper and I took care of Luisana, who was spoiled rotten. One day, she was playing with the Shelly Dolly while Michelle cried. When I said she should share, she secretly emptied the toy box, taking all the toys, one by one to Gerardina's, where she played alone.

With Luisana and Luis gone all day, and Ana Rita asleep most of the time, the kids and I were pretty much on our own. There was no TV during the day and no books to read, so we explored the farm and picked fruit. On rainy days, I'd bake cupcakes or cookies to eat on the veranda, where I'd tell them stories.

We'd only been in Santana a few days. One particular day was cool and sunny, like autumn back home. All of us in sweatshirts I in shorts the kids in jeans, we skirted the nasty pool then galloped downhill toward a shaded brook. Halfway down was a barbed wire fence. Seeing it in time, I guided the kids to one side through the gateless opening.

Galloping past a dead tree, we finally stopped at the edge of the woods, where dappled sunlight danced across a carpet of green and sparkling water shimmered and splashed over the small round stones of a babbling brook.

Something caught the boys' attention a few feet away and they hurried over to see. A gust of wind began to whip the tops of trees and gray clouds swirled in the darkening skies, casting ominous shadows on the forest floor.

"Mama, come see!" Chris shouted.

He and his brother, crouched low, were moving something around with twigs. It was the head of a snake! I moved them away. "Don't touch that!"

"Why not?" the boys said. "It can't bite. It's dead."

"Time to go back," I said. "Looks like rain."

Growing up in Oklahoma, I didn't ignore clouds like the ones rolling in on the springlike wind and getting darker by the minute. "We're gonna get soaked!" I yelled above the wind. "Bet I can beat you guys to the house!"

"Bet you can't!" the boys shouted back.

We raced up the hill and burst into the kitchen laughing.

Gerardina was stoking the stove, when I noticed something moving up my sweatshirt: nearly invisible golden flecks that looked like pollen with tiny legs. Not one to panic, I casually pointed and asked, "Gerardina, what's this?"

Her eyes got big as saucers and a look of horror swept her face. "Garrapata!" she gasped.

I glanced down then back at her. "What's Garrapata?"

"Quick! Out of those clothes and into the shower!" she ordered. "The children, too!"

"First, tell me wha…"

"Do as I say, Doña! Don't let the clothes touch your hair! Don't shake them as you run them to the *pila*. Sprinkle on detergent, let them soak then scrub the kids and shampoo their heads real good!" she shouted as I herded the kids into the bathroom.

I normally stayed clear of water pipes during storms. Cracks of thunder were getting closer.

Removing their clothes and mine, all but my underwear for modesty sake and my socks against the cold concrete floors, I wrapped them in a towel and ran them to the *pila*. Passing Gerardina, who was mopping with disinfectant, I asked her to turn off the water when the *pila* was full, while I bathed the kids.

The icy water took their breath away as lightening flashed and thunder boomed! They screamed, begging to get out, their lips turning purple long before I could shampoo them. I rubbed their color back with towels, wrapped them in dry ones and left them shivering on the bed while I took my turn. When we went to the kitchen for a hot drink to warm them up, Gerardina was still mopping. "Feed the children, Doñita. I'll finish cleaning up."

I asked her about the snake the kids found by the brook.

"Workers kill dangerous snakes," she said, "and bury the head. They should have buried that one deeper. Depending on the snake, it might have killed them!"

We had no phone or car to get them to a hospital!

"Are there many venomous snakes around here?" I asked.

"About four kinds," she said as casually as if I'd asked the time of day.

Staying on the veranda wasn't even safe: where there's frogs, there's snakes. And did we have frogs! Not a few here and there, but a plague of Biblical proportion! What happened next, this city girl is lucky to be around to tell.

Late one night, I got up to use the restroom. Stepping onto the veranda, my bare foot hit something. Jumping back, I shone the light where I'd stepped, expecting to see the raised head of a *matabuey* poised to strike! Instead, it was a frog the size of a dinner plate. I took a deep breath, glad to be alive!

CHAPTER FIFTEEN

GARRAPATA!

Garrapata ("grab [the] foot") or tiny cattle ticks had embedded themselves in my ankles. (I'd left my socks on too long.) Horrendous itching woke me and kept me up half that night. "Looks like you could use some more sleep," Ana Rita said the next day.

"Yeah, I'm beat!"

"Your ankles are red and swollen."

"It's that itching! I thought it'd never stop!"

"*Garrapata?*"

"Gerardina told you."

"No. Did you put alcohol?"

"How does it work?"

"I'm not sure." (If I didn't know how something worked, I wouldn't use it. But why question it? I didn't know how aspirin worked, either!)

I was straightening the veranda one afternoon and spied a tiny white Bible with one corner chewed off. Starved for anything to read in Engish, I opened it. Each page contained a single verse and reference.

"With God all things are possible." Matthew 19:26

"Casting all your cares upon him; for he careth for you." I Peter 5:7

"Behold I am the Lord of all flesh: is there anything too hard for me?" Jeremiah 32:27

"Thou wilt keep him in perfect peace whose mind is stayed on thee, because he trusteth in thee." Isaiah 26:3

"Come unto me all ye who labor and are heavy laden and I will give you rest." Matthew 11:28

"Call unto Me and I will answer thee and show thee great and mighty things which thou knowest not." Jeremiah 33:3

"No weapon that is formed against thee shall prosper." Isaiah 54:17

I wish! I thought and continued.

"God heals the brokenhearted and binds up their wounds." Psalms 147:3

"For God hath not given us the spirit of fear; but of power, and love, and of a sound mind." II Timothy 1:7

Pausing to ponder that one and the one before, I read on.

"For I know the plans I have for you, plans to prosper you and not to harm you, plans to give you hope and a future." Jeremiah 29:11

I laid the tiny Bible on my lap. *Plans to give ME hope and a future? Could this be?*

Chris suddenly leaned over my shoulder. "What 'cha readin'?"

"Something I found in the toy box. Where's the other two?"

"They left me up a tree. I thought they'd be here."

My two little scamps were up to mischief again!

There came a blood-curdling scream! I jumped up as David ran toward us looking scared. "Mama, it's Shell!"

Taking off in the direction Chris had come from, I imagined Shell lying on the ground and a serpent slithering into the bushes. My legs stretched to full stride down the hill. About to yell back at David for her exact position, I nearly stampeded through the barbed wire fence. "Whoa, Nelly!" I said, holding out my arms to slow the boys enough to zigzag them through the gate.

"Mommy, Mommy, they're biting me!" Michelle screamed when she saw me running toward her. Something black was swarming her. Yanking her down from the fork of the dead tree, I tore off her clothes and brushed her until the last ant was off.

"Honest Mama, I tried to help!" David said sheepishly, knowing he'd disobeyed by playing there.

I carried Michelle back to the house, bathed her and applied some lotion Ana Rita gave me. Afternoon was bath time anyway, so I bathed the boys next then sat them all down. "Well kids, we've been here a week and you've learned to leave the calves alone (Chris, who got the wind kicked out of him, had ended up with cloven hoof marks on his stomach from pulling a calf's tail); not to throw rocks at hornet nests, (David was stung on a finger); to stay out of the pasture (the boys threw rocks at the bull the day before, waited until it charged then dove under the fence and rolled on the ground laughing and watched the bull barrel to a stop in a cloud of dust inches away. They were too young to know that a two thousand pound bull can make splinters of a rail fence. Mama always said God watched over children and simpletons); and now you know not to run off by yourselves." The children sat looking up at me in wide-eyed innocence, hands neatly folded in their laps. Behind those angelic expressions, they were already planning their next adventure.

"We'll be good," David promised.

"Yeah," Chris agreed. "Now, how about a story?"

"The Indians and Geronimo!" David interrupted.

"I asked first!" Chris shouted. "Tell about Nelly, Mama."

"How about both in the order they happened?" I said. They loved the family stories I often told, so they wouldn't forget home. Stories helped keep their minds off their world that had been turned upside-down. Since Daddy had related to me all of Grandmother Hoover's tales and could sometimes be careless with their accuracy, I wasn't sure how precise he had been. I'm sure the children didn't mind, but I told them exactly as they were told to me.

"Grandmother Hoover, whose name was Ida Mary, may have been about your age," I said, touching Michelle's nose as she snuggled in close. "She came West in a covered wagon, from Ohio, I believe, with her father, mother, Will, who was first born, and four sisters. They mostly walked. But those whose turn it was to ride were bumped over hills and open fields, through woods and across stony streams as the wagon headed westward with all they owned: feather beds rolled tight, family quilts, farm tools, the china grandmother had given them and two of her rose bushes, seeds and fruit trees to plant, the family Bible with inscribed family history and the guns and ammo Father kept under the wagon footrest to protect us against snakes and wild animals. So, with silver bars in water barrels to keep drinking water pure, gold coins sewn into skirt hems, paper money stuffed inside boots, provisions, family treasures, extra horses, hunting dogs and hearts full of hopes and dreams they made their way West."

"Father was Deputy Marshal in Lawton when soldiers brought Geronimo to Fort Sill. People came for miles to see the famous Indian Chief, except for Ida Mary and her sisters. 'Young ladies shouldn't loiter in front of a jailhouse!' Mother fussed, 'Or even take interest in such things! Besides,' she added, her fan fluttering in agitation, 'seeing that wild Indian will only give them nightmares!'

"'Please, Father,' Ida Mary later begged. 'Will gets to go!' 'Will is nearly a man, Ida,' Father said.

"Ida Mary had seen Indians before. They used to peer in the windows at night. (They'd seen few white girls and were curious.) Later, Father arranged a visit above his wife's objections. She'll be ruined! No decent man will seek her society.'

"'Good grief, woman! She's still a little girl!'

"'Stubborn man! I feel faint. I must lie down. Tell Ida I laid a hankie on her bed, so she doesn't dab at her glow (Mother's word for sweat) with bare fingers, which shows a lack of breeding!' Originally from simple folk, they'd come to this new land to better themselves, so Mama saw nothing wrong with putting on a few airs.

"Ida Mary knew Geronimo would be as frightening and exciting as he turned out to be! He stopped in his cell to stare at the worthless girl the crazy white men brought in, then resumed pacing. His moccasins would eventually wear a ringed trough in the sandstone floor. It was still morning and the jailhouse was like an oven. Ida Mary, having forgotten her embroidered handkerchief at home, wiped away the glow with her fingers, took hold of the bars and pulled herself closer. She didn't know yet, but she would be sick this time tomorrow and had exposed poor Geronimo to the mumps. He got desperately sick."

"But he got better?" said Chris.

"Yes and lived many years."

"Now Nelly!" Chris cried in anticipation.

"Alright," I said. "Ida grew into a beautiful young woman, and William Jessie, with eyes as clear and blue as the Oklahoma skies, had won her heart. Will, who had his own business, saw automobiles (at first considered nothing but toys for the idle rich) as fast becoming the workhorse of industry and traded in his teams and wagons for trucks to haul lumber to building sites.

ALL THE WAY HOME

"'The day of the horse and buggy is over!' he told Ida. 'Autos are the transportation of the future. They're cheaper, too! And just think, no more smelly horses out back, no feed to draw rats; no stalls to clean and no trudging through rain and snow to the carriage house, day in and day out, caring for horses. Best of all, no leather harnesses and buggy seats to polish. I hear autos take care of themselves!'

"The new century was bringing in new inventions every day. And now Ida would have a stylish auto. The changes of modern life were coming too fast for Ida.

"Nelly was with the family for years, and gentle enough for little Ida to ride bareback. Ida kept treats in her pocket. Maybe that's why Nelly loved her best. Nelly and a new buggy were a wedding gift from Ida's parents. Ida wanted Nelly's last days spent grazing in pastures with all the carrots, apples and lumps of sugar she wanted. And now?

"Nelly's last day, it was August and muggy. Ida harnessed her to the buggy, half dazed with sadness. Tiny particles of barn sediment descended in shafts of light onto Nelly's silvery gray coat, and the carriage house smelled sweet with hay and grain and leather. Nervous perspiration popped out on Ida's face. Mama's old-fashioned notion that horses sweat and men perspired but ladies glowed sounded silly in these modern times. Will was right. Things were changing.

"The only change Ida wanted now was to get into a cooler summer frock and get her high-top shoes fastened with that darned button hooker, which took forever! Ida was all thumbs. Ouch! She hadn't stuck herself with a hatpin since she was a girl. She made sure it stopped bleeding so she wouldn't stain the pink silk flowers on her broad rimmed hat or the pink sash she tied under her chin into a neat bow. Glowing as she was made it hard to pull on her white gloves embroidered with pink rosebuds. She'd better take her fan.

"Gliding gracefully to the carriage house, she climbed into the buggy, walked Nelly down the long drive and onto the dirt street. Nelly knew her mistress usually stopped at the post office first and pulled up there on her own. The general store was last. In between, Nelly seemed to know when to stop at the bank, seamstress, hairdresser, drugstore or ice cream shoppe. Ida could even lay down the reins to pin back a fallen strand of hair or bend low to fan air up her floor-length skirt, when no one was looking. Nelly, who never spooked at backfiring automobiles, was a true lady's horse, gentle and steady as they came.

"On the way back home that last day, Ida fanned herself to the muffled clip-clop of Nelly's hooves in the deep soft dust. Disturbing thoughts of losing Nelly, that Ida was to sit in a machine that backfired and that the carriage house would soon smell of oil and gasoline, left her faint. She laid the reins down to dab at her glow with a lace hankie. She didn't want to change how she lived or lose certain comforts, like feeling safe with her horse. Nelly loudly whinnied: they were nearing the turn to the driveway. Inside the cool carriage house, Nelly looked back at Ida for her lump of sugar. Ida removed the bit so Nelly could fully enjoy it and the sweet carrots, juicy apples and extra oats. Nelly's velvety muzzle gently nibbled each morsel from her hand as Ida stood there heartbroken with tears streaming down her cheeks.

"As soon as Nelly was gone the next day, Will's men knocked down the stall and converted the carriage house into a garage. Will told her that the new auto, which resembled her old buggy, could go twenty miles per hour. *Why so fast?* Ida thought. The new auto had a stick instead of reins, which set Ida to thinking, *You drive geese with sticks, not something one rides in!* She preferred the word, 'motoring.' Why, even the brake was all wrong; a pedal on the floor, when everyone knows a brake lever is beside the seat and used with one's hand. How would she ever remember it all? A pedal to make it go, another to stop and a stick for turning. Motoring would be like patting your head and rubbing your tummy at the same time!

"Ida delayed motoring to town that first time until noon. Will had backed the auto to the back steps and closed the wooden garage doors for her before leaving for work. He'd bought her a floor-length white coat called a duster and oversized motoring gloves, both in heavy fabric, already smelling of gasoline, and a hat with itchy netting that tied under her chin and some ugly rubber goggles.

"Standing before the lifeless machine, Ida gave it a pat for luck. A hollow sound echoed inside cold, hard metal. She cranked it up (something a lady should never have to do), whispered a prayer, climbed up on the leather seat and put it in gear. It jerked and she motored away in puffs of smoke from its smelly exhaust.

"Ida's friends stood chatting in the shade of the old tree on the village green. Ida normally stopped and chatted from her buggy. She tried to slow down, but mashed on the excellator instead. The frightful sight of her coming down the street with all the strange sounds and smells sent an oncoming horse and wagon into a ditch, leaving Ida's friends to wonder who that crazy woman was speeding by in a heavy coat in the middle of summer? The August wind hit her like a blast furnace as her cheeks flushed hot with embarrassment.

"She finished her errands in town and got into the auto. *To blazes with delicate words like glow!* Ida thought. She was sweating like Nelly and those rubber goggles kept sliding down her nose. And did she have to wear a corset today? She could hardly breathe! She didn't dare let go of the stick to look for her fan. Drowsy from the heat and barely able to think straight, she wished she could be in her old buggy. Nelly would get her home. Ida suddenly saw she was nearing her driveway. Nelly wasn't out front of the buggy! She jerked the stick to one side and up the driveway she flew. Thinking it was reins in her hands, she pulled back, 'Whoaa Nelly!' and crashed through the garage doors. Will hadn't hauled away that last pile of hay! Flying over the dash, Ida landed upside down, dress over her head with her unmentionables showing."

I changed the ending for the kids, who fretted over Nelly's fate of never coming back to Ida. This was how it went:

"Will had the stall rebuilt and Nelly brought back. And everyone lived happily ever after. And that's why when we make fast stops, our family says," I moved my hands as if directing a chorus, "Whoaaa Nelly!" we all cried together.

That night, the boys were in their twin bed and Shell and I on our cot. I was just drifting off, riding horseback across the green hills of home, when I heard a crunching sound. I lit a candle. Beneath the badly chipped paint of the wood plank walls riddled with holes, were termites munching through their little tunnels. Black ants came from nowhere, possibly the kind that had attacked Michelle, their powerful mandibles crushing the termites inches from my face. Horrified, I ran the flame along the wall. The ants scattered and didn't return. I blew out the candle and went to sleep. It never occurred that I might have sent that whole house up in flames, which must have been a tinderbox! Mama was right. God *did* watch over children and simpletons.

We hadn't heard a word from Roberto since he left six weeks earlier. He could have at least sent a note with Luis. The kids had "cabin fever." The boys teased Michelle mercilessly and she threw David's red chick and Chris' blue bunny in that nasty pool. The Sixaola dry cleaned them, but they were never the same.

On March 26th, I helped the kids bake me a birthday cake. Ana Rita helped them make a homemade card from stationary and crayons. Even Luisana put her mark. We had to wait until after ten p.m. when Luis got home with the ice cream and candles to sing Happy Birthday. Roberto missed another of the kids' cute moments. They hadn't asked about him since we'd been at the farm, Santana.

A couple of days later, I was looking out the kitchen window, about to open a can of evaporated milk to make pancakes, when Roberto

breezed in. "Hi!" he said, stopping at the table that separated us. Startled, I wheeled around. "I've got some terrific news!" he grinned.

We were going home, I could feel it! I stepped forward, can and opener in my hands.

"I got that job!" he continued, "Bet you can't guess what I've been saving every penny for?"

"Tickets home?" I said, relief sweeping over me and arms dropping limply to my sides.

"Costa Rica is our home!"

The only thing that kept me from parting his hair with that little pickaxe was that I couldn't reach him. He took a menacing step toward me, bumping into the table. My hand involuntarily flinched, the can opener still in it. Roberto backed off and continued sober as a judge.

"I picked a furnished apartment in San Pedro, La Granja, a nice San Jose suburb with lots of children. We can also afford a private school. They even pick up and deliver kids to their front doors."

I stood there speechless.

"Look, forget about the States!"

Slamming the can on the metal table, I poised the tiny pickaxe over it like Liberace about to strike one of those big fat chords by Rachmaninoff. "Mr. Showmanship," who could play anything from show tunes to the classics, performed with incomparable flair. Gazing into the camera, he'd wink and smile to the delight of his audience, suspend his hand high above the keyboard and come down on precisely the right chord. Mine was more a Norman Bates smile! Holding the little pickaxe high, I came down on my "keyboard" with bold decisiveness. Whap! Metal hit metal! Gracefully, I returned my hand high over my "instrument" in Liberace's resplendent style. Roberto turned pale. I'd struck the desired chord. I felt quite... musical!

"You're busy," he choked, clearing his throat. "I'll be back Saturday to shop for what we'll need for the apartment." From the safety of the door, he added, "Be ready!" and ducked out.

Ana Rita came out of seclusion and cleared up a mystery. When Doña Lydia was found in a family way and Don Vicente forced to marry her, he took his anger and resentment out on his wife and son. Not until his grandson, David, was born, who looked exactly like him, did he know he'd been wrong. Roberto *was* his son! He rocked back and forth with David in his arms and cried, maybe for all those years he and his wife had lost and the years he'd spent abusing an innocent child.

Ana Rita also cleared up my red, swollen ankles. "Maria, are you still itching?" I don't know why I was so surprised when the alcohol she applied worked. I'd have had relief from both garrapata and a bad marriage by simply listening to advice.

That Saturday, a friend brought Roberto to Santana. I'm sure he wished he still had the wagon we drove down from Tulsa. But typical of many Latino men, he never stopped at stop lights or stop signs. On his way home drunk from a cantina, he hit a cow and totaled the car.

The kids, excited to tell him about all their adventures on the farm, were ignored. We had barely left Santana, when Luisana began fussing for a story. Ana Rita offered to read her one but Luisana wanted her daddy to. Luis calmly pulled onto a wide shoulder, set her on his lap and read for five minutes, which kept Luisana satisfied for the next hour. If only my children's father were this tender. Maybe he never had the example.

Pulling back on the highway, Ana Rita tuned in the American music station. The smooth tempo complimented the car's pace as we floated down the mountain, springlike air blowing the fresh smell of pine through our hair as the Sandpipers sang, "Come Saturday morning, I'm going away with my friends. We'll Saturday spend till the end of the day." My thoughts went to Ana Rita and Luis and how they'd been a

Godsend, offering us sanctuary, how Luis had brought the kids candy from town and Ana Rita made them cakes and special pancakes we'd never tasted. "And I will remember, long after Saturday's over."

It was déjà vu at the new apartment: a modern building on a low hill with five residential streets meeting in front. Exactly like in my dream about Italy a few months before! *Los Apartmentos El Retiro* (retire or withdraw) was a good name. There I could regroup and think of a way out of there! We walked through the covered parking onto polished granite sidewalks that led to each door, past beautifully tended gardens. Roberto fumbled at the lock of number five apartment by the staircase to the second story—five, the number for grace (unmerited or undeserved favor).

The tiny living room's built-in L-shaped sofa was covered in a hideous mustard-yellow Naugahyde, dingy with volcanic ash. A built-in entertainment center on the living room side and china hutch in the dining room separated the combined living areas that had cool granite floors. In a hutch drawer beneath the telephone were dried seahorses; one black, the other coral.

The dining room had a Danish style large table and six chairs, two buffet tables and an outside door to a small garden that was comprised of a patch of grass surrounded by narrow beds of bright flowers. Rising ominously above that splash of fragrant color was an eight-foot cinder block wall painted gray with three lines of barbed wire along the top, reminding me of a prison. Many homes had this or broken glass embedded on the tops of outer walls to keep thieves out. Older homes were starkly plain in front. Newer ones had front yards like in the States, minus yard ornaments or anything that could be carried away in the night. If thieves could see it, they'd try and steal it.

The apartment's kitchen floors were linoleum for easy cleaning, but the kitchen, itself, must have been a contractor's afterthought. There were no cabinets, shelves or drawers! Hence, those two buffets. The tiny turquoise blue electric stove, with the smallest oven I'd ever seen, gave occasional electric shocks and the fridge would need defrosting every week. At the narrow end of the room was a tiny sink, corrugated metal counter tops and a view of that gray wall and barbed wire from a high window.

The utility room door was made of reinforced steel and led to a tiny backyard, again with a gray wall and barbed wire. Clotheslines in the utility room and under the covered patio would be good during the rainy months when it took a couple of days for clothes to dry. The maid's quarters that adjoined the utility room had a three-quarter bath and no closet. A small chest of drawers and twin bed stood beneath high curtainless windows.

The free standing *pila,* or sink, stood against a wall of windows that faced the backyard. I could watch the kids while I washed and ironed. Beside it, there was a metal-top table to fold clothes where the maid could also eat. A coverless wooden ironing board, way too short for me, stood in the otherwise empty end of the room, which would be plenty of room for the kids to keep a toy box and play on rainy days.

Off the living room were two bedrooms and a bathroom with a shower that came with a plastic shower curtain and matching curtains. Best of all, the shower had hot running water! (I knew what I was going to do the minute we moved in!) It was the only faucet in the apartment with hot water, but I wasn't about to complain!

The bedroom and connecting hall floors were hardwood. Closets with mirrored doors covered entire bedroom walls with plenty of hanger and shelf space. The view from the two windows in the kid's room was that gray wall that wrapped around from the back patio. Large elephant ears peeked over the low sills of the master bedroom windows, where a desk stood. (I hated the short, draw-string drapes in ugly dusty turquoise.) There was also a vanity with drawers and a mirror and stool, but no beds. Roberto bought those and used linens at a hotel going-out-

of-business sale. "What do you mean you can't use these?" he said, astonished. "Just wash 'em!" *Men!*

I was starting over with nothing. Aunt Mozy told me her mother had once lost everything.

––––––––

"Mozy, hurry up! We're leaving!" the Old Man shouted.

"Coming, Dad!" she hollered back. Cutting out her dress pattern would have to wait until after supper. She hurriedly shoved the sewing box under her bed. Mozy, who was twelve and old enough to work in the fields with Charlie and Clyde and Glen, scrambled out the door and into the back of the wagon. Her younger sister, Gladys, would stay home to care for Mama, her brother, Little Frank and baby Josilee.

"Charlie and Glen, you're going to the Johnson's today," the Old Man mumbled. "Clyde and Mozy, to the Sawyers. And no talking back there," he said, slapping the reins across the backs of Buttons and Old Blue, "I don't like it." Only the clopping of hooves could be heard down the country road that pre-dawn morning, metal wagon rims grinding ruts to powder like the Old Man crushed the spirits of his seven children.

Mozy and her brothers didn't like hiring out, because Dad just bought another bottle when they needed food, especially Mama. The Old Man would find himself a shady spot to get drunk and nap, while their mother plowed the fields behind two mules. Mama just had a baby and was bedfast with milk leg. Some thought her a saint, because she saw good in everyone, even her no-good husband, Amzie (Am-zee). "He's not bad at heart." she'd say. "Besides, his beautiful tenor solos on Sundays will get him to heaven."

Because of Susan's unfortunate "lazy eye" that drifted to one side, it was hard for her father, Anderson Llemuel Bizzle, to find her a husband. A.L. married his other three daughters off well, and had the money to

set all his children and their spouses up in business or buy them farms. Amzie Edward Davenport was finally convinced to take Susie. Who knew that good-looking boy would turn out to be so mean?

With such a dismal beginning, A.L. should have been just as mean. His father, Stephen, had been on the front lines of the Civil War for two years. Nobody's sure exactly why he went back home. Some say he heard his wife was being unfaithful or maybe it was to get a glimpse of the two year old son he'd never seen. After being home a few days, he returned to his unit, where he was shot as a deserter. He was nineteen. A.L. was beat and abused by his new stepfather until he was nine and went to live with his grandmother. Through her nurturing care, he grew to be a loving and responsible father of eight and a propertied and successful businessman.

A.L. bought Susie and Amzie a farm. With crop money and the sale of some cattle, Amzie bought a race horse named Salem. His son, Glen, who was small, agile and athletic was the jockey. The Old Man did so well, he built a racetrack on his property. Salem never lost a race, so the Old Man bet the farm. The morning of the big race, Glen mounted Salem and knew something was wrong. "Dad, Salem's been drugged!"

"Can't stop the race now. I give my word. Do your best."

Salem lost and everything they owned was auctioned off. Neighbors redeemed Grandmother's china and some other items and gave them back to Susie. Otherwise, the Davenports left the farm with the clothes on their backs, and according to Glen, never lived well, again. When Glen's baseball coach saw how his protégé lived and how the Old Man treated him, he got Glen a small apartment in town over a store where he could work sweeping up after games and practices and support himself. (Fifteen or twenty years earlier, at the turn of the century, you could rent a whole house for five dollars a month, so the apartment was affordable for a kid.) Uncle Glen called this coach's kindness, "his salvation."

Mozelle's salvation came after the last baby was born. Susie had developed milk leg and was confined to strict bed rest. This meant Amzie would have no clean laundry or hot meals. Twelve-year old Mozy was listening behind the door to the orders The Old Man gave to her seventeen-year old brother.

"Yur mama's gonna be down fer a while. I talked tah John Rivers 'bout his daughter, Annie, cookin' and cleanin' fer us but with the boys here, he won't let her stay 'lessen she's married'. Take Ole Blue tah fetch 'er, an stop by the preacher's, who's awaitin'. She'll be cookin' supper tonight, so don't be long. I'm hungry."

"Farming" your children out with family in another town or state was common in those days as times were hard. Suzie's brother, Newt, and his wife, Jessie, took Mozelle in. They had a daughter Edna, who was Mozy's age. Mozy would miss her own family, especially baby Josilee, who she'd named after Mama's grandmothers, Josie and Lee. "Stiff upper lip, Mozy!" Mama said. "Cryin's not our way. We're Pioneer stock!"

But Mozy had reason to be glad, too. There was no outhouse at Uncle Newt's and Aunt Jessie's. Mozy wouldn't have to empty slop jars or share bath water on Saturday nights, either. At home, her brothers would drag the tub in from outside and place it next to the kitchen stove and boiling water. But Edna's folks had a real bathroom! Imagine! Indoor plumbing, a bathroom heater and *real* toilet paper. No more slick pages from the Sears catalog!

And no beating the rooster up to pick cotton all day in the hot sun with hands all scratched and bleeding. Mozy intended to be a lady of quality. Living in town meant she'd have store-bought clothes, sliced bread, Cokes with friends at the drug store, ice cream sundaes at the malt shoppe, go to dances, parties and even picture shows when she had a nickel for admission. She'd get a job, then she'd have lots of nickels!

MARY SUZANNE LOPEZ

Tall and skinny, Mozy had green eyes and red, stringy hair. In town, she could get a perm and buy makeup to cover freckles. No more ugly duckling! She'd be a swan, like beautiful silent star, Gloria Swanson and statuesque Theda Bara. Gladys' blue eyes, porcelain skin and strawberry blonde hair wouldn't even be noticed anymore. The boys would be flocking to Mozelle, the new belle of the ball! But then who cared what a bunch of farm boys from Harrah thought? Someday, Mozelle would marry a prince of a man, who would whisk her away to live in the lap of luxury like a Hollywood star. Then everyone would be sorry!

Mozy's pumpkin shattered that first week. She didn't care so much about not having store-bought clothes. She could sew anything! It's that Mozy loved music and Edna got the piano lessons. Though Edna's parents did all they could for Mozy, she promised herself that someday she'd have money, and plenty of it! Like her heroine, Scarlett O'Hara, would say years later in Gone With the Wind, "As God is my witness, I'll never be hungry again, nor any of my folk!"

Mozy was smart enough to see that the new social status symbol in America was the correct use of the English language and education, the key. Plucky Mozelle was going to be somebody! One day, she'd be dripping in furs and jewels and accepted in the finest circles. Yes, one day!

The only professions open to women were teaching, nursing and secretarial work. As a nurse, she might land a doctor. While studying though, she met Joe Cox. Her ambition and strong work ethic could take his small business to new heights! After marrying, she kept books and traipsed all through the seedier parts of town collecting debts Joe would have left go unpaid. He thought grimy shops no place for women and that Mozy should be home cooking, puttering in her garden or sewing some new frock. But energetic Mozelle, who excelled in multi-tasking, took her added load in stride. By 5:30 each morning, the wash was on the line, vegetable and flower gardens were watered and breakfast was

on the table by six. Since they had only the truck, she left with him to be at work by seven. Within thirty minutes of getting home that evening, she had supper ready with nights to sew, read, knit, crochet or embroider. In late summer, she made preserves and canned vegetables.

World War II's demand for crankshafts had Uncle Sam taking bids from companies across America. And Mozy meant to bid on every job! Joe Cox Grinding Works was her chance to carve out a dynasty. The competition made millions, while Joe undecidedly poked along, calling golden opportunities "risky chances."

Mozy decided to call her own shots and went into real estate. In her new 1959 pink Cadillac (which cost around six-thousand dollars), she went to her bridge club and the Tulsa Opera to hobnob with the local upper crust, dripping in diamonds and furs, dahling! But you know the old saying: "You can take the girl out of the country, but you can't take the country out of the girl." When she'd had enough of the snobby elite, she was never happier than in her Victory Garden on Quebec Street, where she grew everything from azaleas to zinnias and apples to zucchini.

———————

Our living in Costa Rica wasn't nearly as hard as losing everything you owned like Grandmother Susie. Though I had little with which to set up house, I still had the kids. I'd make it. *We'd* make it! We were pioneer stock!

There was much to ponder that last week in Santana. All I'd ever wanted in life was a man who loved me and happy, healthy kids. Guess you can't have it all! But as long as the kids' father loved them, and they were happy in Costa Rica, I could stay... really stay and make the best of it. After all, home was where my children were.

CHAPTER SIXTEEN
LIFE IN THE BURBS

We moved in the week before *Semana Santa* (Holy Week). All week, before Easter, churches were packed and platforms carried through streets bearing elaborate, life-sized statues draped in velvet and lace, mostly of the Virgin Mary in a golden crown with fresh flowers around her feet. As the parades snaked down avenues choked with the faithful, dads removed son's hats and mothers helped tots make the sign of the cross.

An American Easter consisted of Easter Bunnies and colored eggs. Roberto liked our traditions, so I had his blessing *and* his money to comb the city looking for what I needed, while he actually stayed home with the kids. There were no long-handled baskets, so I got some without. As for Easter grass... "You want *what...?*" the astonished clerk asked, "...for *Semana Santa?*" I ended up buying whole 3 x 3 sheets of cellophane from the *librería* (book store): pink for my little girl, Michelle, green for outdoorsy David and purple for Chris' burgeoning artistic ability, and meticulously cut them in thin strips at night, while the kids slept.

I bought some individually wrapped Guatemalan chocolate that tasted American, and managed to find some jelly beans. The surprise was the imported chocolate bunnies in colorful foil I happened upon, the last three on the shelf. After filling the baskets, I wrapped them in

cellophane and tied them with bows. The kids knew nothing of the surprise, high in the closet behind Roberto's gun, while we colored Easter Eggs with food coloring that Saturday. I could hardly wait to see their faces when they woke up on Sunday morning and saw what the Easter Bunny brought!

While shopping for these things, I ran into Tia Nina, a plump woman with a comfortably ample lap for children, who said her sister, Lydia, was still pining over not seeing Roberto and the children since the night we left for Santana. How could I tell Doña Lydia that Roberto never wanted to see her again? As a mother, I'd have been devastated by such news.

Easter was a time of forgiveness and new beginnings. How could I not make peace with her? I admit fear and pride nearly stopped me from getting off the bus at the place I'd once called the doorway of hell. I expected Doña Lydia to slam the door in my face. Instead, she received me like a daughter. I, too, acted like nothing had happened between us and merrily pulled out goodies from my rope *bolsas* to show her what I was putting together for the children. She tried not to look bewildered, wondering what strange, foreign ideas could inspire such purchases. "A *rabbit*...? she stuttered, "...that brings colored *eggs* and candy? You're going to do *what* with those sheets of cellophane?" She was positive and enthusiastic about traditions as hollow as the chocolate bunnies wrapped in pretty foil. As we parted with the traditional peck on the cheek, I accepted her invitation for lunch on Easter Sunday, hoping Roberto would come, too. He did. Pulling me aside, there, Tia Nina beamed through her missing front teeth. "Maria, you have done a good thing taking Lydia's side."

"I did it because it was right," I said. "In families, there *are* no sides!"

I visited several schools for Chris and arrangements were made for him to be picked up and dropped off everyday. Until then, we walked the short distance. It was springlike that first day. Chris was late enrolling, and excited to be in first grade. The sweet *directora* (principal) spoke English and had the kids flitting around her like hummingbirds to sugar water as she escorted us to Chris's class. When I entered the room, the class stood, faced me and in unison said, *"Buenos dias, Señora."* I thought they were addressing the principal, but she was still in the hall with my kids. I was glad the school would reinforce the values I'd grown up with. American schools weren't demanding obedience and self-discipline from students or emphasizing respect for authority anymore. When I was a kid, a paddling from the principal got you a worse spanking when you got home.

What kept Costa Rican students in line, of all things, was peer pressure! The general consensus was that next to love and respect for God, parents, and country, excelling in school was a child's highest duty. Classroom disruption, belligerence and rowdiness not only wasn't "cool" but considered, even by first graders, to be childish. If kids went out to play before they did their homework, they were ridiculed by neighborhood kids. If kids were smart enough to get good grades but didn't even try, they were shunned. It seemed to be in the nation's DNA that a lack of education meant a life of poverty. Maybe because if you failed, there was no welfare to sit home and collect. It was sink or swim!

Peer pressure cured Chris of my having to pry him out of bed every morning and prod him every step of the way to make the bus on time. He missed it one day and had to walk. The whole class teased him in unison. "The covers stuck to Chris, today! The covers stuck to Chris, today!"

Chris' problems weren't the culture differences or learning another language. (I thought I'd learned Spanish fast at three months. Chris was communicating in three weeks!) His main problem in school was writing. Printing and the alphabet were learned in the second grade. Right now it was cursive, and each letter had to be perfectly formed with a regular pencil.

"I can't do this!" he said one day at homework, slapping the paper and rolling his pencil across the dining room table.

I was translating his primer and looked up. "Did you know if baby chicks thought like that, you wouldn't have had eggs for breakfast this morning?"

"What's that got to do with homework?"

"Chicks grow up to be chickens and lay eggs, don't they?"

"Yes, but I still don't get it."

"What if they gave up fighting to get out of that egg, even with the tooth God gave them to break the shell and hatch?"

"A tooth?"

"Yes! Haven't you ever heard of something being as rare as hen's teeth?"

"No."

"You're young. You will."

"Hens have teeth?"

"No, chicks have a tooth."

"Really?"

"Really, especially to break the shell. It can take hours of hard work to get out of that egg."

"I'd break it open for him, so it wouldn't have to work so hard to get born."

"But if you break the shell, the chick will die."

"It will?"

"Uh huh. It's the struggle that makes it strong. That's why what you're doing right now is so important. I could do your homework in

about five minutes, but where would that leave you? To be strong and win, you must sometimes struggle."

"If I gave up, the kids at school would think I was a loser."

"Maybe. Would *you* think you were a loser?"

"I would be if I quit."

"And we're not quitters, are we? We're from…"

"I know, Mama," he interrupted, "pioneer stock!"

We laughed and he got back to work.

I attended class with Chris the first few weeks and translated his workbooks, so he could read English when we got back home. Chris knew practically no Spanish and had entered school a month late, but he worked hard, made the honor roll all four quarters and was acknowledged for his efforts in parent/student assemblies. My little chick was pecking!

While I whispered class lectures to Chris, his siblings colored at a nearby table and recessed with kindergarten kids. I went to recess with Chris and helped him answer his classmates' questions. Foreign languages are no big deal for children. They don't care about sounding good, they just want to communicate. At first, Chris' sentences weren't grammatically correct. Instead of, *"Yo quiero ver"* (I want to see), he'd say, *"Mi quiere ver"* (Me wants to see) and *"Estar hablando"* (to be speaking), instead of, *"Estoy hablando"* (I am speaking). But he got his point across to friends who sweetly corrected him. Latinos are very loving.

First grade had fourteen subjects, including woodshop for boys and needlework for girls. Hammers and needles in the hands of six year olds? Daddy used to say, "It's not what a person has in his hand, but the *person* who holds it." I noticed that kids with self-control and respect for others did right by others. Maybe Daddy was right.

ALL THE WAY HOME

When Chris read aloud in English class, his peers treated him like big man on campus. It didn't matter that he already spoke English. Because these children aspired to higher goals, they would gather around him on the playground to learn all they could. For their Californian teacher, in her early twenties, English class was more of a political forum: *La Raza* this and *La Raza* that. She called herself a *Chicano* (whatever *that* was) and insisted the Costa Rican kids call themselves that, too. Somehow, it didn't feel right. But because I knew so few Americans, I tried to befriend her. She'd already made up her mind she didn't like me. Not only was she abrasive to talk to, she was actually mean and hateful. If the U.S. was sending Little "Miss Razas" all over Latin America to represent the U.S., no wonder they hated us! If this was being funded by tax dollars, then congress was hosing us *again!* (Was *that* anything new?)

First grade boys wore navy shorts, white shirts and black leather, high-top shoes. On morning inspections, if shirts weren't starched, ironed, and tucked in, teeth brushed, nails clean, hair combed and shoes polished to a spit shine, kids were sent home until they were. Chris was sent home only once for having dirty shoes. I remembered what Lelo had said, and never let it happen again.

When Chris was established enough in school and I was home with David and Michelle, I'd stay outside while they played, translating for them with neighborhood children. They understood much of what was said to them now, but couldn't answer back, a common pattern in learning a language.

An Italian family lived next door whose daughters had just come from Rome: eighteen year old Cinzia (Chin-cia), and Monica, who was eleven. Their tall, stout and energetic mother, Erica, had laughing eyes and short hair that curled around her face like Gina Lollobrigida. Though Spanish was our common language, she often spoke Italian when we visited her neighbor friends from Rome. Erica taught me to make pizzas from scratch, even the crust. (And I thought they came frozen in a box!)

Like Don Beh, she was superstitious and said the seahorses should stay in the drawer for luck. Her superstitions became a nuisance when I wanted to make a pint-sized bib apron for Michelle. Erica loaned me some straight pins to pin it together. I was about to run it through her sewing machine, when her husband came home for supper. "Maria," Erica said, stopping me at the door, "you forgot my pins."

"*Mañana.*" I said, trying to pass by with the pinned apron.

"You can't leave with my pins," she insisted.

"I'll bring them back!" I laughed.

"The pins aren't important," she said.

"Then what?"

"Leaving with them will bring bad luck to our friendship."

"You can't get rid of me that easy!" I said, trying to gently push my way out her door.

"I'm serious, Maria," she said, blocking me.

"Alright, I'll leave the apron here with you."

"No," she vehemently objected, "that's bad luck, too! The apron is yours. Leave it here and we could end up enemies!"

We could end up enemies if she kept THIS up! I thought.

Dozens of carefully placed pins went back on the paper. Michelle was disappointed when her apron came back in pieces.

I was sweeping the front walk one morning, when Erica hurried over with an ad from the paper. I invited her in and set the broom against the wall next to the door. Flying past me, Erica grabbed the broom and ran it to the kitchen. "Maria," she said, shaking her folded paper at me, "never invite a friend in with a broom by the door. It means you want them to leave and you'd like to sweep them out! Look at this," she went on, never missing a beat, "'WANTED: Homemade goodies for sale in citywide cantinas and grocery stores.' I'm taking my single size pizza. Why not take your sugar cookies?"

"Think they'd like them?"

"Of course! Be ready by noon. My husband will drive us. Cinzia can watch your children."

They didn't want her pizzas. It was Erica's idea and I felt bad for her. But since pepperoni and cheese had zero shelf life, they took my cookies and *Cajetas,* a popular local candy. I made goodies one day and delivered them the next. Roberto was seldom home until after supper and never knew. When he found out I had extra money, he cut my grocery allowance. (From the pairs of movie tickets I found in his shirt pockets and lipstick on his collars, maybe he needed it to buy his girlfriends popcorn!) I'd saved twice to have my ears pierced, but that went to pay the milk and bread delivery. I finally pierced them myself!

At two thousand colones (three hundred dollars) per month, Roberto's pay was better than most. We rented a wringer washer at sixty colones (ten dollars) a month, when for two hundred, a maid would not only wash, iron, and clean, but also be an instant babysitter. Even the rich had few modern conveniences like vacuum sweepers and floor polishers, so fat chance I'd ever have those to do the work myself. A maid was essential and the word went out.

Vicenta, a wiry little woman with fluffy, salt and pepper shoulder length hair, would do day work for me and go home to her family at night. Her husband deserted her, leaving her with four small children, so she moved in with her semi-invalid mother and unmarried brother. She'd rise at three, iron her brother's work clothes and get the heavy wash on the line. Her ten and twelve year old girls did light wash, ironed their own uniforms and cleaned the house. Vicenta left lunch ready in the fridge for her girls to help her mother throw it together and cleaned the kitchen. Vicenta would then ride the bus twenty miles from Cartago, arrive at six and tackle our laundry. Like Margarita, after lunch, she'd iron *everything* (even my underwear) "to kill germs," she said. She'd leave at five-thirty for a second job, catch the last bus home and start over the next morning.

I appreciated Vicenta's hard work and would give her some of the cookies I baked to take home to her kids. After lunch, Chris played with the chemistry set Roberto bought him, while David played soccer with friends on the lot next door. Michelle was usually sleepy and would sit with Vicenta and me, who were hooked on the popular soap, *"Angelitos Negros"* (Little Black Angels). After Chris went back to school, the other two napped and I'd bake, sell cookies or write letters home. Those activities and grocery shopping were best done in the morning, before it rained. Vicenta was happy to watch the kids.

Young boys waited at the mercado entrance to carry a doña's *bolsas* then take them to her car for twenty-five centimos (3.75 cents). With bus fare ten centimos each way, it was hardly profitable to accompany a doña home, but they did it to help their families.

"Can you take me to vendors with the best prices?" I asked.

"*Sí, Señora,*" one answered.

"And go home with me on the bus?" I added.

"*Con gusto* (with pleasure), *Señora,*" he said with a deflated look.

"I'll pay five colones," I smiled.

You'd think I'd just offered him the British Crown Jewels!

"*Cinco?*" he asked.

"Plus bus fare to and from."

ALL THE WAY HOME

With my height and coloring, it was like I was a flashing neon sign: *Rich American, right here! Get your dollars, while they're hot!* Each week, I spent fifty colones on mercado meats, eggs and produce and fifty at the supermarket for toilet paper, soap, sugar and flour, etc. Pedrito, who saved me enough to buy Miracle Whip for the kid's sandwiches and maple syrup for their pancakes, waited for me at that same place for six weeks then disappeared into the misery of the surrounding slums. I hoped God would watch over him.

Roberto wasn't home much with the children and me as we steadily adjusted to life in Costa Rica.

CHAPTER SEVENTEEN
ANGELS UNAWARE

Instead of giving the kids his time and attention, Roberto bought them things: a chemistry set, bikes, a tricycle. Nice toys weren't part of the harsh world of *los barrios* next to where we lived in *las residencias*. Both *barrios* and *residencias* mean "neighborhoods," but they were worlds apart, separated by high walls topped with broken glass or barbed wire. Hardly a day went by that some poor barefoot soul in rags from *los barrios* (poor neighborhoods) wasn't begging at my door, like that older gal in the dingy apron and blue print dress. Her granddaughter wore a dresses two sizes too big and huge shoes when it rained.

Since begging must have been humiliating, I let her go on about how nice my home was though bland and sterile as a hotel room and how darling Michelle was. She prattled on with unnecessary flattery when I'd intended to help all along. I came to dread their frequent visits. Both had short, bushy hair that fell into large finger curls. I dubbed the older woman Curly Locks.

Other people who needed help came straight to the point, like the gardener's wife. *"Señora, perdón la 'molestia'"* (Ma'am, pardon me for 'bothering' you) she said, using that word that always got my attention, "but I wonder if you can help me?"

"I'll try," I said.

"Last night, my husband found two children in a roadside ditch soaked to the skin. After a hot bath, my husband shared his dinner with them, I wrapped them in blankets and they fell asleep. I washed their clothes, hoping they'd dry by morning, but with this humidity, I'll have to iron them dry. It's so cold out. I wondered if you had some clothes your boys have grown out of?"

"Sorry, but...."

"Anything at all?" she pleaded.

I excused myself to at least look and was surprised to find socks and underwear, play shorts and tees, long sleeve shirts, pants and sweaters, even two pairs of shoes. Gazing at me through tear-filled eyes, the gardener's wife made quick bows as she backed away with her treasure. "*Mil* (a thousand) *gracias. Que Dios le pague, Señora. Que Dios le pague.*"

"May God repay you," a cultural phrase everyone used. I didn't help her to get "repaid." But if some good *was* coming, I hoped it would be soon. Instead, things got worse, like the kids' tummy ache turning out to be stomach ulcers. The doctor prescribed Donnatal and asked about stress at home. I played dumb, in case the good doctor was another school chum of Doña Lydia's. When Roberto was home for meals, he rode them hard, especially Chris, whose compliance and obedience was rewarded with abuse.

Don Beh brought over a typewriter and asked me to translate a local magazine. I wasn't proficient enough to translate from English to Spanish, but with my trusty dictionary, Spanish to English would be a piece of cake! I needed the money and hoped it would discreetly connect me with some kind soul who would help get us home. Six weeks later and still unpaid, I quit. Don Vicente got back from a business trip to

England and never came or called to see how the translation was going or picked up the typewriter.

Spunky Vicenta, who'd saved for years to go back to school, gave me her notice, promising to train someone new and the word went out. I could hardly see the eyes of the fifteen year old who applied beneath her curly hair. As she washed at the *pila*, Vicenta smiled in a proud and wistful way, a network of gold fillings sparkling between nearly every tooth. "I was her age when I started."

Since Vicenta got home so late at night, she'd brought a dress to iron in good light. It was drying in the utility room. That Sunday, her oldest was to have First Communion. Vicenta wanted the dress ready ahead of time.

She and I were waiting at the front door for Chris' bus to pull up, when the new maid burst between us clutching a bundle. Vicenta's face dropped and she ran to the utility room. The dress was gone! She ran after the little thief. That dress, worn by everyone Vicenta ever loved, was made from the best fabric they could afford, had no mended places or stains and was to go to her granddaughters, only now it was gone.

That evening, she looked beat down, but wouldn't stay that way for long. Vicenta was a fighter; a survivor!

Before seven a.m. on Vicenta's last day, a young woman knocked at the door. This time, I was more "Latina," cautious and more cynical, if you will. This kind of thievery would *not* be repeated!

Tall and slender Marta, with large eyes and sleek black hair in thick flowing tresses, was sweet natured with children and outwardly calm. Inwardly, she was a nervous wreck, as evidenced by unsightly nails chewed to the quick. My offer of a five and a half day work week brightened her face, which went stoic again. "I do everything but babysit," she said. With clothing and other kinds of factories springing up all over San Jose, young women could get better hours for twice the pay, so I didn't push it. (I did insist she fold sheets so they looked perfect on my shelves.) She could start that day and bring her personal items and bedding the following Monday.

Roberto helped at *his* convenience. But since the little despot's temper tantrums tended to agitate the kids' ulcers, I didn't push it. When he did watch them, he'd count the minutes, anxious to be gone while his children flitted around him like butterflies, hoping for a rare smile of approval. I'd been so busy with the children and my daily tasks, I hadn't noticed his attitude getting worse as he slipped back into his old ways.

One day, I'd waited all afternoon for him to get home and watch the children so I could go buy groceries. He was late.

"It's five now," Roberto said, looking at his watch. "To and from the mercado takes thirty minutes with an hour to shop. Be back by six-thirty."

People were milling about on a corner a block from the bus stop, many standing on tiptoes to see through the double doors. Above, a sign read, CAMPAÑA ESTA SEMANA. At first, "Campaign This Week" made no sense. From the singing and clapping going on inside and out, I'd say they were having a foot-stompin', pew-jumpin', swingin' from the chandeliers revival! (*Campaña* must mean revival.) When I was young, teens would dance rock and roll to this music across the street from tent revivals, because of the loud electric guitars and drums. The folks at this one had the same spaced out, syrupy expressions like the ones back home. I'd seen American Amish downtown with their beards, bonnets and buggies, but never expected to see Holy Rollers in Costa Rica.

One gave me a "come hither" look I blocked with my umbrella and hurried for shelter beneath the spreading branches of *el higarón* (huge fig tree) at the bus stop. All the way to the mercado, I compared what I'd just seen to the dignified English language services at the Baptist church

downtown, where we attended. I thought attending church might help the kids' ulcers.

At the mercado, I literally ran from vendor to vendor. With no boys to carry my *bolsas,* I must have been lugging around about forty pounds. I could hardly hold the umbrella over me in the rain, on the way to the bus stop. Dashing under occasional awnings, one thing was obvious: tonight, I was going to get wet! Ducking into a doorway, I leaned against the heavy wooden door waiting for the light to change. Crouched in a dark corner on centuries-old stone steps, now shallow troughs of rain water, was a young woman covered in a black shawl, clutching a newborn. She froze like a deer in the headlights, her large dark eyes fixed on mine. Besides my bus fare of ten centimos, I had forty centimos (about seven cents) left. Hardly enough to make a real difference to her. It was late. Roberto was waiting! The light changed and I trudged on. My foot was on the first step of the bus when I remembered that my *bolsas* were filled with fruit, cheese, bologna and tortillas. I could at least give her something to eat. At home, I had dry blankets and a safe place to sleep. Maybe I could take her home and find a neighbor who would give her work. People behind were pushing me to board. I backed up and bucked the crowd in the pouring rain to get back to that doorway. She wasn't there. I looked for her all the way back to board the next bus.

From the relative shelter of *el higarón* (the huge fig tree), I could see the mob still milling on that corner and took another way home. Not only were my clothes heavily soaked in the torrential rain, but the brown paper food wrapping and rope *bolsas* were, too. They were so heavy, I was practically dragging them. The handles had cut off the circulation in my fingers. I couldn't set them down to rest, afraid I wouldn't be able to carry them any more. With my fingers beginning to hurt now, I didn't even set them down to knock at the apartment but kicked the door. I expected Roberto to relieve me and take the *bolsas*. (Now, why would I think that?) He only stared at me then looked at his watch. "It's six fifty-two. You're late!"

"Out of my way!" I said, body shoving him and marching to the kitchen. He must have been in a hurry to get to his party, because I'd have normally been decked for that.

When you think of the month of May, flowers and warm days might come to mind. In Costa Rica, it's cold and overcast. We couldn't put on enough clothes to keep warm in our unheated apartment. Writing letters during naptime, I'd gaze out the window at the gray skies and dream of home. Raindrops, I believed as a child were angels' tears, fell in muffled thuds on giant elephant ears in the front garden. I longed for hearth and home, but wrote cheerful letters. Why worry family back home? Besides, they couldn't help me. What I needed was a hot cup of coffee with Erica.

Erica and I went a few doors down to visit her Italian friends, who had suffered a financial setback. The landlord let them sell frozen *recortes* (scraps) from their door until they were back up. These *recortes* were the end pieces of vanilla ice cream layered in chocolate cake from their fancy party cake business. Nothing like chocolate and laughter to cure the blues!

CHAPTER EIGHTEEN

ONCE UPON A DREAM

Don Vicente brought me a wool skirt from England styled like a Scottish kilt. I wore it to a dinner at his house the afternoon of an incident with Tia Nina that set my teeth on edge. She was squeezing David's pudgy cheeks and calling him "cute," something he couldn't stand. "Leave me alone, you skunk!" he yelled. Tia Nina, who couldn't understand English, laughed and pinched him again. When he spit at her, everyone laughed. Latinos encourage such behavior. But to me, it was disrespectful and against everything I'd been taught. "Roberto, stop him!"

"You're not family," he glared. "Stay out of this!"

Roberto ranted for weeks about hating his job. While leaving for work one morning, he paused at the closet door, pointed at the gun and said, "Why don't you do the world a favor this morning and use that on yourself?" Did this foreshadow the tragic newspaper story on everyone's lips?

The news report said a lively three-year old was left home with her father for an hour. This intelligent, beautiful child knew her dimpled

smile and a toss of raven curls could charm her way out of most any mischief, but not today.

Quickly bored of playing with her, the father spread a blanket on the grass next to the driveway, got her some juice and cookies and went back to waxing and buffing his car. Watching children was "women's work." Cars he understood. *Ahh, my pride and joy,* he thought, glorying in his own reflection on the shiny black hood.

Detailing the rear of the car, he heard a strange sound. He peered around to see the girl standing tippy-toe, baby bottle in hand, dripping juice then slapping the finished hood, leaving gooey cookie prints all over his fresh wax job. He held her hands down on the pavement and grabbed the first thing he found. Blind with rage, he came down hard, time after time. Screaming and writhing in pain, she fought to pull away. "I told you to keep your hands off Daddy's car!" Just then, a moist chunk hit his cheek. Wiping it off, he saw blood. He looked down at his baby's pulverized hands and his eyes filled with tears. Turning the hammer on his car, he struck blow after blow!

Somehow, he called the family, got her to the clinic then raced to a remote hill, where he flailed a bottle of Baccardi at the stars and wept bitterly. Her betrayed look! Her screams of pain! If only he could go back and live today over!

Days later, the young father faced the heartrending results of his anger when his baby reached out to him, her bandaged stubs stained with blood. "Make the doctors put my hands back, Daddy. I'll be good."

His wife, now a shell of the beauty he'd married, stroked the doll in her lap and stared emptily into space. Her baby always fingered this doll to fall asleep. How would she sleep, now?

He had traded his child for some chrome and shiny metal. She'd never hold another bottle to feed her doll, stroke the purple velvet ribbon he bought for her hair or hold the chains of her baby swing,

thrilling as Mommy swung her high in the air. Pudgy fingers would never again chase dry cereal around her highchair tray to press between eager lips or struggle with the oversized doorknob to steal into her parent's room on Sunday mornings to cup her hero's face in dimpled hands and say, "I love you, Daddy."

He fled the clinic, self-hatred blinding him with tears of despair. The deep pits left by the hammer's blows were clearer as he neared his parked car. He stood accused by juice and cookie prints of tiny hands that were no more. Up a country road raced the car with the pocked hood. Unable to forgive himself for what he'd done, he crashed his car into a tree and died.

Like that young father, Roberto made rash decisions when life got tough and mostly ran away instead of solving problems. But I feared he would hurt one of the children and think later. Compliant, obedient Chris took the brunt of the punishment. Defiant David was never touched. But Michelle's first taste of her father's wrath came at the age of three and a half when he punched her. "You'll break her arm!" I screamed, running across the room to her.

At two that morning, I was awakened by the muffled echoes of guitars being gently banged on the stairs under the balcony. I thought it was a neighbor's birthday or anniversary serenade until I heard Roberto ask for a favorite of mine, *"Historia de un Amor* (Story of a Love)." I'd have called the police, but serenades were legal. Besides, to quote Lelo: "Police won't even come to investigate a robbery unless you promise them a fifth of Jack Daniels!"

After the customary three songs, Roberto came in. "It'll never happen again," he pleaded, "I promise." He got undressed and laid down behind me. This was something sex couldn't "fix." Pulling away, I shook him off me. "No, no and no!"

"Como que no, no, no (What do you mean no, no, no)?" he said, trying to lighten the mood. It didn't work. "Look, I swore I'd never do

to my children what was done to me," he drunkenly slurred. "I was correcting the kids when Shell giggled. She obviously wasn't listening and I.... Don't abandon me," he sobbed uncontrollably, using the Spanish term in English meaning, "Don't leave me." "I'll do anything!" He buried his face in my gown and soaked it with his many tears, and I fell for it... again.

In the 40's and 50's, there was a color drawing shown on billboards, in picture shows and later on TV, of a family of four in their Sunday best (father and son in hats and suits and mother and daughter in dresses, bonnets and gloves), walking toward a huge white columned church with a tall steeple. Below was a message as American as apple pie: "Take your family to church this Sunday. Remember, the family that prays together, stays together." Was *this* the answer? "Come to church with us Sunday," I found myself saying to him. "Or let's pray, now," I added. (I didn't even know how!)

"I can't pray while I'm drunk. It wouldn't be right!"

"There's a song in the Billy Graham Crusades called, *'Just As I Am.'* Maybe it's okay not to be perfect when you come to God."

"Tomorrow!" he interrupted, stretching and yawning then pulling me close.

Was he serious this time; ready to be a real daddy and husband? I lay awake for hours going over in my mind what I could say to help him understand.

Suddenly, he was up, dressed, and walking out the door. "Leaving already?" I sat up, shaking myself awake.

"I always leave at this time," he coldly answered.

"What about breakfast?" I asked, jumping up.

"I already ate."

"I thought we were going to...."

"Forget the God stuff!"

"But last night...."

"Last night, I'd had one too many," he said, turning to go.

"But you promised!"

"Look, religion is nothing but a crutch priests invented to keep guilt-ridden people coming back and the money rolling in. I spit on priests! I spit on the church!" I froze in shock. "What are you staring at? I spit in the face of God!"

"You shouldn't say such things," I warned.

"Are you judging me?" he yelled.

"No, it's just that you should respect God and His church."

"I heard a priest once preach about wives submitting to their husbands and the 'natural use of the woman.' Instead of going to church all the time, why not concentrate on submitting to me?"

"Our preacher quoted the Bible last week and said husbands and wives should submit to one another as unto the Lord."

"I don't like you going to that church!" he said, then stomped out and slammed the front door.

Lord, if we can't get away from him, at least get him away from us! If that qualifies as a prayer, a funny thing happened the following week. Roberto got a job flying cargo around the Caribbean and would be away for days at a time.

When he *was* home, he'd try to make us late for church by asking for big Sunday breakfasts. I had bus fare for only one way, so we often walked home. The "Church of the Perpetual Revival" was only a block and a half away, but I wouldn't go because of all the wide-eyed zealots. Our weekly hour of peace was at the little Baptist church downtown.

ALL THE WAY HOME

People seemed happy there, the sermons made sense and exposure to good concepts was making me a better person.

In Latin America, lunch is the big family meal of the day, so visitors and phone calls are rare. I'd just served the kids when there came a knock at the door. How irritating! I ran to get rid of the visitor. It was a tiny old man thumbing a brown fedora, his head full of silvery curls, he humbly bowed.

"May I help you?" I asked, hoping he'd hurry.

He looked up with eyes bluer than the skies of Oklahoma. "*Perdón la molestia, Señora,* but I was just released from the hospital and have been walking home all morning to Cartago."

Twenty miles is a two or three-day walk for this guy!

"I wonder, ma'am, do you have some bread and cold water you could spare?" he asked, wiping the wrinkled, long sleeve of his shirt across his brow then resumed thumbing his hat.

"Wait here, please," I said, closing the door. I sugared my glass of tea and filled my plate with fries, salad, rice, black beans, a buttered *bollito*, my *bifstek* and ran it to the door. When the old man saw the food and ice tea, his blue eyes welled to sparkling pools that spilled, leaving curious clean spots on dusty barefeet beneath the frayed cuffs of his trousers. "*Muchimas gracias, Señora,*" he sniffled. "*Que Dios le pague!*"

"I'll check on you, later," I answered.

I filled my own plate with salad, fries, rice and beans and ate with the children. After a while I thought, *he shouldn't be walking. Maybe I've got some money hidden from Roberto from my cookie sales for the old man's bus fare. Why didn't I think of this before?* I rushed it to him but he'd already gone, his empty dishes neatly placed on the polished granite sidewalk next to the door.

I now had a new peace that even Doña Lydia couldn't shake. I noticed it one Sunday afternoon when they all came over for lunch. My Mom used to make the most beautiful meringue pies, while I stood on a kitchen chair watching. She'd masterfully flute the edges, swirl the meringue into high curlycues then bake them a golden brown. When Doña Lydia saw my pies on the buffet, she insinuated my extravagance with her son's money was what made them so pretty. I answered her in love. I even made her laugh. My attitude was improving, while her son's was getting worse.

He had atrocious timing for intimacy, thinking nothing of showing up during the day, demanding what he called a "nooner." The kids and I had just finished lunch, when he arrived home with that big, silly grin. Did he think he could knock me around and later I'd melt like butter? (How come men don't get it?) The kids, thinking his playfulness was for them, swarmed him for attention. He swept me into the doorway of our bedroom. Chris, who was sitting on our bed, wanted to show his daddy the "A" he got, but Roberto ignored him. After all, a man's needs come first! "There's no lock on our door, honey" I smiled, gently resisting. "Let's wait till tonight." His "playfulness" vanished! Trying to edge through the door between us and get out before the fireworks started, Chris was punched in the chest. He had on his uniform shorts, so his bare legs stuck and screeched, stuck and screeched as they scooted across the hardwood floor. Finally stopping, he leaned back on his hands and looked up at his daddy, afraid to move. "See what your mother did to you?" Roberto said. He left in a huff and stayed gone until late that night.

I comforted Chris first, whose bus was due by any minute, while David stood at the front door, shaking his fist and Shell waved bye-bye and cried.

ALL THE WAY HOME

I'd no sooner gotten Chris gone and closed the door, than there came a knock at the door. Curly Locks? Not now! I was emotionally upset and my kids needed comforting. I slammed the door!

With escaping constantly on my mind, I began having strange dreams: I'd run, but in slow motion, walk in the rain and not get wet; be in my bathing suit on a sunny beach shivering in knee-deep snow, yet feel toasty warm; rooms were dark, yet brightly lit; I'd be in a crowd, and yet alone and people always had blurred faces. Maybe you've had dreams like that.

I had the same dreams over and over. In one, I was going through a desert to meet the kids someplace where we could escape. Riding horseback then running on foot, I dodged cactus, rattlesnakes and wild redskins after my scalp. Upon climbing a summit overlooking a valley, I could see passengers boarding a Flash Gordon-type airship about to take off. I ran down the mountain. *I'll never make it!* "Wait!" I shout, running and holding my aching side. "Don't leave me!" As I get to the boarding platform, the ship rises slowly into the air in puffs of smoke and sparks. *I'm too late!* I watch it circle low. *At least the children are safe, now.* I search the passing windows of the ship for their faces; then it disappears behind a smoking volcano. I'm turning to leave, unsure of where to go or how to get along, when Roberto steps from the shadows, the children in hand. They didn't escape after all! He comes toward me. He's angry. I awake in a cold sweat!

My most prevalent dream took place in the 1800's at a royal ball in some ornate European palace, undoubtedly influenced by Aunt Mozy's incessant tales of princesses dancing nights away in billowy gowns. Faces are blurred and conflicting scenes seem surreal.

In my dream, mirrors reflect the glitter of silver service, shimmering crystal chandeliers and elaborate gold candlesticks as tall as a man. Only the toes of my blue slippers show beneath ruffled pantalets as I descend the staircase of the grand ballroom. My gown, like clouds and sky, is a

ruffled vision of white lace on powder blue. I can understand wearing silk stockings to hide my ankles from the roving eyes of men who are gentlemen in name only, but why a horsehair crinoline on such a warm evening? Mother insisted! I fan myself as I brush by gilded tables lining mirrored walls in the new hoop skirt Father has just bought me. He says whalebone hoops make a softer, more ladylike sound, when going through doors and brushing by furniture, than metal or cane hoops.

My long hair, swept up in back, is fastened by combs with silk, peach-colored camellias attached. Store-bought "English ringlets" cascade down my swan-like neck, where a ribbon holds an Italian cameo pendant to match my earrings.

I dance Strauss waltzes with a dozen blurry faced young men. They tell me, "Prince Charming is here," and I blush behind my fluttering fan, embarrassed by my scandalous thoughts of him. Suddenly, the Prince stands before me. The very air throbs to the strains of Strauss' "Tales From the Vienna Woods." Gliding beneath crystal chandeliers shining in the candlelight, I catch our reflection as we gracefully whirl down mirrored halls, past golden candlesticks tall as a man, he in a dark blue uniform with gold embroidery and I in flurried cascades of powder blue and white.

Is it love or the melodic grandeur of the music? He stares at me, his dazzling smile coming and going in a blur. He opens his mouth to speak of his undying love for me, is tapped on the shoulder, bows and withdraws.

The rough, ill-mannered man, whose face is blurred waves to the orchestra and takes me in his arms. *I can't follow this! Who can? He's trying to waltz to Mussorgsky's "Night on Bald Mountain!"* He's no mountain unfurling its wings who's really the devil, but close. The blurred face suddenly revealed matches the macabre music. It's Roberto's!

Running away, I lose a slipper. Afraid to go back, I kick off the other and bolt into the crowd lining the empty hall. Snuffed-out candles burn,

casting images on opaque mirrors, reflecting a dazzling light. Breathless, I run with ease beneath the glitter of dull chandeliers and diminutive gold candlesticks tall as a man.

The faster I run, the slower I go. My flailing arms and kicking feet produce "wing-lift" and I'm airborne. "Swimming" the breaststroke takes me higher. Roberto jumps and grabs my bottom hoop. I plummet in slow motion. Reaching back, I unhook skirt, hoop and all and let them drop. Covering him like a giant, heavy net, they send him tumbling. He throws it off, raises his fist and curses as I fly away.

Ten to twelve feet high, my feet are still lower than the rest of me. He jumps, his fingers brushing my ankles. I "swim" like crazy to attain greater altitude. There's a staircase ahead, leading nowhere. Landing halfway up, I turn. Roberto runs up the stairs toward me. There's a revolver in my hand. I raise it and fire! The middle of his face explodes in blood and smoke.

I'm shocked awake.

Weeks of sleeplessness from recurring nightmares, that thirty pound weight loss months earlier, compounded by stress and fear, threaten a physical and mental breakdown. Unfit for company, I began keeping to myself just when I needed a friend the most. Then one day I had no sooner sat down on the bus when I heard, "Nice day, isn't it," an American woman said a little too cheerfully then sat down beside me.

"Certainly is," I politely said, trying to be nice.

"Going far?" she asked.

"Mercado Central." My tone was better. "And you?"

"To Sears for some cotton dresses."

"That's nice." I hadn't had anything new since David was born.

"Polyester doesn't work down here, does it?" she quipped.

"Not on hot, humid days," I laughed, lightening up.

"I need cool clothes to help my husband in his work."

As the bus pulled away from *el higarón*, my tone changed to warm and sunny. It wasn't *her* fault I married a jerk! While growing up, "bastard" was said to be a "seven-letter" word like hell and damn were four-letter words. "Husband" was my new seven-letter word. But I'd be nice and use that dirty word anyway. "What does your husband do?"

Practically lying across my lap, she pointed at the "Church of the Perpetual Revival," its store front façade gleaming white in the sun. The banner above its double doors in bold red print read: CAMPAÑA ESTA NOCHE (REVIVAL TONIGHT)!

Crap, a Holy Roller! I knew absolutely nothing about their exact beliefs. But taught to despise them, I turned away and looked out my window.

"Have you visited our church?"

I returned a long silence.

"No," she answered herself. "I'd have remembered you. You'd like it. The blind receive their sight, the lame walk, and the weary find a friend."

I could use a friend all right, but not her!

"The Father loves you," she added.

I must look pathetic for her to approach me like this. "I hate the word 'father!' All mine ever did was beat me!"

"When parents forsake you, the Lord will take you up."

My hateful expression must have said it all, because she stopped talking. As she stood to exit the bus, she laid her hand gently on my shoulder. "Remember, you're never alone. Jesus or His angels are always with you."

No thanks! I thought, returning her smile with daggers. I needed REAL answers, not pie in the sky by and by and make-believe "friends!" Was I ever glad to get rid of *her!*

Waiting in one of the five lines crowding the mercado butcher shop and thinking bad thoughts about that busybody, someone yelled out their order from the back and was served. Thinking this rude, inconsiderate and disorderly, I did what Americans are taught to do from childhood: I kept quiet, waited in line and ignored the other rude people shouting out their orders. When customers did make it to the counter, they were greeted with a cheerful, *"Y como se le ofrece, negra"* (And how may I help you "negra?") I'd heard people call their kids, spouses and friends that as an endearing term. Once the culture shock wore off and I understood how it was used, it sounded so sweet that I secretly wished someone would call me that.

It was nothing personal to merchants, who used it with anyone and everyone all day long. But to me, who desperately needed a kind word, this was the closest thing to feeling loved and accepted I had. So, when the butcher in the bloody apron said, *"Y como se le ofrece negra"* to me, it nearly took my breath away. If not for my pioneer stock stiff upper lip, the tears would have flowed!

CHAPTER NINETEEN
HOPE DEFERRED

Roberto punched Michelle again one day after lunch. She'd been cranky, but that was no excuse. "Daddy didn't mean it, baby," I consoled, the words sticking in my craw. Once I got Chris off to school and the little ones down for a nap, I cocooned myself in the majestic chords of Handel's "Messiah."

Still reeling from Roberto's cruelty, I sat half stunned through the "Comfort ye's," "Rejoice ye greatlys," and "Surely He hath borne our griefs and carried our sorrows." It was "Glad tidings of good things" that made me mad enough to fight back. The only glad tidings I wanted were four tickets home! The next seven minutes of Handel's masterpiece made me mad enough to kill, then dumped the very means to do so in my eager lap!

I was washing my hands in the kitchen to the bass air with a rhythm so perfect for scrubbing, I sang as I lathered and rinsed, making up my own words.

"Why do Roberto and I so furiously rage together?
Why does he imagine such vain things?"

The next chorus reminded me of the Gordian Knot.

"Let me break his bonds asunder,
and cast away his yoke from me."

During the tenor recitative, I sang and imagined God taking hold of "Baron" Roberto and shaking him until his teeth rattled!

"He that dwelleth in heaven shall laugh him to scorn;
the Lord shall have him in derision."

Holding that last note, I sang, "Whatever derision is,... and I hope it's bad!"

The tenor air had me grabbing the basket of clean clothes and marching to my bedroom. With the kids asleep, I could only sing with muffled gusto, picking folded clothes up and slamming them onto shelves in anger to the rhythm to the music.

"I shall break him with a rod of iron;
I shall dash him in pieces like a potter's vessel."

Boy, was I ready for a scrap!

Socks and underwear hit the shelves on beat. The air ended with one sheet left in the basket. Grabbing it, I slammed it onto the stack of sheets high in the closet, my thumb inadvertently sliding into a metal circle on the final note. I knew exactly what I'd hit. *The answer to all my troubles!* I clutched it to me as the chorus singers exploded in song! "Hallelujah, hallelujah, hallelujah, hallelujah, hal-le-lu-jah!" The same glorious music that once brought a king to his feet, had me sinking onto the edge of the bed, my thumb still in the trigger guard of Roberto's Walther PPK.

I was just imagining myself standing over Roberto's body, smoking gun in hand, when Daddy's voice boomed, "I'd better never hear of you shooting someone out of anger, vengeance or malice!" I placed the gun back in the stack of perfectly folded sheets, (obedience, remember?)

closed my bedroom door and curled up in that fetal position I swore I'd never catch myself dead in. *I've been at this for a long time, now. I* thought. *When is the "struggle" supposed to make me strong? When do I break free from all this? Cut the Gordian Knot? What's the use? I wouldn't have the strength! Oh, why was I even born? Esa no es vida, es un bidet!* I shut out the soprano singing about worms eating somebody's dead flesh for a song that offered some hope. "No matter how your heart is grieving, if you keep on…," but I couldn't believe; not anymore.

Later that week, I was out with Nena and mentioned how violent Roberto had been all along and how unhappy I was living in Costa Rica. Of all people, I thought she'd understand. "Maria, if you're so unhappy, why did you ever come here?"

This could get back to Roberto. I stopped seeing friends, hardly ate and began spending much of my day in bed, except for going to the grocery store. And I'd have gotten out of that if I could. But Marta didn't do grocery shopping. I wish she had, because I could hardly function in public now.

One day, a seven-year-old and her little brother stopped me inside the supermarket, asking for *una limosna*. I'd never heard that word. My mind was so muddled with my own troubles, I thought she asked for *un limón* or a lemon. The manager walked up just as I figured it out. "I thought I told you not to come in here and bother customers." They were asking for "alms." I didn't follow them out the door to give them money.

Later, I noticed a missionary we knew in another checkout line sporting a broad smile that sometimes broke into a laugh, trying to engage others in conversation. Housewives and maids, looked at him suspiciously, not making eye contact and hardly giving him a nod or answering his questions. I should have helped him, but I couldn't. I couldn't help those children. I couldn't even help myself.

I'd burned myself out trying to get out of Costa Rica. A verse from that tiny Bible was almost audible: *"God heals the brokenhearted and*

binds up their wounds." If only it were true! Where *was* God? Where had He been my whole life? I'd looked for Him everywhere!

While I was growing up, except for curses, God was hardly mentioned in our home. The first time I heard God's name in a good light was when they put Him in the Pledge of Allegiance and the adults were so pleased. I learned about Jesus in kindergarten. Remember the song we sang after saluting the flag?

> "Jesus loves the little children,
> All the children of the world,
> Red and yellow, black and white,
> They are precious in His sight,
> Jesus loves the little children of the world."

I figured if Jesus loved all those kids, who was I not to? Still, the song was confusing. I'd seen brown people downtown, but never any red or yellow ones. I liked black horses, but couldn't imagine black children. As for white ones, I'd only seen one, (an albino girl) who had white hair and pink eyes. Strange the song never mentioned pink children like me or the brown people downtown. From then on, I decided to be especially kind and understanding to all "white" children from then on. Because as hard as it must have been to be red, yellow or black, having no color at all must be terrible. Poor little things! They couldn't help it!

School was where I also learned not everyone was Baptist. By junior high, I'd seen lots of Catholics but never a Jew. I heard Jews were all rich and looked different. I looked for one, but everyone looked alike. As far as the Jews killing Jesus, Aunt Mozy cleared that one up. "Jews in the Bible," she said, "referred to the religious leaders and priests. Besides, if Christians hated Jews, why pick a Jewish Messiah or make the New Testament out of letters from a rag-tag bunch of Jewish peasants?" Aunt Mozy knew everything! Some said Jews were intolerant of other religions. But Jews in our school reverently bowed their heads and listened

during readings from the Old *and* New Testament before class and following prayers. One covered his head with one hand. No one teased him or objected. Live and let live and respecting our differences was how America was supposed to be.

A parochial school in Alexandria, Louisiana, was where I made my best grades. The nuns expected it! One day, I heard whispers that I was a Protestant and didn't believe in the Virgin Mary. I did so! She was the mother of Jesus! Besides, I wasn't Protestant (whatever that was)! I was Baptist (whatever that was)!

The school was across a field from our backdoor. I went to church every morning before class, only they called it mass. I liked how ornate it was inside; inspiring paintings in gilded frames, lifesized sculptures of Jesus, Mary and the saints, lighted candles and fresh flowers. I'd sit by Sister Mary Frances, who was serious in church and playful everywhere else. When girlfriends told me nuns were bald, she took me inside and lifted her veil. "See? It's just cut short."

She took time to be with me (something my parents didn't do). I believed she loved me. During church, she'd lend me her small rosary and use the one on her belt. I didn't know how to pray the rosary. I just wanted to be like her. At the end of the service, they'd have an alter call. The nuns and kids went forward and the pastor, they called a priest, placed on the tongue of each, a thin white circle called a wafer. Sister said it was the Body of Christ. I didn't know how He got in there, but believed it because I loved her. Not being Catholic, I wasn't allowed to take communion but listened from the pew as the priest held the wafer high above him, speaking words I couldn't understand. I didn't understand the whole service. Sister said it was Latin. My parents spoke Pig Latin to each other when we were little. I could understand their not wanting us to know what they had to say, sometimes. Only why wouldn't *God* want us to know His words?

ALL THE WAY HOME

Inside the cavernous church, echoes distorted every sound. In one part of the mass, it sounded like the priest said, "It-way, Ott-way, Chicken-way." These words must have been very holy, because everyone was quiet and reverent. I hoped God saw I was reverent, too, that I was there everyday and I loved Him, too.

After church, the kids made a mad dash for the prefabs set up for the lower grades, where boxes of doughnuts awaited the faithful. I wasn't allowed those either, but I didn't mind. God had already slipped me the "secret wafer" I'd asked Him for.

As an Air Force brat, we moved a lot. That next year, we were in San Antonio, where I was again alone and friendless. Most of the kids spoke Spanish among themselves, shutting out anyone who wasn't Latino.

A major appliance box in the yard of our apartment, waiting to be picked up, gave me an idea. I'd need crayons for stained glass windows, paintings and "statues" of Jesus and Mary with their crowns and halos, a shoebox for an altar and one of Mama's embroidered tea towels to cover it (I asked first, of course). I didn't ask for the birthday candles and matches, and I don't think she'd have approved of that piece of bread I planned to squash with my fingers into circles for wafers. (I didn't know then that communion bread is unleavened.)

After working all afternoon on the little chapel, I slipped inside to hold my "service," hoping to find the same love I'd felt before. I lit the candles and lifted the wafer high like the priest, repeating his words exactly as I'd heard them, "It-way, Ott-way, Chicken-way." What I really wanted to say was, "Please God, send me a friend like Sister Mary Frances."

Mama must have needed God, too, because she began taking us to church. With their failing marriage more apparent by the time I was twelve, she began dropping us at church to stay home trying to talk some sense into Daddy. Finally, she said what our family needed was baptism. "After all, families that prayed together, stayed together." (We never prayed together. Maybe that's why we didn't stay together.) No one explained the significance of baptism to me, so maybe it didn't "take." But when Mama said *jump*, all you asked was *how high?* I was baptized twice before the divorce. The second time, Mama must have forgotten it was "taboo" to wear the devil's color to church. Climbing the baptistry steps after she was dunked, her red underwear showed through the wet, clinging robes. Poor Mama! No one laughed. I don't think laughter was allowed. Squirming in church was especially taboo. If you so much as reached up to scratch your nose, people either side of you on your pew looked to see who was moving!

By eighteen, I had a lot of questions, like which religion was God's? Aunt Mozy said if you were American and Baptist, you automatically went to Heaven. That's the only thing she ever said that didn't ring true. I tried every religion only to find they were made up of people didn't seem to care about the new kid on the pew. Aunt Mozy said *care* is the most important word in the English language, more important than *love*. She said caring puts action to love. Otherwise, love is just another word.

Aunt Mozy knew a lot about words, even the forbidden "F" word. In the late 50's, rock and roll singer Gene Vincent was supposed to have sung it three times in his hit song, "Woman Love." (I never actually heard it. I was in the eighth grade and not allowed to listen to rock and roll.) But I heard he was fined fifty thousand dollars and forbidden to record or perform for six months. Then in the late sixties and early seventies, like pimple-faced adolescents trying to shock their parents with "adult" words, film markets couldn't get enough "F" words, in movies! Aunt Mozy said the use of that word may have begun back when Pilgrims put people in pillory and stocks for offenses like drunkenness, laziness, breaking the Sabbath and peeping in windows, etc. and posted the offence. One offence was so long and had to be written small to be seen from a distance, it was abbreviated: "For Unlawful Carnal Knowledge." (You figure out the rest.)

Aunt Mozy not only knew lots about words, she knew just about everything else. Why, she drove all the way to Louisiana once to talk Mama out of letting me become a Catholic. Funny, but that religion probably saved my life.

By the time I graduated from high school, Mama, Daddy and Aunt Mozy all had new spouses. I spent that summer "partying" with Latinos from the University of Tulsa. After months of wild living, I came to myself and turned to church. Immaculate Conception was two blocks from Uncle Joe's. Since the doors of Catholic churches were always open, maybe I'd find God there.

That sunny autumn day, tree shadows lining the playground of Immaculate Conception School stretched across the street into the Safeway parking lot. Instead of going to the grocery store, I pulled my coat tight against the cold, fall wind and pressed northward, dry leaves swirling and tumbling past me.

Inside, the church was warm, quiet and peaceful. I liked solitude, the way the light of late afternoon shone through the stained glass windows and the soft glow of prayer candles. I liked the free standing statue of Mary holding the baby Jesus on one side of the pulpit, a solitary Mary on the other and an inspiring, life-sized image of Jesus on the Cross suspended behind the pulpit.

Two nuns were praying up front, so I quietly slipped into a back pew and knelt to whisper a prayer Sister Mary Frances had taught me years before. "Hail Mary, full of grace, the Lord is with thee. Blessed art thou amongst women and blessed is the fruit of thy womb, Jesus. Something Mary, Mother of God, Something, something, something and at the something, something, something. Amen." I'd forgotten!

Determined to relearn that and more, I decided to join the church. The Irish priest wouldn't let me slide through the infallibility of the Pope (who was fallible before he was Pope) and that you had to pray to Mary to get to Jesus to get to God. I flunked catechism five times, but carried

my two rosaries for months, as they had a crucifix and I was scared of vampires. That October was the scariest Halloween night I'd ever seen. The fall air was cool, a huge full moon hung low among leafless, gnarled oak branches and thick fog crept along the ground threatening to swallow you up.

Along with the Latino students, I'd also met some from the Middle East I never dated. One kept phoning. It was a dark February evening when the bus reached my stop from the downtown uniform shop I managed. There were two and a half blocks to walk in that fierce storm of '62. The sting of sleet numbed my face and legs as I trudged up the hill toward Country Club Drive. Halfway there, a car pulled up. "Get in. I'll take you home," a voice called from inside.

I was surprised to see Mohammed, who was either from Iran or Iraq.

"I brought my friends to meet you. Get in."

I looked in at the two young men with the scowling faces in back. Something inside me said no. "Thank you. I can walk."

"Nonsense, you're freezing!" The one in front jumped in back, leaving the door open. "You can't walk in this! Get in!"

I *was* freezing! Mohammed had phoned me lots of times and seemed nice, so I got in. "That's my uncle's house," I said as we pulled around the corner. "Wait, we're passing it!"

No one spoke. A block before Immaculate Conception, I tried to open the door and jump. The guy in back reached up and stopped me. The two in back jabbered angrily away. I didn't have to understand their language to know I was in deep do-do! I pulled out my black rosary, fingered the beads and silently prayed. *Holy Mary, Mother of God, pray for us sinners now and at the hour of our death, hour of our death, hour of our death, hour of our death…. God, where are you? Help me!*

ALL THE WAY HOME

We drove into the hills over Tulsa to an empty field off a lonely country road. Mohammed parked and turned off the engine.

He'd watched me with my beads from the corner of his eye and said something to his friends that made them furious! I don't know how they heard his soft voice over their yelling. He turned the engine back on and drove me home in silence.

Did my beads remind Mohammed of Islam? Did my calmness and quietness remind him of his mother, sisters or grandmother? Had his parents taught him the virtues of decency and honor? Whatever it was, I was thankful.

———————

I didn't tell the kids when the Fourth of July came around. Besides, fireworks were only sold at Christmas, and I forgot to buy any for the Fourth thinking we'd be back in Tulsa. We couldn't have done fireworks anyway with all the rain. A damp chill hung over the city much of that month. David and Michelle caught colds, Marta went home with the flu so her mother could take care of her and later, I'd be sick, too. Roberto wouldn't be much help even if he were there! (So what else was new?) The pot of soup I'd made and the sandwich fixings would get us to Monday when Marta returned.

It was Saturday and just getting dark. The kids were out playing and I was finishing preparing Chris' uniform for Monday, when I felt someone behind me and turned. No one was there. Unable to shake the feeling, I kept turning and looking and finally saw a figure shrouded in black filling the doorway. I blinked and it vanished.

I spent all day Sunday sick, and was wiped out by bedtime. Shell had been waking me up with tales of monsters walking on the wall outside their window. I'd already told her it was a possum and hoped she wouldn't wake me tonight. I must have had a high fever, but all I had were some baby aspirin I was saving in case the younger kids, who

had slight colds, needed it. I spent the night in cold sweats, which soaked my gown and sheets.

Chris was well, so I packed him off to school Monday. It was still dark when his bus pulled away and I stumbled back to bed. While closing the bedroom door, I glanced up in the open closet and recalled Roberto's taunting words. "Why don't you do the world a favor this morning and use this on yourself?"

Why not? I thought. *It's the only way I'll ever get out of here!* I can still feel the coolness between those sheets as my hot hand searched for the gun. Fevered fingers touched cold steel and shocked me back to reality. *My children will be left with a monster!* I thought. *The last memory of their mother will be my brains splattered all over the wall! I can't do it!* The gun went back among my perfectly folded sheets.

Crawling back in the damp bed, I pulled cold covers to my chin and searched beyond the ceiling, where God's supposed to be. *Where are you?* I thought and whispered the holiest words I knew, "It-way, Ott-way, Chicken-way," then waited and listened. Nothing happened. David once said, "If you want something from God, maybe you're 'possa ask, first!" Okay, here goes!

"God, if You're real... if You really exist... help me!"

A silhouette appeared against the ugly teal drapes that dawn's light always made a pretty blue. Was it a man? I dabbed away the blur of tears with the sheet. It *was!* Roberto wasn't going to like this at all! (I'd hit a new low. I was more worried about what he'd say than my own safety!) The figure had white hair, a burnished gold beard and glowed hot white all over. He was leaning across my middle on one arm like someone visiting a sick friend. We began moving upward like on an elevator. *I must be dead, and didn't even need a gun!* I thought. *If I am, my body will still be on the bed.* I wanted to look down but couldn't. His eyes shone like stars and in His gaze I felt enveloped in love. Just above the ceiling, we stopped. *Did he change his mind? Am I being sent the "other way?"*

I stole a glance downward. *It's me! Am I...? I don't feel dead!.* My eyes searched His for the answer.

"Do you want to go home?" He said telepathically.

"Oh, yes!" I answered the same way.

"Would you believe me if I said you'd be home soon?"

"Yes, sir. I mean, look who You are!"

"Then you'll be home on Thursday."

Dreamy-eyed, I looked past him and sighed, "Home!"

"That's right. Now, smile big for me!"

I beamed back.

"Now laugh!" He said.

"Sir, I haven't laughed in a long time."

"I know. Do it for me."

Mama had always quoted the Bible verse, "A merry heart doeth good like a medicine." But I'd never heard, "The joy of the Lord is my strength." I now think He was trying to get me to laugh so I'd get better. Then He cracked a one-liner and I was horrified! I couldn't laugh at HIM! He kept cracking one-liners. I could hardly keep a straight face. The last one finally got me. My head went back and I belly laughed. When I pulled myself together, He was gone and I was back in my body. *Rats! I didn't get to ask that "important" stuff I always wanted to know, like why men don't "get it," why God gave them all the upper body strength and why I married that turkey in the first place?*

My fever was gone. I sat up on the side of the bed. What happened couldn't be real. I'd been delirious with fever. This was just another weird dream.

I didn't think about it again. A few days later, Roberto, on one of his rare days home for lunch, accused me of smiling too much. "You're trying to kill me aren't you?"

"What?" I said, taken aback.

"You found out that slowly increasing arsenic in my food will give me a heart attack, didn't you?" He went through every shelf and drawer. "If you think you're going to put a hole in me like you did that rock in Coto," he said, emptying his gun and sliding the shells into his pocket, "you can forget it, hot shot!" He left and I got the ulcer medicine for the children, who were upset and crying.

One evening, a week later, Roberto happened to be home when the phone rang. What made him run for it was his own guilty conscience. "For you," he said, disappointed it wasn't my "secret lover." Instead of staying to listen, he went outside to watch the kids play. Watch the kids play? Put *that one* in the miracle column!

"Hello?" I said above the usual static.

"Mary Sue?" came a scratchy voice, crackling on the wire.

"Aunt Mozy?"

"No time to chit-chat. This is costing me a fortune! In the past week, I've had three dreams that you're dead or dying. Are you all right?"

"No," I said, letting it drop. I wasn't about to humiliate myself by begging for tickets again!

"Do you want to come home?"

"Not without my kids!"

"That's four tickets isn't it? Where do I send them?"

Not knowing whether to be dumbfounded or flabbergasted, I finally stuttered, "The Pan Am office in San Jose."

ALL THE WAY HOME

Audrey Mozelle, the skinny girl from an obscure little Oklahoma farm town. Mozy, the freckled-faced kid with stringy red hair the fancy girls didn't befriend. Mozy, the ugly duckling boys wouldn't date. Mozelle, the girl with the fancy French name who dreamed of being "somebody." Mozelle, whose name is the feminine version of Moses was to be our deliverer.

Roberto was home again for lunch a week or so later, when the phone rang. I sat closer to it, but he jumped up and ran around the table to answer. "Señora DeBenedictis, por favor."

"This is Señor DeBenedictis," he answered in Spanish.

"Tell her her four tickets to the United States may be picked up at the Pan Am office at her convenience."

He'd turned red plenty of times before, but never purple! A huge vein wormed its way down his forehead and two up the sides of his neck thick as a finger. I used to love the way Ricky Ricardo's eyes bulged when he was mad on "I Love Lucy." Roberto's eyes were bulging, now only I wasn't laughing, and neither was he!

"How dare you go behind my back? I've half a mind to hire some goons to give you the bum's rush up the side of the Irazú and toss you in!" (He had half a mind, all right!) His threat wasn't original. The papers had reported a man doing this to his wife a while back. "I'm supposed to be the provider! I'm supposed to do these things!" *Why don't you then?* I thought. "You're my responsibility! I'm man of this house! Return those tickets. If you want to visit the States this bad, I'll borrow the money from Tia Soledad. (*His responsibility?* And his aunt *pays* for it?) From now on," he continued, "I read all letters to and from the States."

Maybe God was looking out for me when I returned those tickets. I'd forgotten about the Patronato paper and would have been arrested.

A week later, Aunt Mozy called nearly hysterical. "Mary Sue, Pan Am called! You returned the tickets! What happened?"

"Roberto found out."

"God, no! What can we do?"

"I've been thinking," I said. "I've crossed into Panama several times without papers. Send the tickets to Panama City."

"Do you think you can still cross?"

"I know of four ways: by boat from Golfito to Panama's Puerto Armuelles, which I can also reach through the jungle by jeep or motorcar. The fourth way I'll only attempt if Roberto blocks the others: through the swamps by mule."

"Is there no other way but by sea or jungle?"

"No ma'am."

"You mustn't! It's too dangerous!"

"I'll work out the details. Meanwhile, make sure you only write me about everyday subjects in your letters, like the weather, your health, Mom's travels, etc. Put the 'real stuff' on a separate sheet of paper that I can destroy. Roberto is reading everything."

The next months were spent in careful planning. Nothing must be allowed to go wrong. She wrote regularly, then I didn't hear from her. She was old. What if she...?

November 23, 1971.

Dear Aunt Mozy,

I've waited to hear from you. I wrote a long letter two or three weeks ago about a plan I have to leave. With no word from you, I wondered if you got my letter? I MUST know if you did! Down here, tampering with the mail is no big deal. When I took

your letter to the post office, the clerk who took it said, "Ah, Mrs. Roberto DeBenedictis," like he'd made prior arrangements with Roberto to intercept my mail. I know it sounds farfetched and melodramatic, but I wouldn't put it past him. I simply don't trust him!

In your last letter, you said, "not to lie" about all this. Your letter hurt me. I have not written any "untruths" nor "exaggerated" in the least. Roberto is a complete monster who's treated me like a prisoner since I've been here! I don't think you realize how cruel some people can be. You wouldn't believe the things he's said and done to the children and me. As for your question, "Am I sure, this time?" The only reason I ever told you I was going to stay was that I got tired of begging him to let us go, figuring, if you can't beat 'em, join 'em! When he began hurting the kids, I knew it was impossible to stay with someone I can't even stand to touch me. It's hard to explain these details on paper. (I was afraid the letters were being read.) I hope I'll soon be there to explain everything, including the (new) faith that this horrible nightmare won't go on forever. I should be there after December 1st. Wish me luck. You don't know how scared I am! Crossing Roberto is like crossing the Devil, himself!

The kids are fine. They remember you and talk about you and your house and the Indian beds (you made them) all the time. They don't know about the plan. I won't tell them till we're far from Costa Rica and nearing my "T-town" (Tulsa). God help us!

Love to you all. Hoping to see you soon!
Mary Sue

Sure I was planning something, Roberto showed up at odd hours to search the house. "What are you hiding?" he demanded one day, taking me by the throat. David was outside, jumping his bike on construction site hills across the street or both boys would have jumped in. Chris stepped forward and Roberto punched him in the chest, knocking the wind out of him.

Next day, I left the little ones with Marta, while they napped. The embassy receptionist asked my business. "I'd like to see the Consul on private business."

"He's busy. Can the Vice Consul help?" She ushered me into an office where a portrait of President Nixon hung over a large desk with American Flags on either side, fringed in gold. I stared at Old Glory until the Vice Consul entered. "Good afternoon," he smiled, reaching for my hand. "May I help you?"

"Sir, over a year ago, while I was at work, my Costa Rican husband took our children from the States and brought them here. I came after them and he promised to send us home, but now he's keeping us against our will. He's violent and getting worse. I need the embassy's help to get us home. We'll sit on the floor of a military transport. Just please, get us out!"

The Vice Consul paused; his finger tips came together at his lips, as if in prayer. He was troubled by the embassy's policy and what he had to say. "There's nothing I can do."

"But we're American citizens!"

"I'm sorry," he said, his expression kind, but stern.

I sighed, collapsing backward into the leather wingback.

"Political repercussions over domestic disagreements can cause international incidents," he continued. "Your situation is not uncommon. Three months ago, twin girls were stolen by their Argentine father and taken to Argentina. The mother's gotten nowhere with that government or her husband, who has political connections and has barred her from entering the country. She might never see her girls, again."

"Can *nothing* be done to help her?"

"Women don't realize these difficulties when they marry foreign men. Our hands are tied."

"Even in cases of extreme violence?" I added.

"What do you mean?"

"Before I feared for my life. Now, it's the children's."

"Are they on your passport?"

I shook my head and lowered my eyes, thinking all was lost.

"Can you get photos taken of you and the children?"

A few days later, I was back for my newly issued passport. The kids' picture was more like a mug shot: Chris looking downtrodden, Shell lost and forlorn and David ready to bite anyone who came near him!

"What I'm about to tell you now is confidential," the Vice Consul said. "If you tell anyone and push comes to shove, in other words, my job's on the line, I'll say you're lying about all this to your face. But if you can get to any border and bribe the guards, they'll let you through." He reached out his hand. "Good luck."

Why didn't I think of that? Bribes grease about every transaction in Latin America! At home, I wrapped the passport in tin foil and hid it in the sugar sack, since going home was sooo sweet! Aunt Mozy couldn't send bribe money. I'd long since applied for work translating letters into English in one place and as a foreign phone operator in another. We might have to delay our departure, so I scribbled Aunt Mozy a note.

December 2, 1971.

Dear Aunt Mozy,

    I told a pastor my problem. The U.S. Consul recommended him. He and his wife are helping me. They say they might be able

to take me to the Panama border and (help) bribe the guards to let me through. That's what I needed the money for. I could leave next week or the week after, depending on when Roberto flies.

You just called, so you have the pastor's address (to wire the money). He's safer than a bank, 'cause everyone knows Roberto's family and would call and tell them I just received a large amount.

I must confess I'm a little scared. I just have to put myself in the Lord's hands. He's given me the faith and the courage to come this far. I suppose He means for me to go through with it.

Happy Birthday to Uncle Joe this Sunday. I'll be thinking of him on "his day," and of all of you and when we're together.

I love you.

Mary Sue

SUBSEQUENT LETTER FROM AUNT MOZY TO MOM

Josilee,

I underlined some of her letter because I needed to copy info about the ticket. She didn't do it.

If you write, make it newsy about nothing, but don't mention anything that might foul up our plans. He reads everything and might kill her if he knew.

I must go through all the ticket getting again. Airlines sent us back money after 30 days, but don't tell her. She thinks its simple, but they won't hold more than 30 days. I have a phone (new number) LUther 3-4040 if you want to call.

Mozy

I was afraid once more, but for the children. Restless one night and unable to sleep, I saw something I didn't expect; something that left me totally startled! I know how you may react when you read this, because

if you told me what I'm about to say, my eyebrows would be higher than yours are about to be!

He came back! You know… Him! I knew who He was without seeing the nailprints in His hands. Roberto lay there next to me! What if he woke up? Jesus was now in transparent form, colorful Biblical clothes with darker hair and a beard like His pictures at church.

We "talked" telepathically (Roberto never stirred) and He sat on what seemed to be a short stool, but I never saw any legs. I guess if He can walk on water, He can sit on thin air! These "visits" were natural and relaxed. I took them for granted, thinking they would go on forever and that I had plenty of time to ask those things I always wanted to know. There were other things more pressing now, like that shrouded apparition in the doorway of the utility room that night.

"Oh, those," He said matter of factly. "They only come to frighten."

"Why?"

"Because fear gets your mind off of faith."

"But why come to me? I'm nobody."

"You don't know your power yet! That kind is scared to death of you!"

"Me?"

"Yes. Someday, you'll put a thousand of those to flight! And don't say you're nobody again. You're somebody to me."

No one had ever said things like this to me.

"Your faith protects you, so beware of that kind. He'll try and divert your attention to stop seeds of faith from putting down roots and growing strong as an oak."

"Do I have faith that can be that strong?"

"If you want it."

"What if I lose it?"

"It's not like losing your car keys. Faith is a choice. To lose it, you have to turn your back and walk away."

"Should I be afraid of those things in black?"

"Not those."

"Good, 'cause I'm more scared of Roberto and his gun."

"Haven't you heard? No weapon formed against you shall prosper. And don't you know? God has not given you a spirit of fear but of love and power and a sound mind."

"From the tiny Bible in the toy box!"

He didn't use Elizabethan English "thee's" and "thou's". His was a voice from home with an "Okie" accent. And if I'd been French, Chinese or Bulgarian, he'd have used one of those.

I'd never heard of omnipresence (the divine ability to be everywhere at once). One evening as He sat by my bed, I was embarrassed to be taking up his time, thinking He had better things to do. "Sir, you don't have to stay here. I'm okay tonight." (I called him sir, I guess, because of my Southern upbringing.) "Shouldn't you be talking to Billy Graham or the Pope or someone?"

"I'm with them everyday," He said. "Right now, I want to be with you." No one in Costa Rica wanted to be with me. I thought my heart would melt.

He didn't come around anymore after Thanksgiving. And by the second week in December, I hadn't seen Him for three weeks. His last words were, "Don't leave Costa Rica until I give you the signal." Only He never said what the signal was.

CHAPTER TWENTY

"GATORS AND TIGERS AND SNAKES, OH MY!"

Both companies where I'd applied for work weeks earlier called offering me a job. We were leaving in a few days, so I turned them down.

Roberto was due back any time. I was worried he might put one of the kids in the hospital this time. I'd tried everything. But you can't reason with a monster.

I'd need more than Mom's strength and charm and Aunt Mozy's tenacious will; more than Daddy's military discipline and cunning and Suzy's grit and determination to get us home again. If I could only see some maps and take notes. But if I went to the library, someone might recognize me and call Roberto's folks. I'd have to make do with what I remembered of the Coto area from eight years earlier. Getting out would be a long shot. Could I gamble like the Old Man? He'd lost the family farm! *I'd go crazy if I thought about that now! I'd think about it tomorrow.*

Marta was waxing floors with the same paste wax Mama used when I was little. It smelled like home. I *had* to leave! I needed that signal! In desperation I went room to room whispering, "Sir, where are you? What do I do? What's the signal? Give me a sign. Anything!"

Before I knew it, I was halfway to the pastor's house to get my bribe money and passport. Maybe taking action was the sign! It was the first time in years I hadn't kept my code of obedience. I couldn't ! I had to get out of there!

"This reminds me of during the war," the pastor reminisced, "when I helped Vietnamese refugees escape the Vietcong into Thailand by sneaking them across the border at night through the jungle. What an adventure, like the one you're about to take!"

Adventure? I smiled as pleasantly as I could. *Maybe in thirty or forty years. Right now, it's life and death!*

"God be with you," the pastor and his wife concluded.

Never just say, "thanks," Aunt Mozy had always drilled into me, it shows a lack of breeding. "Thank you for everything," I said hugging them, then raced into the night.

Aunt Mozy said to leave everything, that traveling with luggage would draw attention. But when did I listen to advice? Besides, we'd need our clothes when we got home.

I wanted to see Roberto's family one last time. Don Vicente loved the kids, especially David. They looked so much alike! He beamed when friends who hadn't seen him for a while stopped him to ask his "son's" name. I called, but Doña Lydia was the only one home. To keep her from popping in unexpectedly the next day, I said we were going to a church picnic and wouldn't be back until late. I hated to lie, but if Roberto called her looking for us, it might buy us some time.

ALL THE WAY HOME

This is what I also told the kids. Being "chips off the old block," they didn't ask why we were taking suitcases.

You wouldn't think so, but that night I slept like a baby; no nightmares about running from Roberto and barely escaping.

The alarm went off at five. I forgot Vicenta was coming that day for lunch and to fill me in on her progress at school. I'd have called her, but she had no phone.

I needed some music, but had packed my LP's. I reached for a 45 I'd been playing a lot. With no automatic replay on that fancy turntable, I'd have to stand on the sofa arm to put the needle back and restart the song each time. I must have played it a dozen times as we got ready. I even sang along. "I'm leaving on a jet plane. Don't know when I'll be back, again. Oh babe, I'm *glad* to go!"

I called a taxi then went to tell Marta good-bye, paid her a month and a half severance and warned her to get out before Roberto returned. "Take some sheets. There's plenty!"

I checked through the house one last time. Michelle's childsized shopping *bolsa* lay on the end of her bed. The kids' clothes were packed except for Chris' high-top school shoes, uniform, book bag and books. I hated to leave the primer I'd translated into English, but we couldn't take everything. The jet planes had to stay along with the bikes and tricycle Roberto just bought them. David would miss his bike most of all.

I checked my purse again. In it was my new passport, money, sunglasses, coloring books, crayons, story books, tissues, a damp wash cloth wrapped in tin foil (there were no disposable wipes or Zip Locks), extra panties for Michelle, band-aids and a bag of my sugar cookies.

"Leaving On a Jet Plane" was ending again when I left the kids' room, so I put the record back and checked my room again. This apartment with its gray prison walls and barbed wire had been home. My eyes welled up. It shouldn't have ended this way! Maybe I'd expected too

much. Glancing around one last time, I removed my wedding ring and laid in front of the kids' picture on the vanity atop the Gideon Bible he stole for me from some hotel. Maybe he'd find some answers there.

"Doña Maria," Marta called from the living room, "the taxi's here."

With Murphy's Law's impeccable timing, I jerked my purse off the bed to run to the door and the strap broke, its contents flying to the other end of the room. The kids were opening the front door! If someone saw the suitcases, they'd tell Roberto. "Marta, shut the door!" I called from underneath the vanity, shoveling things back in the purse and looking frantically for a substitute. Shell's *bolsa!* Everything fit but the books and crayons, which I put in my make-up case. What about Roberto's gun? So what that he had the bullets. I didn't plan to shoot it anyway. I just didn't want him using it on us! Have you ever done something you wish you hadn't then prayed later like crazy for God to pull your fat out of the fire? "Don't take the gun," came a near-audible voice. "You won't need it." I froze a moment. *Yeah... right!* I grabbed gun and silencer, wrapped them in diapers, stuffed them in the bottom of the *bolsa* and handed Marta the bag of cookies as we hurried to the taxi.

Roberto and Don Beh knew people at the airport. Would I be recognized? Towering over everyone in a world of brunettes, we stuck out like sore thumbs! So, I don't know why I bothered with an assumed name at the ticket counter or wore sunglasses in that dimly lit terminal, which must have attracted attention.

Destinations within Costa Rica's borders didn't require passports or *Patronato* papers. A table and chairs beneath a stairwell was a safe enough place until our flight call.

Because of the sunglasses, I never saw the male officer searching men and female officer searching women passengers until we walked outside. If I'd been the fainting kind, I'd have fallen over right there! "*Su bolsita, Señora.*" I stared like a deer in the headlights at the lady officer, who was no taller than my eight-year old Chris.

"Let's see what's in the bag, Ma'am," she said in Spanish.

My God, the gun! She picked through things on top then her hand dove to the bottom, wiggling fingers nearly visible out the other side. She checked my carry-on, patted me down and waved me on. "Next."

Hadn't she felt the weight and wondered what was in there? I hurried the kids down the long stairway and across the tarmac. The tail of our C-46 sat low, its nose in the air. The stench of crated pullets welcomed us aboard.

As we banked over San Jose, I whispered into my window, "I'm cutting the Gordian Knot!" I would miss all those I was leaving behind. "Thank you, Marta, for all you did. Vicenta, your sacrifice and study will pay off someday. Erica, I hope you don't take my leaving without saying goodbye as bad luck, but I couldn't take a chance. Hope you see your Rome, again! The seahorses are in the drawer. Dearest Nena, I wish you peace and happiness. Don Vicente, I loved you. Sorry about taking the kids from you, but I can't stay. Sandrita, I miss you already! Carol, you were like a sister to me. Anna Rita, Luís, you were our family. Thank you for taking us in. Margarita, be well. You were like a grandmother to Chris. I'll never forget you." We banked south to music only I could hear as tears streamed down my cheeks. "I'll never forget any of you! 'And I will remember, long after Saturday's over....'"

I never flinched as we landed at Golfito's one-approach airstrip to that "certain smell" in back, now increased by jungle heat. Cabbies shouted and motioned to us from taxies lined along the runway. A raised hand brought one running. Scared of the sea as I was the jungle, I had yet to decide which route I'd take: sharks or snakes! Passengers were pushing from behind. There were no *matabuey's* on boats. But there *were* sharks in the water and the kids couldn't swim. A choice between the lesser of two evils, I was leaning more toward the land route. With each step down, I chanted to myself, *"Gators and tigers and snakes, oh*

my! Gators and tigers and snakes, oh, my! Gators and tigers and snakes, oh my! My hand shot up and motioned to a cabbie. "Oh, taxi!"

A cabbie bolted from the crowd. "Coming, Señora!" His cab looked like all the rest, held together with bailing wire and chewing gum. "Where to, Señora?" he asked in Spanish.

"The border," I casually answered. This was common and he didn't blink.

Getting there then on to David (Da-VEED) might take three, maybe four hours. I think it was nearly ten. The kids had eaten a big breakfast. We'd grab lunch later. This was an emergency! We'd barely passed the last brightly painted house in town with flower and vegetable gardens in front, when the engine sputtered and died. "Wait here, Señora. I know the part I need. It's at my cousin's garage," the cabbie called over his shoulder as he ran toward town. I nervously shifted my weight. Were border police already on the look-out for four gringo runaways?

"Mommy, why didn't the driver say, 'Whoa, Nelly,' when he stopped the car?" Michelle asked.

"Because he doesn't know our story."

"Why not?" she asked, smearing sweat across her cheek.

"Because Grandmother and Nelly," I said, opening the doors to let in some air, "lived in the States where we're...." Stopping myself, I let it drop. "Tell us about Nelly," she said, settling into the stained upholstery of the disabled taxi.

"Sure, Shelly Belle." Their color books were locked in the trunk. A story would help pass time. They'd been so good.

"Once upon a time, when Grandmother Hoover was little...."
"...So, when we make fast stops, our family says...." I motioned for them to yell, "Whoa, Nelly!" and we laughed.

ALL THE WAY HOME

I twisted around and looked behind. Where was that driver? The kids were already fighting over the next story. "About Geronimo!" Chris pleaded. "No, the tiger!" David shouted over his brother. My Dad, Kirk, was alone in the motor pool one Sunday morning in India during World War II and was cornered by an eight hundred pound Bengal tiger. "Then the one where he nearly crashed!" David added, excitedly. Daddy went joy-riding, buzzed a tower of the Taj Mahal and nearly hit it. (I have a letter from his CO, chewing him out for it!) I hadn't yet told them about their grandfather flying reconnaissance during the war in his L-19 and being shot down three times. I'd made those other short stories longer to kill time. This would be even shorter! Daddy hardly ever talked about his war experiences.

"Mommy, I'm tired. I don't feel good," said Michelle.

"You don't feel well," I corrected her. "Food tastes good; people do or don't feel well." I was still killing time.

Mouth open, she gazed up at me with a confused look.

"I'm hot," Chris sighed.

"I'm thirsty," David complained.

I looked out the back window again. We should have lunched in Golfito. "What's the first thing you want when we get back to the States?" I slipped.

"Are we going home?" Chris asked.

"Maybe someday," I lied.

"Ice cream!" Michelle perked-up.

"A big glass of milk!" David sighed.

"I want to see a movie!" Chris said.

"All in the same day?" I kidded to keep their minds off being hot, tired and hungry. "Hope admission's still a dollar!"

"How much were movies when you were a kid?" Chris asked.

"'Picture shows,' as we called them, were a dime in summer and a nickel in winter, to get people out on cold evenings. There was no TV, so there were no Saturday morning cartoons. The theater opened at ten a.m. for Saturday matinees that lasted all day. They began with a serial or two."

"Cherrios, Rice Crispies?" Chris asked.

"Not the kind you eat. A serial is a movie in chapters. Every week, the hero would drive over a cliff or fall out an airplane. The next Saturday, we'd see how he escaped certain death. I liked Clyde Beatty of the jungle, an animal trainer and his big cats." I was enjoying going back in time. "'Movie Tone' brought us the news we now get on TV. Then came a couple of cartoons and a double feature. Mama would give us each a quarter, drop us off and go grocery shopping. A dime to get in with pop corn, a candy bar and pop a nickel each."

"Is a nickel a lot of money?" Chris asked.

"Even a penny was back then. You could get candy or bubble gum two for a penny. Sometimes five for a penny! Ice cream bars and doughnuts were a nickel each. When we spent weekends at Grandmother Hoover's, she'd give us each a whole dollar! We'd walk down to the little mom and pop store and spend it all on goodies. You'd have liked my grandmother, and she'd have liked you."

"Where is she?" Michelle asked.

"In heaven," I answered.

"Tell about Nelly!" Shell cried.

"I have a story you've never heard about a little girl just like you."

"I'm hungry," David yawned, already bored with a "girl story." "When do we get to the picnic?"

"I'm hungry, too," Chris said.

"Be strong, kids. We're pioneer stock."

"Can we go home, now?" Michelle whined.

"Soon, baby, soon."

"Can we have a cookie, now?" David asked.

"May we," I corrected him looking again out the rear window. I turned back with a smile not wanting the kids to know how scared and worried I was.

"Okay, may we?" he said.

"I'm sorry, honey. I had to leave the cookies."

"Any bread in your purse?" asked Chris.

"I never carry bread in my purse."

"Yes you do," Chris assured me. "I found some wrapped in paper napkins. We got weiners from Grandma Lydia's ice box, hid under the table and ate hot dogs when she wasn't looking."

My children had stolen food to survive! Now, *I* needed a story to keep *my* mind off things.

One weekend at Grandmother Hoover's, a friend of hers was there to visit from far away. She brought some old books with frayed cloth covers (possibly original prints). The Walt Disney hit film, "Song of the South," told the same story about a kindly old colored gentleman who'd lived his whole life as a slave and had every right to be bitter and hateful. Instead, Uncle Remus, as he was called, helped the grandson of his former owners, a lonely and confused boy, find some answers to life through his imaginary friends, Br'er Rabbit, Br'er Fox and Br'er Bear. My favorite of the books the lady brought was, "Br'er Rabbit and the Bucket of Butter." Because the books were in the slave vernacular, I couldn't read them. Her delightful Southern accent flowed like honey like no one I'd ever heard.

I begged this lady of the Old South to read them again. Smiling her beautiful smile, head white as snow, blue eyes sparkling with mischief, she graciously agreed in her old-timey way. I was fascinated. I now believe she was older than my grandmother, though not as wrinkled. Of course at seven, everyone looked old to me!

When I asked her to read them a fourth time, she placed the books on the table beside her, gracefully crossed her ankles, straightened her skirt and folded her hands in her lap. 'I know a story you haven't heard, a true one. May I tell it?'

"'Yes, ma'am.' I said. Sitting at her feet, I arranged my skirt over my bare feet, folded my hands in my lap, looked up and she began.

"Once, there was a little girl about your age, who lived in a big house with her mother and father. One day, Father said he wanted her to meet someone very important the next day.

"Mrs. Flanagan arranged Mother's hair, while young Molly dressed the child. Little Emily was to wear her Sunday best. 'One's attire must fit the occasion,' Mother always said. The only thing Molly didn't pin up, tuck in or tie back was Emily's hair that hung in cascades of bouncy ringlets. With Emily ready and Mother meticulously dressed and coiffed, Father summoned the carriage.

"The family rode down wide avenues past houses grander than theirs, past churches with tall steeples, sprawling manicured parks and immense public buildings with white columns that Father pointed out were in the Greek style. Finally stopping in front of a fine home, liveried servants ran out to let down the carriage step and escort them in. After taking their hats and coats, they were shown up a staircase next to the entry hall. Mother was disappointed not to take the grand staircase, having heard of opulent marbled halls lined with gilded tables, ornate

ALL THE WAY HOME

parlors and stately salons with servants at every doorway, vases of flowers in the middle of winter, dozens of lighted candles in chandeliers and a blaze in every fireplace.

On the second floor was a yellow room. Ladies in lovely day dresses and gentlemen, some soldiers, cutting a dashing figure in their dark blue uniforms, milled about or stood before the crackling fire. From a large desk surrounded by officers, the host saw the little family come in. He rolled up a map they were looking at and walked over to welcome them.

"Good, we're all here. Jeremiah, bring my chair close to the fire, so I can get acquainted with our littlest guest. Have your daddy put you on my lap." Her father complied.

"How old are you, dear?"

"Six, sir."

"And what's your name?"

"Emily Victoria, sir."

"What a polite little girl," he said to the other guests, who nodded and cooed in agreement. "And what a pretty name! Do you know you're named after a queen?"

"Yes, sir. Queen Victoria of England."

"How quick you are! Do you go by Emily or Victoria?"

"Emily, sir. It's my grandmother's name."

"She's so grown up!" he commented to his guests. "And this, her first tea. Tell me Miss Emily, do you have a favorite doll?"

"Yes, sir. Anne Marie."

"Any pets?"

"Yes, sir. A puppy named Muffin and Snowball, my pony. Daddy's teaching me to ride sidesaddle."

"Well, isn't that just fine. She'll be the finest little horsewoman in Virginia! Tell me Miss Emily, do you take tea or milk with your cake?"

"I'm not allowed tea, sir."

"Then milk it shall be. There's a small table next to the fireplace especially for you. Jeremiah, fix Miss Emily's plate with some finger sandwiches and a slice of cake. Jeremiah will see to your needs today, Miss Emily. My dear wife regrets she cannot be with us, nor our sons, due to our boys' illness. Mrs. Beasley, will you pour?"

Three years later, Emily came in from an early ride to find the servants crying in the kitchen. When they couldn't tell her what was wrong, she ran upstairs to find Mother, who lay across her feather bed, weeping inconsolably in its deep billows. Emily wept, too, thinking something terrible had happened to Father until he came in to see what all the fuss was about. Emily jumped into his arms. "Oh Father, I thought you were hurt or…!'"

"No, no, I'm fine, but someone we know died this morning."

"Jim!' his wife sat up on both elbows to object."

"She'll find out, anyway. The whole town's draped in black."

"Find out what, Daddy?"

"Remember your first tea and the nice man you met?"

"The tall man who sat me on his lap?"

"Yes, honey. Well, last night somebody shot him."

"James!" Mother exclaimed in horror.

"This is history,' Father said. 'She must always remember this day and tell her children."

The lady from the Old South telling me the story paused." "I did what he said and told it to my children. You see dear, James was my father. I'm Miss Emily and that nice man who died was Abraham Lincoln."

ALL THE WAY HOME

I don't think the kids understood the significance of that story. I know I didn't when Miss Emily told it to me. I wish I'd asked how Mr. Lincoln really was, but I was only a child.

Turning around, I saw the driver hurrying toward us out the back window. He'd been gone three hours. "Sorry to be so long, Ma'am. We called everywhere! That part won't be in for three weeks."

I gave him the twenty dollars he would have earned driving us to the border (he looked like he needed it) and he walked us to a house on the edge of town to call another cab.

Roberto had never been gone more than three days, and today was the fourth. I should have waited! And did I have to be so dramatic and leave my ring by the kids' picture? He's probably back and looking for us right now! If we can just get to Panama! By tomorrow morning, we'll be on a jet plane. My stomach turned. I'd left "Leaving on a Jet Plane" running on the turntable!

"Mommy, I'm hungry," Michelle whined.

"Me too," the boys echoed.

"We'll be there, soon," I said, wishing I still had the cookies.

An hour and a half later, we passed the big red Coke sign at the Villaneily intersection. About thirty more minutes to the border. Would the guards take my bribe? Would they "buy" my story? What story? I didn't even know what I was going to say! Knowing that in Costa Rica it was better if a man spoke for a woman; I tapped the cabby's shoulder. "Sir, I need your help."

"*Sí, Señora?*"

"Sir," I spoke hesitantly in Spanish, "I'm Maria De Benedictis...." Remembering the "magic word" in Latin America was "Mamá," my story was born. "My mother lives in Panama...," I paused, my conscience screaming, *Liar, liar, pants on fire!* "...and hasn't been well."

"I'm sorry to hear it, *Señora*."

"I bought tickets and had our kids put on my new passport," I said, pulling it out to show him. "This morning, I was to get our exit visas, so we could fly down to see her this Saturday. They called last night. Mom's had another heart attack. If I don't get there today, they say I might never see her again!"

"*Dios mio* (My God)!" the cabbie sympathized. "Can I help?"

"My husband, who flies cargo around the Caribbean, said he'd meet me in Panama. Can you convince the guards to let me take the children across without visas or the *Patronato* paper? I can give you a little for your trouble," I added, slipping twenty dollars plus the fare over the seat.

He pulled the car into the shade and went in the customs office. The minutes that followed felt like an eternity. He finally appeared accompanied by two officers, a skinny private bringing up the rear. The one in the lead was obviously career military; all spit and polish, his silver handcuffs sparkling in the sun and shiny patent leather visor pulled low on his brow. He never smiled but stiffly opened the door in military fashion and stood almost at attention. "Are you Señora De Benedictis?" he asked in Spanish.

"Yes, sir." *How does he know my name?* I wondered, forgetting I'd told the cabbie. *Has Roberto's family called the border?* Roberto had friends with access to helicopters and planes. *Has he called a pilot friend to help him pick us up?* "Are these your children?" the officer asked.

I managed a pleasant nod.

"Gather your things and follow me, please."

I'm arrested!

Trooping into the customs office, the children were seated on benches along the wall by the door, while I was motioned to follow him. He slapped his cap on the counter and went behind it to a desk. Without looking up, he poised his hands over the keys, ready to type. "Your name... your nationality... address... phone number... height... weight... age."

Next comes a mug shot and locked cell!

Folding his arms, he leaned back in the squeaky, wooden executive chair. By his smirk, I'd say he was trying to give me enough rope to hang myself by catching me in a lie. "He says," he glanced at the cabbie then at me, "you want to take these kids into Panama. Is that correct?"

"Yes, sir," I said, trying to sound truthful.

"He says your mother lives there and is sick or something."

"Yes, sir."

His tone changed and his smirk broadened to a grin. "And just *how long* did you *expect* to be in Panama?" he said as if saying, "Lady, the only place you're goin' is to jail!"

"Three days?" I answered timidly.

"And your mother just had a heart attack?"

"Yes, sir!" I answered more convincingly.

"Better make it eight then," he said, typing it in.

Ba-BOOM, Ba-BOOM, Ba-BOOM, went my heart!

"Now, all I need is your *cédula* number." He looked down, his hands poised over the keys. I'd forgotten about that! The jig was up! Before I could explain why I didn't have one, he typed in a number. "Don't *preocoop*," he said to the room full of officers. "She's upset, because of her mother."

Ba-BOOM, ba-BOOM, ba-BOOM!!

Ripping the papers from the machine, he gave me the blue copy. "There, let's go! It's after three. Get to David by five and you can catch the last flight to Panama City. Anything to declare?"

"No."

"Medications, drugs?"

"Vitamins," I said.

He came to a screeching halt, causing a pile-up in the narrow hallway. "Vitamins?" he echoed with second thoughts.

"Only vitamins," I answered, with a look as pure as the wind driven snow.

"Come on then," he said, "the bus leaves any minute!"

We hurried past a touring bus full of people, their bags open, awaiting inspection. The officer waved to the Panama side as we ran toward them, "She's okay, let her pass!"

Panamanian guards took my luggage from the Costa Ricans, and loaded them for me. We crawled in behind the driver in a minibus that seated about twelve. Two-middle aged women sat in back. "Where to?" the driver asked.

"David (Dah-VEED)," I said.

"That's what Grandpa calls me! Mommy," David asked, "where's Panama?"

I forgot he and Michelle could understand a lot of Spanish now. "It's where we're going," I skirted the truth.

"Is *that* where the picnic is?" Chris asked. "I hope there's lots of food. I'm starving!"

"Me, too!" David huffed in agitation. "I'm gonna eat it all!"

"Are not!"

"Am too!"

"Are not!"

"Am too!"

"Are n...!"

"Boys, boys, there'll be plenty. Let's enjoy the scenery."

"I'd rather eat." David liked getting in the last word.

"Did you know we're in a *real* jungle?" I said with an animated expression. "Up in those trees!" I pointed, "Is that a monkey?"

"Where, where?" They stumbled over me to get to the window.

"I don't see it," Chris said.

"There's no monkeys here! Just a bunch of trees," David said, somewhat let down.

"It's like a pretty garden," Michelle said.

They chattered and I stared into space, recalling the courtyard garden of that hotel. If I knew its name, we could stay there tonight. Why were we going so slow in a country where cars fly like bats out of you know where? "Sir," I said, leaning forward as he pulled over to pick up two more passengers, "how far to David?"

"About two hours," the driver said.

"It's three-twenty now, and the last flight to Panama City leaves at five. Can you drive a little faster?"

"*Señora*," he said, twisting around as far as a fat man could dare, "I have eight kids. This is how I make my living!"

In the States, we're taught to shut-up, stand in line and wait our turn. It took me ten minutes to remember that I'd only paid seventy-five cents, American for each of our seats! Time for some *mercado*-style haggling! "How much are the rest of these seats?"

"Ten dollars," he said (They use American dollars in Panama).

What a thief! I thought. "Get us to David in time and you'll get double."

Eeeeeeuuuuummmmmmmm... his engine raced as off we sped! In David, we pulled into a parking lot where a bus and several cabs were unloading passengers. The airport terminal, the size of a two thousand square foot house and four feet off the ground, had a covered, open-air counter running its full length. Through open double doors down the short hallway, I could see four small jets on the runway out back. We hadn't missed our flight! I hurried to be first in line. The driver huffed and puffed behind us with our bags, mumbled "thank you" and counted his money on his way back to the cab. A man behind the counter stepped toward me and smiled. "May I help you, Ma'am?" he said in Spanish, his Panamanian accent sounding so different. "Four tickets to Panama City!" I said, slapping the counter with the palm of my hand. "How long's the flight?"

"About an hour, Ma'am." Pulling a small box from beneath the counter, he thumbed through five by seven cards then looked up. I have two left. How many did you say you needed?"

"I'll take them," I smiled my prettiest. "My oldest can hold his sister, I'll hold David and we'll strap ourselves in real good." In Latin America, these things were done every day.

"I'm sorry, Ma'am," he answered, "that's not allowed."

"Please?" I begged, batting my eyelashes. It's hard being coquettish with three kids pulling on your coattail and whining. "Mommy, mommy, we have to go to the restroom!"

"Ma'am, there'll be plenty of seats on the eight o'clock flight tomorrow morning," he said.

"But I have to get there tonight!"

ALL THE WAY HOME

The kids were jumping up and down in place and holding themselves. (They'd been such troopers!) A bribe might get us two extra seats. I'd get the money out in the restroom. "I'll be right back. Don't sell my tickets and don't go away!"

"I can't!" he said as I disappeared into the Ladies Room. "I'm the only one here, today."

When I came back from the restroom, there was a different clerk I've come to call "my angel." "Where's the other guy?"

"What other guy?"

"Never mind! I've got to have those tickets to Panama City, tonight!"

"One moment, Ma'am." He got out the same box, thumbed through it, pulled out tickets and held them up. "I have four left. How many do you need?"

"I'll take them!" I said, slapping the counter for effect.

We arrived in Panama City at six, worn out! But before finding a hotel, I rushed to the Pan Am desk to claim my tickets. I wanted them in my hands! The children curled up on cloth upholstered chairs. After giving the young clerk the confirmation numbers Aunt Mozy sent me, he went back to check.

Was Roberto in Panama that night? His company's desk was about thirty feet away. Every few minutes, clerks, luggage handlers or flight personnel burst through black vertical flaps behind the counter leading out to the tarmac. Roberto would be surprised to see me, then turn purple with rage! I'd think about that one tomorrow!

Heavy boots on linoleum floors drew my attention left to six soldiers marching toward me, helmets shadowing eyes over expressionless faces. Nightsticks swaying from belts and cuffs softly sparkling in the dim light, they wore long side arms with machine guns over one shoulder for good measure. Men armed to the teeth marching straight for me! Why

couldn't the ugly tile floor just open up and swallow me whole? *Don't worry,* I consoled myself! *We're safe in Panama!* They turned forty-five degrees and marched away. I was just beginning to feel safe again, when six more started toward me.

Fourteen months earlier, when coming to get the children, skyjackings to Cuba were in reprieve. I didn't know it yet, but they'd begun again and airport security had been beefed up all over the Americas.

All of a sudden, it hit me! Roberto's cousin was married to the nephew of the President of Panama! Roberto and his family could have Costa Rican officials alert Panamanian authorities and it would all be over. I should have had the tickets sent to Nicaragua! For the next two hours, vertical flaps burst open to my right and soldiers marched to my left. The clerk finally emerged from the tiny room behind the Pan Am desk. "Sorry, ma'am but I can't find your tickets. This is Mother's Day and most of us are off. Come back tomorrow morning."

"What time does the first flight leave for the States, tomorrow?" I asked.

"Ten-twenty, Ma'am," the nice looking young man with the tired face answered. "Be here by eight and we'll get you on."

Remind me to never fly in or out of Panama on December the eighth again, assuming I get out this time! I thought. Gently shaking the kids awake, I got them in a cab and to the hotel restaurant. It was nine-thirty or ten before we got our fried chicken, and nearly midnight before the kids were bathed and bedded down.

Unable to sleep, I called Aunt Mozy about the tickets. Her phone rang and rang until after one a.m. Because Mom traveled in those days, I didn't think she'd be home, but tried anyway. "Mom? It's Mary Sue. We're out of Costa Rica..."

"Oh, thank the Lord!" Mom interrupted.

"…but not out of the woods! They can't find our tickets! Yes, I gave them the names and confirmation numbers. They don't know us from Adam! I can't wait a day or two, Mom! We've got to get out tomorrow morning. Raise Cain on your end and I'll do the same here. We'll be careful, Mom. I love you, too. Bye. Lord willing, we'll see you tomorrow! I'll call from Miami."

I always thought it sounded so "Scarlett O'Hara," putting things off until tomorrow. Now, tomorrow was all I could think of. When would this warlike experience be over? In longing and fear, I imagined I was Scarlett looking out at the rain at Aunt Pitty's. "When the war's over, Ashley. When the war's over." With war's end on my mind, I fell into a fitful sleep.

CHAPTER TWENTY-ONE

WITH YOU

By eight the next morning, we'd eaten and were at the Pan Am desk. Now and then, someone would pop out from in back to verify information. Was I being set up? Were they stalling until the police arrived?

Vertical flaps behind the desk of Roberto's cargo company burst open every few minutes and armed soldiers marched around. Keeping a poker face, definitely not my forte, was getting harder.

It was ten o'clock when they found my tickets; barely time enough to load our luggage on the plane. We were hurried down the main corridor to a long, narrow hallway with floor to ceiling windows looking out on the runway. A few feet away sat the 747 that would take us home.

Ahead of us were four families, the last having about eight members, many of them children. I kept my kids busy, not wanting to risk them inadvertently saying something that might cause suspicion. Inching forward, we were just another family on vacation, jabbering away and having the time of our lives.

What was taking so long? When I came down fourteen months ago, all I did was flash my passport, hand them my ticket and board. With so many there, I had to step out of line and rubberneck to see the exit and the woman sitting on a tall stool taking tickets and checking passports.

ALL THE WAY HOME

The other woman, a stewardess in a dark blue uniform, her pointy cap askew to accommodate a perfectly coiffed beehive, was running a pistol-style hairdryer up and down each passenger. *Hair dryer?* Was this one of those metal detectors I'd been reading about in the paper? In 1971, few had heard of them, much less seen one. *Oh no, the gun!* We'd just passed a big green trash barrel. Having a gun on me was bad enough, but a silencer? I had to get rid of them! Digging for the cloth bundle in the bottom of my *bolsa,* I looked behind me to see how far I'd have to step back to nonchalantly drop it over the side. That barrel was hell and gone from where I was!

The last members of the family ahead were being checked with the "hairdryer." Running all the way back there to throw away that bundle might attract attention. It looked exactly like the bundles of cocaine on the news that drug dealers had stacked in some jungle. This was it. I was had!

The stewardess motioned me forward I gazed out the window at freedom gleaming silver in the morning sun. We'd almost made it! Why didn't I toss that gun in the jungle or leave it in the hotel trash? *Dear Lord, don't let them find....* Two hands were suddenly patting me down, groping in my purse and the metal detector run up and down me, but didn't go off. It didn't go off! I was handed my passport and waved on. My head was spinning as I all but stumbled out the door.

When the plane banked after takeoff, I pointed to the ships below, so the kids would remember flying over the Panama Canal. At lunch, the kids commented how tender the meat was and creamy the milk. When I said Tulsa food was even better and we'd be home for supper, they couldn't believe it!

"Will it be snowing?" David asked.

"It doesn't usually snow till January. But you can pick out our new sled." This drew a broad smile to his chubby cheeks. He looked out at the clouds and dreamed of snow.

I can't have slept much, when they announced we were over Cuba. I woke the children for a bird's eye view, for the same reason as the canal, I wanted them remember. After landing in Miami, they stuck close and kept up with me like little troopers. I couldn't believe customs officials said nothing about my not having Costa Rican exit visas stamped on my passport. If *that* had only been my biggest obstacle! Then I saw something I'd never seen, and knew immediately what it was. A walk through metal detector *"Oh well,"* I sighed, *at least I'll be in an American jail!"* When it didn't go off, I sprinted for a phone. "Mom? It's me. We're in Miami! We're safe!"

"Thank God," she sighed in relief! "Everyone's all right?"

"We're fine."

"Thank the Good Lord! When do you get home?"

Home! How good did *that* sound? "Miami to Dallas on Pan Am then Braniff to Tulsa, landing at 6:30 p.m."

"We'll be there!" Mom said. "Glad you're safe, honey. See you tonight." We hung up too soon, but we'd catch up tonight.

After changing the last of our colones to dollars, we ate then browsed through shops decorated in red and green. Santa's elves, in velvet suits with pointy shoes and ears, greeted us along with furry near lifesize reindeer and cheery snowmen standing on fake snow.

On our way to our plane down a different hall, I hadn't counted on another walk-through metal detector. Why hadn't I thrown that gun away in the restroom we were just in? Maybe because I wasn't used to "packing heat!" *Please, Lord, don't let it go off! My family won't know what happened to me!* I gritted my teeth and walked through. It didn't go off. Did these things *ever* work? Either it was faulty techonology, or somebody up there was riding shotgun for me.

ALL THE WAY HOME

The children wouldn't experience the dipping and pitching of our plane through the severe thunderstorm forming over Dallas' Love Field. After the lunch trays were removed, they would fall asleep and be whisked to a land of elves, sugarplums and playmates made of snow.

Now, a storm on the way to Costa Rica to get the kids in AND one on the way home is overkill! My romantic inclinations would have had us flying off into the sunset, but since that's only in the movies, let me tell you how it really happened.

The children were asleep when I saw lightning off the wing. Roberto said it often strikes a plane's nose, sending a fireball down the aisle and out the tail. I moved my feet away from the aisle. We were still having turbulence, when we suddenly dropped hundreds of feet, reminding me of why I don't like rollercoasters. I watched the worsening storm out my window. Had God brought us this far to crash in a grassy field in Texas? We circled Love Field for an hour and a half, finally landing, only to scramble to our next flight. (Why is it they land you at Gate 2 with only minutes to run to Gate 39?)

The Braniff plane was smaller with two seats on each side of the aisle. Chris and David sat on the left about two rows from the front with Shell and me on the right. Two nuns sat behind us. It's strange, but it felt good to speak Spanish. I was homesick for Costa Rica. (Not for Roberto, for the others.) The Guatemalan sisters and I talked until we couldn't hear each other above the roar of jet engines, then settled in for our forty-five minute flight to Tulsa that was already two hours late.

Dallas wind shear is notoriously treacherous, and I was nervous. We were still having turbulence at cruising altitude, when drinks and snacks were wheeled out on the cart. That's when I saw Him standing in the aisle in His transparent form. He smiled and "spoke" telepathically. "Hi!"

"Oh, hi!" I answered, trying to look casual, so no one would notice. I'd never spoken to Him with anyone around but Roberto, and he'd

always been asleep! I guessed the same rules applied: I could see and hear Him, but no one else could.

"I came to tell you a couple of things," He began. "They're about to divert your flight to Denver due to sleet in Tulsa."

This was no hardship! My sister lived in Denver.

"But don't worry, they won't," he added.

Darn!

The announcement came immediately over the speaker: "Ladies and gentlemen, due to weather conditions over Tulsa, our flight is being diverted to Denver. Comfortable accommodations for the night have been...."

I didn't listen to the rest. If *He* said it wouldn't happen, it wouldn't happen. I avoided looking straight at Him in case someone was looking, and casually glanced through a magazine. "And the other thing you came to tell me?"

"I came to say goodbye."

"Good-bye?" The plane violently shook as my eyes riveted to His. "What do you mean?"

"You won't see me like this again."

The plane dipped. Gripping the armrests, my natural voice rose above the roar of the engines, "No!" All around me, heads turned. There came another series of bumps.

Cradling my elbow in her cool hand, the nun behind me whispered gently in Spanish, "Fear not little daughter. The Lord is with us."

I patted her hand. *Boy, if she only knew!* I stared back into the magazine and tried to appear calm. "Sir, these months, you've been my strength, my courage, my peace and joy but especially, my hope. I can't live without those things, and I can't live without You!"

"I'll always be with you," He softly said. "You just won't see me again with your natural eyes." He changed the subject. "Will you do something for Me?" He asked with that mischievous, infectious grin.

"Of course," I said, half-grinning back.

"Tell people what happened."

"You mean how we got out of Costa Rica?"

"More."

The grin faded. "About You?"

"Uh-huh," He smiled.

"They won't believe me."

"Some will, some won't," He said matter-of-factly.

"But I stutter sometimes, and lose my train of thought."

"Don't worry, We've dealt with that before."

"Okay, what do I say?"

"Tell them they're loved and We'll always be with them."

"Where do I begin?"

"With your family."

"They sure enough won't believe me! They saw me dance around, pretending to be a Mouseketeer."

"A prophet is without honor in his own country," He said.

Not knowing what that meant, I came back with what sounded logical. "I know! Tell me the ones who are likely to believe and the rest can... well, you know."

"Doesn't work that way," He smiled. "Everyone gets a shot."

"But Sir, I don't have the courage."

"You've got courage. You got this far."

"I got it from You."

"I offered courage. You accepted it and used it."

"Can't you ask someone more worthy, Sir?"

"It's not for you to decide who's worthy and who's not."

"But You don't know the awful things I've said."

"The profanity? Isaiah was a man of unclean lips."

"But I don't just have a potty mouth, Sir. I've done things I'm so ashamed of; things I can never undo!"

"I know. We watched and wept as your future was altered, as you dabbled in sin and threw away the life We had planned for you. You know, people make a big deal over the word sin. It's just an archery term that means, *missing the mark;* missing God's best for your life. We sent you the wife of the pastor of the church you laughingly call, 'The Church of the Perpetual Revival.' She'd have explained this and more. "She was to be your friend and help you."

"I'm sorry, Sir. If I'd only known!"

"You're not supposed to know everything!"

"If you send another, I'd be nicer next time."

"There'll be no next time… with her. You'd have liked her. She *will* always pray for you, though."

I'd failed Him. I lowered my eyes as waves of remorse swept over. "You've wasted your time with me. Why didn't you go to some woman who's spent her life on her knees? Why me?"

"We never waste Our time. And I came to you because I know the real you. I know your heart."

That was the problem. So did I! An unseen force lifted my chin until my eyes met His.

"Do you think all those ugly words and deeds caught Us by surprise? We've known you since the foundation of the world. Isaiah said some awful things and became a prophet. King David was an adulterer and a murderer, yet a man after God's own heart. Moses killed a man, but became the Deliverer. Peter was an uneducated fisherman, whose prejudice against Gentiles could have destroyed what We had planned for him and the world, yet he yielded and became their shepherd. Rahab the harlot's sins were red as scarlet, yet she became the great-grandmother of King David. Which was more worthy than you?"

"If I'd only known," I said, "I'd have lived better."

"That's what the Bible and church are for."

"Where was God all those years? I searched for Him!"

"You didn't search with all your heart."

"Couldn't you have come to me sooner? I'd have believed."

"You've seen Me many times."

"No, Sir. I'd have remembered."

"When you fell off Tony, that old cowboy kneeling by your side?"

"That was you? With that atrocious grammar?"

"No matter what your Aunt Mozy says, perfect grammar isn't a prerequisite to heaven. Remember the boat paddle your father broke over your head?"

"Yes."

"I weakened it."

"I always wondered about that."

"How do you think you crossed the border yesterday without paying a bribe?"

"But I didn't see You."

"You didn't see Me either, when I kept your bus from sliding off that mountain road. I was the lamp on the hill of that Mexican village that got you off the unfinished highway in time; I was with you before you asked in the conscience of the Muslim boy on that dark, country road; I was the fish that swam by your leg and scared you back to shore before you ran into real sharks. I was the sick old man just out of the hospital you gave your lunch to; the homeless boys you clothed, the young mother and infant in the doorway that rainy night...."

"But I went back!" I interrupted. "Why didn't you wait? I'd have taken you home, given you a place to...."

"You also slammed the door in my face."

"Curly Locks?"

"You see? You've seen Me and My messengers many times."

"And that Valium thing?"

"I was there."

"But why me?"

"Because there's something I want you to do. Remember the things I've told you. You *do* trust Me don't you?"

"Yes, Sir."

"Then do as I ask. Soon, the Comforter will come to you."

What's He saying? I don't need a blanket!

He smiled, knowing I would soon learn of these things and went on with what He had to say. Time was short. "I promised you'd come back

home and that I'd be with you all the way, didn't I? And so will I be with you," He said, pointing heavenward, "all the way home."

He was still smiling that beautiful smile, His eyes like stars as He faded from view. I thought I'd always have Him with me and now He was gone. As the plane banked our final approach into Tulsa, my stare shifted from where He'd stood to the runway lights outside my window in the shape of a cross. He *was* with me.

We deplaned exhausted and disheveled, lacking only tags hanging from our lapels to look like refugees. Dressed for the tropics, we stepped into the cold winter wind, sleet stinging our bare arms and legs as we made our way down the air stair and across the tarmac.

I wanted to get down on my hands and knees and kiss the ground. But somewhere behind the terminal's dark glass was my mother, whose queenly dignity wouldn't have approved of such theatrics. So, I smacked the air as I walked and whispered, "Love ya', Tulsa!"

Soon, we were all hugging, kissing, laughing and weeping, when I remembered my promise. I gulped hard and blurted out, "Mom, you'll never guess!"

"What?" she smiled.

"We didn't come alone."

Visibly shaken, she leaned way out to peer around me, expecting Roberto to walk through the door behind me.

"Not him; Him," I said, indicating upward with my eyes.

"Whom?" Mother said.

"Him," I said, glancing up, again.

"God?" she said, hesitating and also indicating upward.

"No, Jesus."

"Christ?"

"My God," Aunt Mozy said to Gordon, "she's gone over the edge! She's been through too much. She needs my Valiums."

"No I don't! I just talked to Him a few minutes ago." Chins hit the floor. "I know it sounds weird. He first came when I was sick. But it didn't look like Him. He had white hair, a gold beard and glowed all over. We rose above the ceiling, kind of like on an elevator, and talked a while. Actually, we talked lots of times," I said wistfully. "The last time wasn't quite twenty minutes ago." The blank stares nearly made me doubt myself. "Honest! Doesn't anyone believe me?"

"*I* believe you, Mommy," Michelle yawned. "Now, can we go home?"

"Yeah," Aunt Mozy's new husband, Gordon broke in. "If we hurry, I can still catch the last of Bonanza."

Incensed he was thinking of TV at a time like this, Aunt Mozy rebuffed, "Bonanza's on Friday night. This is Thursday."

Thursday! The day He said we'd be home.

Mom took over. "Let's feed the kids, tuck them in and you can tell us all about it."

Walking up the concourse toward luggage, I tried to recall His face. It was already fading; that beautiful smile, those eyes. But His words, like Cinderella's slipper, were mine to keep.

"I'm with you always. I'll never leave nor forsake you. Lo, I am with you... all the way home."

EPILOGUE

We'd barely arrived at Uncle Joe's from the airport, where there would be more room for us, when I got a phone call. "Hi!" Roberto cheerfully greeted me as though nothing were wrong. "Guess what happened at El Coco this morning?"

"I don't know," I replied. Wasn't it only yesterday, at that same international airport, I'd been overwhelmed with fear when that officer's tiny arm shot into my purse and her fingers wiggled up the other side? Were we actually home? Were we really safe, now?

"Some guy tried to skyjack a plane to Cuba!" Roberto went on, ignoring my grand silence. "The President finally went down to the airport, slapped the skyjacker in the face and took his gun!"

Yesterday, I'd had a gun and so much could have gone wrong.

"Leaving like you did was dangerous," Roberto said then stopped himself. He could wait until I was back in Costa Rica to really chew me out, but felt justified and quickly added. "Didn't you think of the kid's safety at all?"

"Their safety is why I left!" I soberly emphasized each syllable.

Mom took the phone. "This is Josilee."

"Josilee!" he exclaimed, cheerfully donning his mantel of charm. "I can't imagine why Mary Sue left like that! I had her set up like a queen with a modern apartment in a beautiful neighborhood and anything she needed or wanted!"

"Show your face in this country again," she calmly said, "and I'll have you thrown back in jail so far, you'll never see the light of day!"

My Tulsa attorney later sent new divorce papers. Roberto wouldn't sign for a year, because I refused to send the children to Costa Rica every summer for "visits." (Was he nuts? I'd been there, done that!) Costa Rican friends wrote that he remarried six months after the kids and I left. When I wrote Don Beh that the new wife might object to Roberto not bothering to divorce me first, he signed.

Twenty-two years later, Roberto phoned to "see how the kids turned out." (Where was he when they were all in braces?) He said he spent ten years wanting to come up and shoot me. But hate was eating him like a cancer, so he gave it up. I didn't tell him about the years of premonitions I'd had of watching TV from my recliner, and having him suddenly appear at my screen door, gun in hand. Ever try "rolling" out of a recliner in a hurry? Doesn't work in premonitions, either!

He said for years he'd crawled around on his belly in the jungles of Nicaragua fighting for Daniel. *How strange,* I thought, with Daniel Ortega a flaming communist and Roberto a nasty Nazi! I'd often heard Roberto and his family speak fondly of Mussolini and their intellectual relative with the pen name, Gabriele D'Annunzio, who had influenced Il Duce's political views on Italian Fascism.

In reference to that "prophecy" *la bruja* said over Roberto when he was a baby, if there *had* been a communist take over in Costa Rica, did Roberto think Ortega would be his shortcut to the Presidential Palace? And if Roberto's wife lived with him in Nicaragua a while, I wondered what sent her packing, Roberto's hair-trigger temper or adjusting to life in "The People's Paradise?"

Roberto said he'd owned a successful cargo company but that all three of his C-46's were confiscated by U.S. customs in Miami and he is now barred from reentering the United States. Had "fighting for Daniel" included gunrunning, drug smuggling or both? Roberto was disillusioned with communism (international socialism) when Ortega's regime didn't reimburse him for the loss of his planes. I asked if he was going back to fascism (national socialism)? He said he didn't know, yet.

What he *did* know was that if he was ever placed in charge of what he called, "the next Jewish Holocaust," he would spare Barbara Streisand. When I asked, "Why?" he contemplatively paused with a far away look then answered, "Because she pleases me." In almost the same breath, he said he'd like to someday "talk" with Sylvester Cat, the cartoon character. (Pistol-packin' Yosemite Sam seemed more his type!)

Roberto liked shocking people. And though you might think saying "I spit in the face of God" was his worst, he hit a new low just before our escape with "I shit in the mouth of God!" As both are shocking, especially in print, I wouldn't have used either had they not illustrated the grace (undeserved/unearned favor) of God. Personally, I'd have struck him with lightning! Guess that's why God hasn't put me in charge of any prodigals.

I don't know who wrote it, but there's a saying that kind of fits Roberto. "No one is a complete failure. They can always be an example of how NOT to do things." He taught me that not everyone who smiles is nice, that those with pretty faces and smooth ways don't always mean you well and that his precious hate and fear only alienate and divide. Roberto even changed the way I vote. I learned it's not enough to want peace. Everybody wants that. But there comes a time when you must draw a line in the sand, when you shout "That's it—no more!" when it's okay to fight back!

Roberto's inability to deal with the abuse he'd suffered growing up left him sad and confused. I hope he's happy now and has found some inner peace.

Don Vicente passed away about thirteen months after we left Costa Rica, God rest his soul. I loved him.

I hear Andreina's and Gilberto's Lydiana is now a doctor and that Sandrita is married and living somewhere in the States. I hope she reads this and contacts me.

I had lunch with Carol before leaving Costa Rica. She told me that she and Roger, who had two cute little blonde kids, were divorcing and that she was beginning a new business. With her beauty and dynamic personality, I'm sure she was successful.

Last time I heard about Lelo and Carolina, they were living somewhere in Florida.

Carl and Sunny, who live in Tulsa with their five children and many grandchildren, were planning a family trip to Coto but advised against it, because the mosquitoes there are bad now. They've let the plantations go back to jungle, but *somebody* must live in Coto Valley, because Villaneily (Neily Village) is now Cuidad Neily (Neily City.) People no longer go to Panama to shop for American goods. Golfito is now a duty free port. (Possibily a great move by some smart Costa Rican politician!) And with that long dock for unloading merchandise, I'm surprised Walmart doesn't already know about it and has set up a store there!

Speaking of politicians, I hear that ambitious boy in Coto, who snagged a job washing helicopters and was sent to mechanic school in the states, is now in Costa Rica's congress and that his American wife, Billie, has all but forgotten English. Before coming to Costa Rica, she was in a child custody battle with her child's grandmother. Two weeks before Enrique graduated in Tulsa, he sent Billie and Angel to his parent's in Costa Rica then lied to police. Billie had named her daughter Angel because of her white-blonde hair and sky-blue eyes, but because Angel is a boy's name in Latin America, they changed it to Angelina.

After Vivian passed away, Daddy moved out east of Tulsa and began building model airplanes inside the house. His house was filled with valuables like mason jars of gold and silver coins, thousand dollar model steam engines imported from England, and replica muzzle loading pistols and rifles he made himself. He also made twelve cannons he'd lend to the Tulsa Philharmonic each summer that the percussionist would wire to a keyboard for performances of Tchaikovsky's "Battle of 1812" at the city-wide Forth of July picnic. One woman complained that falling cinders set her hair on fire. She'd refused Daddy's warning to step back from the cannons, but Daddy's part was cancelled anyway.

In 1988, Daddy had a stroke that left him in a coma for weeks, his right side was paralyzed and his speech severely slurred. When they told him he might never regain his beautiful speaking voice, he died only weeks later. I never thought he'd give up like that. While hospitalized, those he trusted most ransacked his house, taking everything of value. We didn't tell him. He'd have dragged himself home, gotten his gun and gone after them. They also had his beloved cats euthanized, which would have broken his heart.

Aunt Mozy passed away at eighty-two never having made her peace with God. Years earlier, her pastor had stated in his character letter, the last requirement for her to adopt a baby, that she was nervous and high strung and would make a poor mother. She couldn't get over it and never went back to church. I don't blame her! (Some people are so spiritually minded they're no earthly good!) Wonder how many "perfect" mothers sat in *his* pews? But Aunt Mozy, being of good pioneer stock, was a mother to all her nieces and nephews. There was no more tender mother. And she did more than love us, she "cared!"

MARY SUZANNE LOPEZ

On December 4th, Aunt Mozy's birthday, about six weeks before she passed away, her birthday gift was a 24" Christmas Tree I'd made from silk pink poinsettias with a cherub-like angel on top. She got tired while I was there and asked to be taken to bed. As I helped her there, she corrected my grammar. "No Mary Sue, 'farther' denotes distance: I'll walk with you farther, but won't speak of this further," then she collapsed. During her lucid moments the next few weeks, I told her that except for my children, she was the one I wanted to see most in heaven. I hope in some private moment she made her peace with God, because early on the morning of January 19, 1993, she slipped into eternity.

Mom followed ten years later at the age of eighty. Now that I'm older, I think I understand why Mom's words were often so bitter and hurtful. She never got over all those years of abuse at the hands of her father. She never sought help. Her generation didn't air "dirty laundry in public" but took their secrets to the grave. Linda and I tried to get her to talk about it, but she couldn't. She did make her peace with God and was happier her last years. It was good to see her laugh.

She didn't laugh much when we were little. She stopped cuddling and reading to us when I was about four; about the time we moved into the new home Granddaddy built us. I have a photo of Linda and me on the front porch with our knees bandaged. We accidentally fell on some screen. Mom was surprised I could remember back that far and amazed at what I recalled in my manuscript. (She read much of it before she died and was my biggest fan.) I can go back as far as eighteen months of age, when I burned my feet on that floor furnace. At twenty months, Mom and I moved to Tulsa weeks before Linda was born. It was night and heavily snowing when our train pulled into the station built with big stone blocks that looked like a castle to me. While writing my story, I often wondered why my memory was so vivid at such an early age. I may have discovered why at Mom's funeral.

ALL THE WAY HOME

A cousin said when I was about a year old, Mom and I came to see them. I was given something to drink and spilled it on their brand new rug. Mom yanked me up, ran me to the bathroom and started spanking me. When my aunt heard the commotion behind the locked door, she ran out back to get my uncle, Mom's brother, who banged on the door and ordered her to open up. He was about to crawl through the tiny bathroom window, when Mom opened the door and calmly walked out. My aunt rushed in. There was something wedged between the wall and the back of the commode. My cousin saw it, too. It didn't move. It was me. They thought I was dead. I believe this and other episodes awakened in me a more alert consciousness of an older child and out of self preservation, I became more aware of people and situations around me.

Some family members say Linda and I grew up by accident, that mom should never have had children and that I have every "right" to be angry. Yes, I could hold grudges and whine the rest of my life. But that can cause all kinds of health problems like cancer. Do I *really* want to end up bitter and sick? Life's too short! Neither parent was evil by nature or intentionally malicious. I forgave Mom when I was twenty-five. How could I not? I have a lot to be forgiven for, too. ("But if you don't forgive people their trespasses, neither will your Father forgive yours." Matthew 6:15) Why suffer a lifetime of offences, real or imagined, only to end up in an eternal time out? The panic of trying to get cool during a hot flash was enough to convince me I wouldn't like hell at all!

Mama never played with us. (I don't think she knew how.) Daddy, played with us two, maybe three times. I prefer remembering the good things they *did* do; the igloo he built us in the front yard and the times he took us sledding. I wanted to put on a play with our big front porch as the stage, so Daddy filled the front yard with folding chairs to seat the neighborhood and Mama made tons of free popcorn. A leopard escaped from the Oklahoma City Zoo and officials thought it might be lurking in the woods behind our housing edition on the edge of town.

The neighbor men went out with rifles and bows and arrows to hunt it down and Daddy took me along. I felt so grown up. I was the one who spotted paw prints along the creek bed, probably of a large dog. But what an adventure!

Then there was the time Daddy was ordered to Wyoming on bivouac with his National Guard unit and took his family along. While he was off "soldiering," I rode Duchess and Mama, Bonita. I can't remember the name of Linda's horse. Some of my best childhood memories were of learning to saddle a horse at that dude ranch and riding every day.

Mama didn't like roughing it, so this was no vacation for her. She had to work twice as hard cooking on that old stove, keeping feather beds fluffed, block ice in the ice box and mopping up the melted mess. A deer named Doe-doe (who turned out to be a buck) would come to the owner's cabin and take milk from a calf bottle. Mama even fed him. She enjoyed that.

I remember walking home from school, pausing at the top of the hill on our block, smelling cupcakes or pies and knowing it was Mama baking our desert for that night and our afterschool snack. The Nelson's TV show came on Friday nights (I believe), and she'd bake chocolate chip cookies for us. And did I tell you that she walked to school in a blizzard to bring us our galoshes and wool leggings? (Girls never wore pants at school, but "leggings" beneath dresses to walk back and forth in cold and snowy weather, which were hung in the cloak room with our coats).

I remember the silk fans porcelain dolls Daddy brought us from Japan and the set of china and Mikimoto pearls he got Mama. I remember a Fourth of July when the neighbor men each bought a large grocery sack (each cost five dollars) full of fireworks to set off from our backyard. While letting me light a small bottle rocket, it must have tilted, because it went into the crowd and straight for the next door neighbor's elderly mother, who was in a chaise lounge. It left a half dollar size burn hole where her chest had been. I never saw a woman her age move that

ALL THE WAY HOME

fast! Daddy could have sent me to the lilac bush for a switch, (any of you ever do that?) or at least humiliated me but he didn't. Our parents were cool in emergencies like when I fell off Tony.

Still, I don't think our parents knew that the definition of discipline was to correct, not beat a child half to death. Grandmother Hoover stood between us and a lot of the "discipline." She made all our clothes, sewing ruffles on everything when there was no wash and wear. Before Mama ironed, she had to cook the blue starch on the stove to the consistency of pudding, dip clean clothes in, squeeze them out, hang them out to dry, bring them in, sprinkle them with water, put them in plastic bags in the fridge so they wouldn't mildew then spend the day ironing. Her hands turned red. She never complained. And although exhausted from all she did, she still had enough energy to walk me around the neighborhood and help me sell my Girl Scout Cookies.

Perfect childhoods are rare. Some spankings I deserved, the actual abuse is another subject. But do I hate my parents? I hate how they acted at times. I hated we weren't closer. Now that I'm older and know some of their life experiences, I'd like to think I understand. My parents weren't perfect (who is?) but I believe, Mama especially, did the best she could with what she knew. Maybe they weren't the best parents in the world, but your parents are your parents, warts and all!

Toward the end, Mom often spoke of wanting to go back and do things over. I wouldn't mind doing a few things over myself. Who wouldn't? At the top of my list would be to laugh and play more with my kids, instead of trying to be perfect and cleaning all the time. But this was what I saw my mother do day in and day out. I'd have even treated Doña Lydia with more tenderness and tried to help her more, now knowing how she must have suffered in what seemed to me, a loveless marriage. I would have encouraged Aunt Mozy more, who thought she'd so miserably failed in life. And I would certainly have been more understanding with Mom.

Once, Mom was telling me how she'd failed Linda and me. "I'm not worth the bullet it takes to shoot me!" she lamented. "Yes you are, Mom!" I blurted out. We stared at each other. It's funny how laughter can change an awkward situation.

Mom didn't like being touched, while I was used to the Latino way of greeting and saying goodbye with a kiss. The first time I tried it, she recoiled. It took years before she allowed it. Then she got sick and died. Mom so wanted us to be like her "touchy/feely" friends (as she put it) and their daughters. And we were getting there!

Mom's vivacious personality drew people to her like bees to honey. She was so beautiful she could have been a movie star. With all those pages of rituals she memorized later in life for her lodge work, learning lines for a film as a young woman would have been a snap. She would never have consented to be a pin-up girl, but with her classic 1940's look, she could have been. Silk flowers nestled in that gorgeous red hair piled on top of her head, in a bathing suit and looking over one shoulder, she'd have given Betty Grable a run for her money! Mom was certainly a star at USO dances. Aunt Carrie (wife of Little Frank, Mom's brother), who accompanied Mom to dances (nice women didn't go places alone), said Mom could really Jitterbug and Swing dance. Dancing must run in the family. Aunt Gladys won many first prizes for the Charleston and Black Bottom.

Daddy's flamboyant behavior made him seem more confident than Mom, but he was as self conscious as a school boy. He seemed to crave the limelight, yet hid from it. Strangers used to walk up and tell him he looked like John Wayne (which he did), so he grew a full beard, dressed in buckskin and hung out at muzzle loading meets, where he was the life of the party. Before he died, he had a goatee and mustache and looked very much like John Wayne in "The Shootist."

Searching through an old trunk of Daddy's, I found World War II letters he'd written home to his mother and old photos, one of a bombed out city, where he'd scribbled, "Poor Palermo!" Sadly, until then, I didn't know he had tender feelings. He always hid them, keeping Linda and me at a distance. His friends seemed to love him and he married four times, but I don't think he knew how to be close to anyone. I wish I could have known him, *really* known him. He never talked to us, even as adults, but lectured, usually on the "War Between the States." As a Civil War buff, he knew so much, it was like he'd been there! In his own way, he was amazing!

Now that I've mentioned Linda, I must relate what happened to her just before her son, David, was born. Her husband, Dave, took her out in a small sailboat that capsized off the coast of Florida. Knowing he couldn't let the current take the boat out to sea, he swam off to retrieve it, leaving her to tread water. Because she was five or six months along, she couldn't get up on her back and float. She was barely keeping her head above water, when she suddenly felt swirling sand beneath her feet. Before she knew it, she was standing on solid ground. As Dave sailed back and got close enough to easily reach her, the sand began swirling again and the sand bar disappeared. She says it's as though her son, David, was meant to be born. He's been the joy of her life. He married lovely Becky, a beauty queen and they're both in theater. They have two beautiful children, Sarah and Will.

Speaking of joys, let me tell you mine! A.L. Bizzle began life with his father shot as a traitor in the Civil War but fought becoming bitter and tried to make his children's lives better than his had been. Mama's life was better than his; mine better than Mama's and my kids' were better than mine. I still believe in respect for authority but that authority can be respectfully questioned. Where my personality and dreams were routinely squashed and I was never allowed to question, my inquiring and exuberant grandchildren, who have near ideal childhoods, are free to become everything God intended them to be. My faith in God and that I'm watching my grandchildren grow up happier and with greater advantages than I had is my greatest joy and why I've been able to leave the past behind.

Grandmother Hoover, was born in the horse and buggy days of 1875, yet lived to see satellites launched into outer space. In her day, if a man saw a woman's ankle, he was obligated by honor to marry her. She told me that one summer day, she was sitting in the shade on the wall around their well with her dress pulled to her knees to keep cool, when a stranger suddenly appeared on horseback, riding past the row of cedar trees out front. She was only about thirteen, but flew into the house before he saw her! She said back then even the roughest men never used bad language around women or children and that references to the human anatomy (especially a woman's) were taboo. A table leg was a limb, and when eating chicken, one asked for white or dark meat, not a leg or a breast! No one wants us to go back to our grandparent's day. Still, I wonder what she would think of things today.

My generation can remember when there were no electric refrigerators and block ice cooled our ice boxes; when milk came in glass bottles with the cream on top and both were delivered in horse-drawn wagons; Some laugh at the forties and fifties, but maybe the joke's on them. We didn't have to lock our front doors and murder was extremely rare. Children could lie out under the stars on their own front lawns and no one dreamed of bothering, much less hurting them. (Now deviants break in and take our children from their very beds!) It was a time when the law was sure and justice swift; when people obeyed the law, not because of surveillance cameras, but because it was right; when children could safely play out past dark; when parents could drop kids off at the movies for a day of clean fun or take them to any film Hollywood cranked out and didn't have to explain the so called "adult" situations; a time when the main offences students commited in schools were shooting spit balls and talking in class, not assault, rape, bombings or shooting up the place; back when parents and schools taught children the same values; when kids knew right from wrong and respected authority. When teachers didn't have to sit at the end of every row to keep high school kids under control during graduation. (Have you gone to one lately?)

There were no malcontents looking for a reason to be offended and take you to court; no political correctness, so that what *needed* to be said, *could* be said. In fact, words still meant something and bad behavior wasn't cloaked and excused. It was a time when you didn't "rip someone off," you stole from them; you didn't "hook up," you had illicit sex; you didn't get "plastered," you were drunk; you didn't "get wasted," you drugged yourself; you didn't "snuff" someone, you committed murder; you weren't "gaming," you gambled your family's rent and food money away; and you didn't "spin" the truth, you lied.

Aunt Mozy said one reared children but raised animals. Today, it's the other way around. The smutty "entertainment" we wink at is now called "edgy." Now, five-year olds can recognize obscenity and sixty-year old judges can't; one is not "aimless," but *finding* oneself; not a "failure," but *misunderstood;* and not a "loser," but *directionally challenged.* In this "what's in it for me world," free speech is any thing you want to say or do; marriage is optional; children an inconvenience; honor unnecessary; happiness something owed us; and everything else depends on what the word "is" is.

Some say evil is a condition of the heart, others that there is no such thing; and that wrongdoing can be eliminated through education. Politicians who are supposed to make laws to protect us, tell us these issues are "complicated." What's so complicated about right and wrong? If "education" *is* the key, why do robberies occur in the United States every minute and a murder every thirty-four? Why are there 1.3 forcible rapes of adult women every minute? Why are hundreds of children kidnapped by parents and strangers every year?

Our children live in a "girls gone wild" world of filthy language, suggestively dirty dancing performed at high school proms, wardrobe malfunctions on live TV and they think it's all normal! Immodest and confused young women are our kid's roll models, mothers are written into sitcoms as "desperate housewives" and men can now play video games where they beat women to death with baseball bats. Roberto's unpredictable temper and volatile personality were scary enough! If he'd grown up in today's culture, would I even be around to tell my story?

I'm glad I grew up then and not now. Films like *The Wizard of Oz* taught me "there was no place like home," and "the next time I looked for my heart's desire, I wouldn't go farther than my own backyard," *The African Queen* taught me that "Human nature is what we're put in this world to rise above," and the 1943 version of *Miracle On 34th Street* that "Faith is believing in things when common sense tells you not to."

The visitation, special as it was, didn't insulate me from bad things that sometimes happen in life. I wish I could say I rode off into the sunset and lived happily ever after, but I had poor health for nearly twenty years. (Doctors couldn't pinpoint it. I now suspect food allergies.) More devastating than that was losing family members which sent my health into a worse tailspin and left me angry at God for years. And to think I knew where to find peace and didn't go get it!

I've been up to here in do-do more than once in my life, but never saw myself as a victim! These were merely problems that needed solutions. As far as rescuing my children, I did what any mother would do. I made many errors rearing them, not out of maliciousness, but from pure ignorance. (Too bad kids don't come with an operator's manual!) But I guess we wouldn't be human if we didn't make mistakes.

I didn't intend to ever remarry until I met a kind and gentle man named Arnaldo, a college graduate with a master's degree, who is hard-working and self-sacrificing. Together, we had three more beautiful, intelligent children: Anthony, Ben and Albert. We're proud of all six! They've worked hard and achieved their goals. Most of all, those who are married are great spouses and wonderful parents to their children.

Chris, a big movie fan, who now goes by Robert, should have been in film work, as he did some pretty advanced movie tricks with the camera my sister gave me. Sadly, I didn't know how to guide him into what he should study to achieve this. He didn't either. But taking the bull by the horns, he found something he was good at, put himself through school and is now a master auto technician like both his grandfathers (the best in a four-state area) and a genius with anything electronic. He married sharp and talented Tracy, who is like a daughter to us (I love all my son's wives). Their good-looking teenage son, Cameron James, who's smart as a whip, is already being scouted by a prestigious eastern university.

David, who still loves the outdoors, is in construction. He married a wonderful girl named Kay, and they have two lovely teenage daughters, Shelby and Brooklyn.

Michelle, who played tag football with her brothers until she was sixteen then discovered she was beautiful, modeled in Tulsa, Los Angeles and New York. She is now a TV assistant Producer and has a precious son named, Tyler.

Anthony (Arnaldo Antonio), is an advanced Neuromuscular therapist, married a sweet girl named Pammi. They have four children: Theresa, Natalie, Anthony (Arnaldo Antonio III, after my husband) and Carina Suzanna, after me.

Ben (Alfredo Ruben), a cardiovascular anesthesiologist on staff at a prestigious Houston heart hospital, enjoys surfing and world travel.

Albert (Alberto Jose) got a degree in motion picture and television at a California university and is realizing his dream career in writing and film making.

As for me, with the children grown and gone, I'm realizing a dream of my own in writing. If you've got a dream that's been on the back burner too long or a mountain seemingly too high to climb, don't give

up! You can make it! Always remember, you're not alone. I'll bet He's standing there now, loving you with that big smile, His eyes bright as stars. A course, you're 'possa ask first. But if you like, He'll be with you too ... ***All the Way Home!***